American Folklore Studies

AMERICAN FOLKLORE STUDIES
An Intellectual History

Simon J. Bronner

University Press of Kansas

1888-89
AMERICAN
FOLKLORE
SOCIETY
CENTENNIAL
1988-89

A Centennial Publication

Published by the University Press of Kansas (Lawrence, Kansas 66045), which was
organized by the Kansas Board of Regents and is operated and funded by Emporia State
University, Fort Hays State University, Kansas State University, Pittsburg State University, the University of Kansas, and Wichita State University

Library of Congress Cataloging-in-Publication Data
Bronner, Simon J.
  American folklore studies.
  Bibliography: p.
  Includes index.
  1. Folklore—Study and teaching—United States—
History. 2. Folklore—United States—History.
I. Title.
GR46.B76   1986   398'.07'073   86-9292
ISBN 0-7006-0306-9
ISBN 0-7006-0313-1 (pbk.)

Printed in the United States of America
10 9 8 7 6 5 4 3 2

To Bill McNeil, who helped chart the waters

Folk-Lore has become a subject of the day. . . . Folk-Lore is not merely a study of the survival of decay, it is the demonstrator of the possible and probable in history, the repository of historical truths otherwise lost, the preserver of the literature of the people and the touchstone of many of the sciences. . . . But if Folk-Lore, in its extent, embraces the matter of the sciences, by the quality and the degree of knowledge it expresses, it differs from them all.

—Fletcher Bassett, address to the Third
International Folklore Congress, Chicago, 1893

Contents

Illustrations

Preface

In the word *folk* have been bundled various attitudes toward continuity and change in society. During the last one hundred and fifty years, folk was at first used to characterize a past primitive tradition; then it came to characterize the cultural inheritance of ethnic, regional, and occupational groups apart from the mainstream; and then it predominantly described an informal, communal way of learning and doing things that can be found in all groups. Used to describe life and lore, folk is the driving mechanism of two important nineteenth-century intellectual inventions—the words *folklife* and *folklore*. Folklife arose to describe the traditional way of life shared by peasant and ethnic communities; folklore arose to describe the traditional artistic expressions of tales, songs, and crafts held onto by common people. As society felt itself transformed suddenly into a modern industrial age, a new professional, the folklorist, helped it to understand what it was leaving behind. The folklorist collected and explained the lore of groups still operating with preindustrial ideas. In the twentieth century, the meanings of folklore and folklife shifted to a feeling that tradition and modernity existed as part of each other, and as these meanings changed, so too did the work of the folklorist change. Folklore and folklife remain significant for a modernizing society. The words are still instruments of major intellectual movements in the society.

My effort in this book is to present the succession of folkloristic ideas in their historical and cultural context. To describe this body of ideas, I use "folklore studies," following common usage in the United States, as my umbrella term for professional studies of folklore and folklife. I find that in its one hundred and fifty years of professional existence in America, folklore studies has followed the trends—currents, if you will—in modernist thinking about culture. During the nineteenth century, a preoccupation was uncovering a longer past than theology had taught. Thus, cultural studies opened up the past for a secular present. The next trend was to expand the present's dimensions. Against the background of revolutionary changes in mechanical transportation that occurred in the late nineteenth and early twentieth centuries, cultural studies turned to charting time and space. Rapid changes in communication have dominated the years since, and society's preoccupations have become increasingly oriented toward the future. Folklore studies has responded by using models drawn from the structure of communications media to understand how traditions come to be. These interconnections, or intellectual currents, reveal folklore studies to be an intrinsic part of a broad intellectual history—a history of the beliefs that Americans have held about tradition and culture. This kind of history goes beyond mere chronology to raise issues; it becomes intellectual criticism. My purpose is, not a celebration of folkloristic achievement, but an interpretation of it. My goal in this book, therefore, is not to present a vista of the discipline's waters; rather, it is to give an exploration of some of its currents in the United States.

I can clarify my theme by noting the influence of three works. First, I wanted to combine the records of what scholars have done and the ideas inherent in American civilization. Writing in *New Directions in American Intellectual History* (1979), Murray G. Murphey offered an important insight toward this goal in his chapter on "The Place of Beliefs in Modern Culture." He pointed out that scholars have had an influence on the beliefs that society holds and are subject to them. In a modern culture marked by professionalism, it is fruitful to approach the criticism of complex ideas through the specialties that use them. Especially in folklore studies is found a conscious effort to create a specialty that reveals perceptions, modern and traditional, of society's character. Thus I have looked at folklore studies to illustrate its professional distinctiveness and its broader connection to the circulation of ideas on tradition and culture.

Ideas are, of course, subject to translation into terms. When terms expand with meaning—causing admiration, hostility, embarrassment, and study—they are keywords. *Folklore* and *folklife* are keywords that fitted into the mood of the times. Modern life provided the standard by which folk life was measured. *Folk* described the others—communities, persons, and artistic expressions—that did not conform to progressive views of modern industrial life. Folklore represented the hidden roots from which modern life sprang. Yet folklore and folklife consisted of materials commonly collected in the midst of modern life. They were part of yet apart from modern life. They therefore raised questions of the state of the times and its progressive standards; they were both the basis and the antithesis of modern life. The words folklore and folklife, then, were commonly used against the background of the thinking of the times about itself.

By examining keywords, such as folklore and folklife, as vocabulary, as socially constructed artifacts, it is possible to move past the circulation of ideas to study the construction of ideas. For this, I am indebted to Raymond Williams's work, especially *Keywords: A Vocabulary of Culture and Society* (1976). Keywords, he points out, are rarely agreed-upon terms. A keyword is "bound up with the problems it was being used to discuss." Keywords are "significant, binding words in certain activities and their interpretation; they are significant, indicative words in certain forms of thought. Certain uses bound together certain ways of seeing culture and society."[1] Although Williams devoted considerable space to *elite* and *popular,* he did not cover *folk.* Yet to the same, or a greater, extent, *folk* signifies changing ways of seeing culture and society.

The third work is *The Discoverers: A History of Man's Search to Know His World and Himself* (1983), by Daniel Boorstin. If Murphey opened the depths of a profession to wider cultural scrutiny, Boorstin announced the breadth of discovering knowledge through time. But among Boorstin's discoverers, folklorists were absent. Yet I would argue that they were important figures for his categories of both "opening the past" and "surveying the present." Folklorists rose as Western society became more aware of differences between rising modern ways of doing things and threatened traditional life. The ideas that arose, as chronicler Lee J. Vance noted in 1896, were explanations and justifications of "the progress of man in culture." As late as 1980, a leading folklorist, Richard Dorson, was still touting the study of folklore as a parable of modern life. "Through folklore," he wrote, "we learn much that is otherwise concealed about the human condition."[2] Here I fill out the record of folklore studies and retain Boorstin's attention to relating the search for knowledge with changes in technology.

The neglect of folklore studies in these three works is not a sign of the discipline's lack of importance. It is, rather, a sign of its lack of historiography. The few histories of the discipline are in dissertation form, and then they usually fail to link events in the discipline with broader intellectual themes. I drew from those histories and owe a debt to them, but I planned to do something different here. I planned to write, not a chronological or biographical history, but an intellectual history, connecting folklore studies with broader intellectual and cultural movements, and examining the changing perceptions of tradition and culture. My outline of change from the nineteenth century to the present is not meant to suggest a stepladder chronology of folklore studies; it is meant to show the direction of major intellectual currents.

In this regard, I found instructive Richard Dorson's warning that American folklore studies has taken less the shape of a simple story line than the form of "episodic chapters, passing currents, and arresting personalities."[3] Yet consistent underlying intellectual themes can be found by going beyond the bibliography of folklore studies to the social worlds where folkloristic ideas were used. The statement of these themes—the hidden usable past, the professionalization of time and space (surveying the present), and the era of communication—provides my division of chapters. The first theme is evident during a period stretching from 1830 to 1910, the second lasts from 1880 to 1960, and the third extends from 1920 to 1980.

And where were folkloristic ideas used? For the social worlds of folklore studies, the events may be conferences and congresses, presidential addresses and special lectures; for the society, it may be world's fairs and public celebrations, welcoming addresses and political speeches. For the writing of folklore studies, the evidence may be its journals and leading books; for the society, it may be its novels and magazines. For the organization of folklore studies, the evidence may be its associations and schools; for the society, it may be its factions and professions. In my chapters, I use this evidence of events, writings, and characters that held significance for the period under discussion to bring out the fundamental ideas connecting folklore studies to the society.

The opening chapter on the hidden usable past of folklore introduces the importance that the process of prolonging the past, brought by evolutionary theory, had for the ideas of the nineteenth century. I trace the development of the terms *folk, folklore,* and *folklife* in scholarship, and I survey the topics that arose during the early period of professional folklore studies. To show how folklorists' investigations of the past were part of the social issues of the day, I discuss the relation of folklore studies to industrialism and feminism during the late nineteenth century. In the ensuing photographic essay I introduce people and places that were important in the rising profession at the turn of century, and I chart some of its winds of change.

The development of a professional study of folklore and a shift from natural history toward ethnography, with its emphasis on shrinking time and space, provide the focus of the next chapter. Whereas natural history stressed the specimens of a single cultural past, ethnography emphasized the observable behavior of groups in the present. I discuss the "arresting personalities" of Franz Boas, Stith Thompson, Bronislaw Malinowski, and William Bascom in this chapter to emphasize the intellectual character of the period of this shift and the perceptions that it raised. These perceptions inform my discussion of the "passing currents" of evolution, diffusion, and function.

The final chapter covers what historians have called "the big change" in American history. The introduction of new technology, especially for communication, dramatically changed the ways that Americans lived. Both the reporting of events and, consequently, the way Americans viewed them changed. Folklore studies responded to this change, and it became a discipline independent of anthropology. Indeed, after a fallow period in the 1910s and 1920s, folklore studies enjoyed renewed public attention in the 1930s as a result. Theories diversified, and new topics entered the scope of folklore studies. In this final chapter, I survey the range of theories and topics that arose and show their connection to a vigorous era of communication. Most of the new theories shared the keyword of *communication;* following the simultaneousness of several prominent media in modern society, the new theories stressed simultaneous, multiple ways of seeing and structuring society—an emphasis that I call a "multiple perspective," in contrast to the singular perspective of the nineteenth century. I conclude with a look back at the continuity running through the history of folklore studies and a look ahead to changes on the horizon.

I close the book with a bibliography, to show the sources for my intellectual history of American folklore studies. As well, it is an invitation for further exploration of the subject.

This book is for folklorists and other students of tradition; it has been equally informed by them, although they should not be blamed for my opinions. I begin foremost with a tireless historian and a valued friend, William K. McNeil. I dedicate this book to him for extending to me his wide knowledge, unceasing encouragement, and good humor. I am also indebted to others who stepped forward to discuss their views on the history of cultural study. They, too, deserve recognition: Richard M. Dorson, Wilhelm Nicolaisen, Wayland Hand, Louis C. Jones, Warren Roberts, Rosemary Lévy Zumwalt, Frank de Caro, William Wilson, Ellen Stekert, Howard Marshall, Susan Dwyer-Shick, Dan Ben-Amos, Kenneth Goldstein, Linda Dégh, Sandra Stahl, Bruce Jackson, Edson Richmond, and Marta Weigle.

For their expertise in anthropology, I owe Roger Janelli, Elliott Oring, Michael Barton, John Vlach, and Stephen Poyser. For offering insights on intellectual history, I am grateful to Stephen Stern, Eugene Metcalf, Roderick Roberts, William Mahar, Robert Bresler, Charles

Townley, and John Patterson. For discussing problems of psychological interpretation, I thank Alan Dundes, David Hufford, Michael Owen
Jones, C. Kurt Dewhurst, Lee Haring, and Henry Glassie. For clarifying
points of sociological theory, I thank Gary Alan Fine, James Hudson,
and Herbert Hunter. For discussing ideas on ethnography, I am
grateful to Roger Abrahams, Jay Mechling, and Ronald Baker.

I also have acknowledgments for those who saw the book through
with me. Deborah Bowman was family—and colleague, companion,
and confidante while I was writing this book. Then there's Peter
Voorheis, appropriately from a town named Friendship, who discussed
with me all the above topics and more. In Harrisburg, Pennsylvania, I
was lucky to have a lively group of folklorists nearby to provide
intellectual stimulation: Priscilla Ord, Kenneth Thigpen, Yvonne
Milspaw, William Aspinall, Thomas Graves, and Shalom Staub.
Thanks are especially due to Sue Samuelson and Frederick Richmond
for their caring and tolerance.

Many libraries, archives, and museums cooperated with me to
make available the documents I needed for my research. I extend my
gratitude to the staffs at the Indiana University Folklore Collection, the
Folklore Institute at Indiana University, the Van Pelt Library of the
University of Pennsylvania, the University of Pennsylvania Archives,
the University of Pennsylvania Museum, the Archives of the Folklore
and Folklife Department at the University of Pennsylvania, the Historical Society of Pennsylvania, the State Library of Pennsylvania, the
University of Pennsylvania Museum, the National Anthropological
Archives, the Brooklyn Museum, the American Philosophical Society,
the Henry Francis du Pont Winterthur Museum, the New York State
Historical Association, and the Smithsonian Institution. Librarian Ruth
Runion, at the Heindel Library of the Pennsylvania State University–Harrisburg, was especially helpful in tracking down my nineteenth-century sources.

Indeed, the Pennsylvania State University at Harrisburg helped
make this book a reality. Students posed hard questions and asked for
answers in a book. The Center for Research and Graduate Studies at
Penn State–Harrisburg helped to prepare the manuscript. Editorial
assistant John Drexler and archivist Iris Wood helped to check it. I
extend special gratitude to William Mahar, division head of humanities, for supporting my research. And thanks to the secretaries from
the divisions of humanities and behavioral sciences—Kathy Ritter,
Louise Morgan, Donna Horley, and Loretta Reigle—for graciously
handling my correspondence.

I might also acknowledge an artifact that provided me with
inspiration during the writing of this book. My copy of *The Blithedale*

Romance, by Nathaniel Hawthorne, inscribed with "To Elsa from Aunt Linda, Kansas, 1904," has a clipping pasted in the front which reads: "At the age of 16 years Hawthorne had formed his ideal in life, and he wrote to his mother: 'I do not want to be a doctor and live by men's diseases, nor a minister and live by their sins, nor a lawyer and live by their quarrels. So I don't see that there is anything left for me to do but to be an author.'"

I have not changed my ideal in life—to live by men's traditions and to write about them. Having devoted previous books to traditions in the field and in the library, I here turn my attention to intellectual movements devoted to them in the academy and in the profession and, indeed, in the society.

1

The Usable Hidden Past
of Folklore

In 1887 the middle-class intellectual magazine *Open Court* carried an account of a new science. Entitled "Folk-Lore Studies," the article by Lee J. Vance chronicled the rapid rise of this science in the nineteenth century. He traced its roots to the tale and legend collecting of the brothers Grimm in the early nineteenth century. "From that day until this," Vance wrote, "the by-ways and hedges of all Europe have been more or less ransacked by keen-eyed and inquiring disciples of Grimm, eagerly taking down the marvelous stories as they fell from the lips of the peasantry. What was thus taken down, not only found its way in print, but found thousands of readers. And now the lettered were willing to sit at the feet of the unlettered. Folk-Lore societies were quickly established for the purpose of collecting and preserving these fanciful legends, and its members are now numbered by the hundreds."[1]

Vance then asked, "What have our American students of Folk-Lore done toward contributing their share to the History of Culture?" If America did not have its brothers Grimm, Vance argued, it did have Washington Irving and others who had collected legends at the same time as the brothers. And now it had its avid students of the subject and would soon have a professional society to carry on the work of this science, which is so important, he stressed, toward the understanding of "the history of progress."

Surveys that followed Vance's ran a similar course: they note the surge of public interest and professional activity, and they describe the leading figures and their theories. As a basis for the rest of this book, I have added another dimension—that of intellectual criticism. Why did

1

this surge occur? What relation did the rise of professionalism and cultural theory have with society's thinking?

Theory is often given as a model for an objective explanation of reality. Here I consider it as an outgrowth of a subjective dialogue on social conditions between members of the professional middle class and their changing society. During the nineteenth century, many members of this class who called themselves folklorists or, more broadly, "scientific men and women" unearthed a usable past which had been hidden by the rapid material transformation of the present. For these Victorians, folklore was a body of material set squarely in the past, even if it still could be heard on the lips of the "backward portions of society." And the past was directed forward. In a period marked by often-paradoxical combinations of, on the one hand, spreading imperialism, industrialism, and militaristic masculinity and, on the other, utopianism, antimodernism, and feminism, *folklore* and *folklife* became keywords in a new scientific awareness of the past which would, in turn, furnish the emergent social order.

For Victorians who were reading and studying folklore, the upwardly aspiring present required a past by which to measure its accomplishments. The yoke of theology had previously restricted the past. Many theologians used the Irish prelate James Ussher's scholarly decree of 1654 that the creation occurred in 4004 B.C. When Charles Darwin proposed in *The Origin of Species* (1859) a longer past for humankind than theologians had thought possible, the past became new territory to explore and control. The territory needed to be usable, mapped in terms of the immediacy of the "civilizing" present and the pleasing prospect of the forward-moving future brought by science. The past of nature appeared as an evolutionary line from simple organisms to complex humans. Soon, other evolutionary lines were drawn, from superstitious beliefs to scientific observations, from primitive societies to modern industrial nations. Scholarly debates over the origin of nature and culture spilled over into the popular press. Nineteenth-century magazines such as *Open Court, Monist,* and *Popular Science Monthly,* which regularly carried surveys of folklore, arose to reconcile religion and science for their middle-class audience.

Opening up the past of nature suggested that creation might also be similarly defined for humanity, and hence for culture. With the past apparently remote, however, specialized practitioners with esoteric "scientific" skills became necessary to uncover the past for the public. The social side effects of such changes in thinking were significant. For one, a shortened theological past meant that changes in nature and man were necessarily large ones. The opening of the evolutionary past suggested that the world's beginning was not a literal wholesale creation, but was a metaphor for slow and constant change. While the Victorians were feeling that transformative changes were occurring during their time, the new world view provided the security that their era was, not a cataclysm, but a climax of growth.

The longer evolutionary past suggested that man had control of cultural growth, for in such a past, nature was not predestined. The longer past described a changeful world, filled with races struggling to ascend the cultural ladder. For many writers, this was not a rejection of theology, but was a revision of it. After all, studies of the evolutionary past were intended to shed light on the creation and the nature of man. But it also allowed for the secularization of culture, because it set social growth in human and natural terms. The present, rather than the beginning, became the standard. Sources of change were earthly, and

John Fanning Watson (1779–1860) in a photograph taken in 1860 (courtesy of Henry Francis du Pont Winterthur Museum, Joseph Downs Manuscript Collection, no. 58 × 29.17).

the lines of growth led to what seemed to be a distinct segment of time and culture—the industrial present.

I can illustrate this view of culture in the United States by giving the example of an early collector of American folklore who opened up the hidden past—John Fanning Watson (1779–1860)—and describing the influences on him. In April 1824 he submitted the article "Recollections of Ancient Philadelphia" to *Poulson's American Daily Advertiser* to awaken the public "to the utility of bringing out their traditions and ancient family records." His research flowered six years later in the publication of his book *Annals of Philadelphia and Pennsylvania in the Olden Time* (1830). Reaction was swift. The *Germantown Telegraph* declared, "We can scarcely imagine a work that would be sought after with more avidity, and read with higher satisfaction." The *Daily Advertiser* (Philadelphia) announced that "such a book, we may safely affirm, *has never before* been produced in the United States" (emphasis in original). The *Village Record* (West Chester) made special reference to the folklore in Watson's collection: "The author has been at much pains to collect a mass of traditionary lore, which but for him, must soon have passed into oblivion. . . . It seems to convey us back to other times—we see things as they were—*minutely* and *particularly*—and not as presented by stately and buskined history, *in one general view,* vague, glimmering, indistinct, and but too often partially coloured" (emphasis in original).[2] Drawing raves from leading newspapers and enjoying brisk sales, the book went into several editions before and after Watson's death. Watson followed his annals of Philadelphia with a similar collection for New York and with a set of *Historical Tales* for each of the cities.

These cities received antiquarian attention because their past seemed to give way before the industrialism that had begun to spread through a corridor from Philadelphia to Boston. In the 1790s, more than one-third of all exports of the United States came from Philadelphia. In 1795, Oliver Evans introduced his automated gristmill in the Philadelphia area; to the amazement of the public it received raw material and delivered a finished product on a large scale with little human intervention. Similar transformations were occurring in the printing, cloth, leather, and iron industries. The factory system began to take shape in these technological advancements; artisans and small farm operations, a mainstay of the economy in the Middle Atlantic States for more than a century, felt squeezed out by more mills and iron furnaces. By 1800 at least 167 furnaces and forges had been established in Philadelphia, and their owners represented the economic and civic leadership of the city. In the early nineteenth century, Philadelphia led the nation in manufacturing and population; New

York was its main competitor and by 1820 had become the biggest shipper.[3]

The cities became more aware of their folk past. In 1827 the *New York Mirror* noted the demolition of New York's seventeenth-century Dutch houses with regret. "We cannot but view them with deferential regard," the writer stressed, "and whenever the spirit of innovation and improvement which is abroad among us is stirring energy, levels one of them to the ground, the noise of the trembling structure falls upon the ear of the sensitive man with a sound somewhat akin to that of the earth, as it rattles on the coffin of an old and long-known friend."[4] In the early nineteenth century, Sir Walter Scott's (1771–1832) romantic writings about the folklore and antiquities of a vanishing country folk in Scotland sold especially well in Philadelphia and New York and influenced New York writers Washington Irving (1783–1859) and James Kirke Paulding (1778–1860) to draw inspiration for their fiction from native folklore. "Rip Van Winkle" and "The Legend of Sleepy Hollow," from *The Sketch Book* (1819/20), took from native Dutch folklore and became Irving's best-known stories. Paulding, himself of Dutch ancestry, published his tales in New York and Philadelphia magazines. He gained renown for these tales and novels, such as *The Dutchman's Fireside* (1831), before Edgar Allan Poe and Nathaniel Hawthorne had drawn attention to their fictional adaptations of folklore.

Many of these authors were also drawn to histories of everyday life in the past, which took in folklore and folklife. Irving wove humor into his *A History of New York* (1809), a takeoff on S. L. Mitchell's *The Picture of New York* (1807). Earlier in Philadelphia, Benjamin Rush (1745–1813), a doctor and advocate for American independence, produced *An Account of the Manners of the German Inhabitants of Pennsylvania* (1789). By manners, according to a common usage then, Rush meant, not a code of etiquette, but traditional ways of doing things from farming to dining. He recorded his random observations to argue that the lessons of German heritage should be retained in the creation of the new nation. Although this early literature set the stage for studies of folklore and folklife, it was Watson's annals that became exceptional for its sweeping collection and devotion to a field of inquiry.

The past events and customs described by the early-nineteenth-century accounts were called "antiquarian" lore. Watson added the collection of orally told legends and beliefs to offer what he called "traditionary" lore. By contemporary standards, Watson was not discriminating. He published everything from changes in the prices of food to proceedings of witchcraft trials. With additions made by Willis

Hazard in 1891, the annals of Philadelphia had grown to three volumes. This sweep of information, Watson wrote, "is an effort to rescue from the ebbing tide of oblivion, all those fugitive memorials of unpublished facts and observations, or reminiscences and traditions, which could best illustrate the domestic history of our former days." But in seeking evidence that "others had overlooked or disregarded," Watson made a contribution by including folk objects, beliefs, and legends in his collection.[5]

A banker and railroad official, Watson became well known by the 1830s as a specialist in such lore. He took to collecting local history and folklore in southeastern Pennsylvania and was honored by Dickinson College's Philosophical Society for "unearthing old legends and old bones." The *New York Evening Post* encouraged more collections like Watson's: "Our Historical Society has done well in making Mr. Watson an honorary member; and we hope that the strange things which he has thus brought to light, *will be further pursued*" (emphasis in original). With his own ears attuned to local legends and beliefs, Washington Irving wrote of Watson, "I hope the author *will continue to explore the vein* which he has so successfully opened;—be assured that while he is gratifying himself, he is doing an important service to his country, by multiplying the local association of ideas, and the strong but invisible ties of the mind and of the heart which bind the native to the paternal soil" (emphasis in original).[6]

Using the motto "To note and to observe," Watson sought to recover remembrances in the form of artifacts, legends, beliefs, sayings, and documents from aged informants. Elaborating on his motto, Watson, like Irving and Paulding, used Scotland's Sir Walter Scott for inspiration. Watson admiringly wrote, "When a young man, Scott was wont to make frequent journeys into the country, *among strangers,* going from house to house, with his boy George,—and particularly seeking out the residences of *the old people,* with whom he delighted to enter into conversation, and exciting them to dilate upon the reminiscences of their youth" (emphasis in original). Like Rush, Watson wanted to show the useful inheritance of the past that was hidden by the changeful present, and like Scott, Watson also viewed his work "as a repository from which our future poets, painters, and imaginative authors could deduce their themes, for their own and their country's glory."[7]

Watson began his collecting by distributing questionnaires about the "practices and narratives of olden time," but he soon came to rely on visits to informants. For Watson's final motto became "If any man were to form a book, of *what he had seen or heard himself,* it must, *in whatever hands,* prove a most useful and interesting one" (emphasis in original). "I am of the same opinion," Watson wrote, "from numerous facts known to me in my researches among the aged for reminiscences and traditions."[8]

In addition to admiring Scott, Watson looked to other British antiquarian folklorists for equivalents to his searches for oral tradition. He read William Hone's *Every-Day Book* (1826/27) but criticized its reliance on printed sources. Watson praised Robert Chambers's *Traditions of Edinburgh* (1825), claiming that it "has much the spirit and purpose of my own book." The common thread running through the works was an unearthing of a hidden past. Watson strikes the theme in the first sentence of his annals for Philadelphia: "The same affection which makes us reach forward and peep into futurity, prompts us to travel back to the hidden events which transpired before we existed. We thus feel our span of existence enlarged even while we have the pleasure to identify ourselves with the scenes or the emotions of our forefathers."[9]

Although seeking European models, Watson declared in the annals that collecting "traditionary lore" in America was unusual. "A single life in this rapidly growing country," he wrote, "witnesses such changes in the progress of society, and in the embellishments of the arts, as would require a term of centuries to witness in full grown Europe. If we have no ruins of Pompeii and Herculaneum to employ our researchers, no incomprehensible Stonehenge, nor circle of Dendara to move our wonder, we have abundant themes of unparalleled surprise in following down the march of civilization and improvements,—from the first landing of our pilgrim forefathers to the present *eventful* day!" (emphasis in original). The events promised improvements that would lead to a powerful land of plenty. "In less than twenty years," wrote Watson, "our exports have grown from twenty to eighty millions. Our navy, from 'cock-boats and rags of striped bunting,' has got up to power and renown. Our private law, commercial code, and bold diplomacy, have grown into a mature and learned system. Our inventions and improvements in the arts, which began but yesterday, make us, even now, 'a wonder unto many.'" Watson then contemplated the "topics" of progress and the role played in it by his searches of the past: "If topics like these,—which enter into the common history of our growing cities, may be the just pride and glory of an American, must not the annals, which detail such facts . . . be calculated to afford him deep interest; and should it not be his profit, as well as amusement, to trace the successive steps by which we have progressed, from comparative nothingness, to be 'a praise in the earth!'"[10]

By the mid nineteenth century, the tide of industrialism that first hit the Northeast spread west and south as transportation and commerce improved. If Americans felt that their technology developed rapidly, they could still trace their cultural progress as civilized beings in a long evolutionary line back to the early civilizations. Native American and other aboriginal groups drew attention for showing the antiquity of humankind. The long evolutionary past had the appeal of supplying a rational order to what seemed like a chaotic present that was going off, as the rhetoric of the day announced, "in all directions" with the quickening tempos of trains, mills, and ragtime tunes. Friedrich Nietzsche, in *The Gay Science* (1882), for example, reflected on the new pace by asking: "What were we doing when we unchained this earth from its sun? Whither is it moving now? Whither are we moving? Away from all suns? Are we not plunging continually? Backward, sideward, forward, in all directions?" In this world, historian Erich Marcks observed in 1903, "everything pushes and bangs together." Marcks yearned for the "few traces of the unprejudiced harmony of basic ideas."[11] Evolution sprung into social, political, and cultural discourse because it provided unity and structure from one such basic idea. Darwin's metaphor of natural history telescoped the past into the present. It expanded to a natural history of civilization. The civilized present was industrial and material; it was filled with new inventions and goods, and more of them, than ever. It was shaped especially to the needs of a consuming middle class which was seeking a stable, "natural" claim to a rising status in this changeful world. As lawyer and publisher Lee J. Vance (1862–1942) noted in 1896, the end of the nineteenth century "will be marked by the rise and growth of a new science,—the science which studies mankind from the time when the earth and the human family were young down to the present time. This science (whether called Anthropology or Comparative Folk-Lore) studies the progress of man in culture. It reveals the evolution of modern culture from the beliefs and usages of savages and simple-minded folk. Now folk-lore is concerned more particularly with the 'survival' of primitive or ancient ideas and customs in modern civilization: that is to say, our study traces the development of tribal custom into national law; of pagan custom into Christian ecclesiastical usage and popular festivals; of sorcery and magic into astrology, and finally into astronomical science; of song and dance into Greek drama and poetry; of nursery tales and *Märchen* into the epic and the modern novel. Again, the end of the nineteenth century is remarkable for the immense number of books devoted to the Folk—to people who have shared . . . least in the general advance. These people are, first, the backward races, as the natives of Australia and our Indian tribes; then the European peasantry, Southern negroes, and others out of touch with towns and schools and railroads."[12]

During the late nineteenth century, industrial advances seemed to have brought a culture of abundance. In the middle-class perception, there was an abundance of new goods ready for consumption and an abundance of culture ready for collecting. Consumption was a major theme of Edward Bellamy's utopian novel *Looking Backward* (1888). It sold more than 125,000 copies within a year of its publication and grew to be an international best seller. The novel used the cornucopia as the symbol of a twenty-first-century utopian industrial order that offered a pleasant culture of consumption, the same symbol used by Sears in the nineteenth century. Ralph Waldo Emerson's plaint of 1851 that "things are in the saddle, and ride mankind" was still being echoed during the 1890s, but the fascination with displays of things from department stores, art museums, and world's expositions continued among the educated middle class. The volume of items became an index to the level of culture. The Victorian interior was overstuffed and layered, filled with manufactured accessories such as layers of drapes and many pillows, plants, and exotic shells. Theodore Dreiser's heroine in *Sister Carrie* (1900) leaves the sparse country for the city in search of more than fortune. She wants things; she wants "culture." This is an ironic twist, because the word *culture* originally carried the connotation of "tillage," or closeness to land and nature. Her introduction to the symbolism of the new order is a man who is "successful" in "manner and method." What marks him? "Good clothes, of course, were the first essential, the things without which he was nothing. A strong physical nature, actuated by a keen desire for the feminine, was the next."[13] The 1901 Pan-American Exposition at Buffalo reinforced the middle-class perception of the nature of things with its central Fountain of Plenty in the Court of Abundance. Near the court was the anthropology building, which housed a "grand prize" exhibit of "objects illustrating folklore"—an exhibit of many small items packed into closed glass cases. Whether oral or material, folklore studies used the artifactual metaphor to play on the appeal of appearance, detail, and cultural layering. Folklorists looked to the past and the remote present for eye-catching, accumulable evidence.

Dreiser's connection between the city's materialism and the feminine is not gratuitous. The city's attention to appearance and cosmetic detail suggested the feminine advice of popular manners books, catering to a genteel middle class. Indeed, the American Civic Association, founded by Mira Dock of Harrisburg, Pennsylvania, in 1904, was designed to infuse good taste, recreation, and "contact with nature" into cities. The availability of structured leisure brought to mind the association between women and sentimental activities. Women, it appeared, had leisure and sentiment; men had their industry and science. In the nature of things, science controlled sentiment; technology controlled nature; the present hid the past. But because of the rapid changes during the late nineteenth century, much that had formerly been clear socially was being challenged; many technical and class divisions seemed blurred. The headlong rush to the future was coupled with a longing for the past. The challenges, polarities, and blurs underlay compensatory images of heightened order in the codes of the manner books and in the models of culture.

Folklore was spiritual, while modern life was material. As professionals providing an ego-reassuring service—as cultural therapists for an age that was "nervous" from rapid change—folklorists read the stable past with specialized knowledge. Folklorist John Fiske (1842–1901) commented, for example, that "whereas our grandfathers, in speculating about the opinions and mental habits of people in low stages of culture, were dealing with a subject about which they knew almost nothing, on the other hand, our chief difficulty is in shaping and managing the enormous mass of data which keen and patient inquirers have collected. . . . Railroad, newspaper, and telegraphic bulletins of prices are carrying everything before them. The peasant's quaint dialect and his fascinating myth tales are disappearing along with his picturesque dress. . . . It is high time to be gathering in all the primitive lore we can find before the men and women in whose minds it is still a living reality have all passed from the scene."[14]

The appeal of the primitive in folklore to turn-of-the-century moderns came to the fore in a widely circulated article, "On Being Civilized Too Much," by Henry Childs Merwin, published in the *Atlantic Monthly* in 1897. Merwin bemoaned the loss of "closeness to nature" and the weakening of primitive instincts in the new industrial civilization. Merwin pointed out that the greatest literature—that is, the literature with the most feeling—was created by those who were close to nature. Furthermore, he wrote, "Savages and children have a natural love for good bright colors. Everybody knows that these colors tend to raise the spirits, and therefore to improve the health. . . . This natural, healthy sense of color may of course be cultivated and trained, so that those who possess it can learn to appreciate the beauty of more delicate shades; and in such persons there will be a happy union of natural taste with cultivation." But alas, this is vicarious, because "city people hire others to do for them, but country people know how to shift for themselves." Merwin pleads with his audience to "consult the teamster, the farmer, the wood-chopper, the shepherd, or the drover. You will find him as healthy in mind, as free from fads, as strong in natural impulses, as he was in Shakespeare's time and is in Shakespeare's plays. From his loins, and not from those of the dilettante, will spring the man of the future." The country, the children, and the savages constituted the line-up of the Victorian's "folk," whose anachronistic "expressions" and "productions," as the author called them, were necessary for the health of the overcivilized man and woman.[15]

What Merwin had stated abstractly, folklorists made more concrete. Folk was a clear label to set materials apart from modern life. Folklorists displayed tales, rituals, and artifacts equally as material specimens, which were meant to be classified in the natural history of civilization. Tales, originally dynamic and fluid, were given stability and concreteness by means of the printed page. Although at once local and individual, the tales came to "belong" to a country or to the specialized collections of Jacob and Wilhelm Grimm (Germany), Charles Perrault (France), and Aleksandr Afanasyev (Russia). Beyond tales, folk became attached to other present-day cultural labels. The American Otis T. Mason, for example, stated in "The Natural History of Folklore" (1891): "Without doubt, there is also a folk-speech, folk-trades and practices, folk fine art, folk-amusement, folk-festival, folk-ceremonies, folk-customs, folk-government, folk-society, folk-history, folk-poetry, folk-maxims, folk-philosophy, folk-science, and myths or folk-theology. Everything that we have, they have,—they are the back numbers of us."[16]

William John Thoms (1803–85) in his study (from *The Academy*, 11 November 1899).

To illuminate some of the social meanings of this rhetoric, let me trace the use of this yeasty term and its most popular attachment to lore and life, especially as it related to the United States. The use of *folklore* to signify traditions and their study dates back to 1846, when the Britisher William John Thoms (1803–85) proposed a "good Saxon compound" for what had previously been referred to in English as popular antiquities and literature. In a letter to *Athenaeum,* a leading weekly review of literature, science, and the arts, Thoms described folklore both as a connected whole—"the Lore of the People"—and as separable parts—"manners, customs, observances, superstitions, ballads, proverbs." He wanted to accomplish for the British what the brothers Grimm had done for Germany, and he claimed: "The present century has scarcely produced a more remarkable book, imperfect as its learned author confesses it to be, than the second edition of the *'Deutsche Mythologie:'* and, what is it?—a mass of minute facts, many of which, when separately considered, appear trifling and insignificant,—but, when taken in connection with the system into which his master-mind has woven them, assume a value that he who first recorded them never dream of attributing to them."[17] In the next issue of the weekly magazine, a department of folklore was established, with Thoms in charge. During the 1850s, books began to appear using folklore in their titles: Thomas Sternberg's *The Dialect and Folk-Lore of Northamptonshire* (1851), Jabez Allies's *On the Ancient British, Roman and Saxon Antiquities and Folk-Lore of Worcestershire* (1852), and Thoms's *Choice Notes from "Notes and Queries": Folk Lore* (1859). By 1876, Thoms was signing himself An Old Folk-Lorist, giving a name to the student of the subject; the next year, the term was given sanction by the formation in England of the Folk-Lore Society.

The self-consciousness with which folklore came into vogue is evident from a review in 1866 in the popular nineteenth-century British periodical *Littell's Living Age.* Signed "From the Christian Remembrancer," the unusually long review took up twenty-eight pages, thus implicitly underscoring the importance of the subject. The reviewer considered five books, led by William Henderson's *Notes on the Folk Lore of the Northern Counties of England and the Borders* (1866). "Folk Lore is a modern word," the reviewer began, "telling in its very construction of the period of its formation." The writer continued to hurl praise on the sound and content of *folk lore;* the writer found the word appropriate to an expanding, enlightened age. The review continued: "We feel as sure that [folklore] belongs to the stratum of the Teutonic Archaism as we do that 'Popular Superstition' is of the Latin Deposit. Even the former, in comparison with that of its lengthy synonym, is a proof of the different estimation it has attained.

The monosyllables give dignity, the polysyllables cast a slur. *Folk,* as connected with the great conquering Volken, are ancient and honourable; but *popular,* and *vulgar,* albeit from the same root, have both deteriorated in significance in their transit through Latin. Lore infers something to be *learnt* and sought out; superstition is the excess of belief, and implies that it ought to be discarded and forgotten." Emphasizing the value of using the word *folklore* to encourage collecting by the "educated classes," the writer declared: "In effect the beliefs and customs that fell under the stigma of superstition were driven to such remote corners under that opprobrious title, that now they have become *lore,* and scholars and philologists perceive their value, contempt for them has become so current that their repositories among the peasantry are ashamed of them, and it requires no small amount of address to enable an educated person to extract an account of them, more especially since, strange and interesting as they may be to the antiquary, many are far more honoured in the breach than in the observance." Showing a bit of ambivalence toward the obsolescence of this folklore, however, the writer concluded, "Parson, doctor, and schoolmaster, must blame and condemn them in practice, even though the next generation will lose much that is racy and amusing."[18]

The distinctive round of life belonging to the peasants found special attention on the European continent. The emphasis on *life* implied a concern for traditions of subsistence (*lore* emphasized traditions of imagination) and the isolation of traditional cultures. Nonetheless, overlaps existed between studies of lore and life. The use of the Swedish word *folkliv* (folklife) can be traced to 1847, when it appeared in a Swedish book, *Folklivet i Skytts harad,* or *The Folklife of the Jurisdictional District of Skytt.* The German equivalents of *folklife* were *Volksleben* and *Volkskunde,* which regularly appeared after 1806. The prefix *Volk* as a term to describe tradition had been in print thirty years earlier.[19] It is likely that Thoms's term was derived from the German usage. Indeed, practitioners of folklife and folklore equally invoked ethnology—studies of preindustrial cultures—although their studies stressed ethnic societies within industrialized culture. Early on, however, German usage stressed the overarching "culture" of the folk, while English usage stressed the surviving materials of the folk. The British *Handbook of Folklore* (1914) explained, for example, that folklore "has established itself as the generic term under which the traditional Beliefs, Customs, Stories, Songs, and Sayings current among backward peoples, or retained by the uncultured classes of more advanced peoples, are comprehended and included." George Laurence Gomme (1853–1916), in *Ethnology in Folklore* (1892), underscored the point he had made in an earlier version of the handbook:

"The essential characteristic of folklore is that it *consists* of beliefs, customs, and traditions which are far behind civilisation in their intrinsic value to man, though they exist under the cover of a civilised nationality" (emphasis added).[20]

American writers on beliefs, customs, and traditions tended to be most influenced by the English view of folklore, although a strong nod to the German notion of *Volkskunde* was prevalent in Pennsylvania, as a result of the interest in German scholarship spurred by the area's German heritage. Folklore studies in America were not all imported, however. An American Indian agent by the name of Henry Rowe Schoolcraft (1793–1864) stirred scholarly excitement for Native American lore in 1839 with the publication of *Algic Researches*. In 1842 he helped to establish the American Ethnological Society. In 1846 he made a proposal to the newly organized Smithsonian Institution for "the investigation of American ethnology." He argued that the object of studying American Indians from the standpoint of ethnology and folklore was "to discover and fix the comprehensive points of their national resemblance, and the concurring circumstances of their history and traditions; to point out the affinities of their languages, and to unveil the principles of their mythology." Special recognition to American folklore and historical research came in 1851 at the 169th anniversary of William Penn's landing at Chester, Pennsylvania. Schoolcraft was honored for his work among the Indians; for his work among the European settlers in America, John Fanning Watson, the other great figure of pre-Civil-War-era collecting was also honored.

Schoolcraft was a harbinger of the special attention of post-Civil-War anthropological folklorists to language and mythology. The subject attracted professionals such as lawyer Horatio E. Hale (1817–96) of New Hampshire and physician Daniel Garrison Brinton (1837–99) of Pennsylvania. From before the Civil War through the end of the century, these two men published between them scores of books on folklore and ethnology. Admitting in 1895 that anthropology had been perceived as a pursuit "suited to persons of elegant leisure and retired old gentlemen," Brinton pushed for professionalism in anthropological studies, which, he announced, took in folklore.[21] He made a proposal for a department of anthropology at the University of Pennsylvania, and in 1886 he became its first professor of anthropology. He helped to establish the Department of Ethnology in the University Museum and brought in merchant Stewart Culin and industrialist Henry Mercer, whom he encouraged to become full-time ethnologists with specialties in folklore. Mercer wrote on the folklore of Bucks County, Pennsylvania, and began a collection of Pennsylvania-German art and tools. Culin responded by creating a "folklore museum" at the university, by founding a Philadelphia chapter of the American Folklore Society, and, together with Brinton, by hosting the first meeting of the American Folklore Society in 1889. In the following year, Brinton was elected president of that organization; Hale followed as president in 1893; Culin, in 1897.

The first president of the American Folklore Society, organized in 1888, was a Harvard professor, Francis James Child (1825–96), who gained renown with the publication of *The English and Scottish Popular Ballads* (5 vols., 1888–98). Child provided distinction, as well as a following of others who were interested in European folklore and balladry, such as George Lyman Kittredge (1860–1941) and John Fiske (1842–1901). Although their interests were literary, the anthropological connection was still evident. They debated the origin of primitive ballads and folk songs and the survival of them into the present day. Still, the ballad scholars often considered their material and study to be separate from folklore. The literary critic Francis Barton Gummere (1855–1919) reported that ethnology provided evidence for a communal origin of balladry, but he took ethnologists to task, particularly William Wells Newell, who proposed that an individual author was originally responsible for most ballads. Writing in *Modern Philology* in 1903, Gummere declared: "To tell a man, or mankind itself, about huge strides of progress, is to flatter and please; to use this progress for inference about beginnings is altogether odious." After Francis James Child, another folk-song scholar was not elected president for two decades. In 1898, Henry Edward Krehbiel (1854–1923), who had strong connections with the Cambridge group, moved for the creation of an independent American Folk-Song Society. In response, Newell created a separate Musical Section within the American Folklore Society, which appeased the group.[22]

The core of folklore research during the late 1880s was reported by a lawyer-turned-professor, T. F. Crane (1844–1927), in the *Nation* for 1890. He reviewed seven books, covering tales, customs, artifacts, and games. As the author of *Italian Popular Tales* (1883), however, he showed some self-interest in promoting his turf. "It is quite natural," he offered, "that at first greater interest should be taken in one particular class of folk-lore—popular tales—for they appeal to both the learned and the unlearned, and may be equally enjoyed by those who see in them sun-myths or survivals of savagery, and by those who find in them only an interesting phase of human fancy." Separating public response from professional activity, Crane announced that "the interest in folk-lore seems to be steadily increasing in this country, if we may take as a proof of it the large number of works on the subject which have recently been published here, and the substantial support rendered to the American Folk-Lore Society."[23]

The organizer of the American Folklore Society, former schoolmaster and minister William Wells Newell (1839–1907), of Cambridge, Massachusetts, acknowledged that the Folk-Lore Society of England provided the model for the American society, but he eagerly pointed to the significant publications of Continental European organizations for further inspiration. He noted the special contributions of American scholars to the collection of, first, old English folklore—ballads, for example. Second, he mentioned the folklore of southern blacks; third, American Indian myths and tales; and fourth, the folklore of French Canada and Spanish Mexico. With his allegiance to "anthropological ends," Newell cited the purpose of the society "for the collection of the fast-vanishing remains of Folk-Lore in America" and "for the study of the general subject, and publication of the results of special students in this department." But he stopped short of proposing an independent discipline of folklore. "American students," he claimed in 1892, "will prefer to confine the name to a body of material, and to consider the comparative examination of this material as a part of anthropological science."[24]

Without university support for "anthropological ends," many anthropologists came to the American Folklore Society and similar "learned" organizations for professional sanction. They came from museums, governmental agencies, and professions. To be sure, a line of professional folklore interest already existed among philologists, medieval and classical scholars, and scholars of literature and languages. They tended to have places in the university—Child and Kittredge at Harvard, Gummere at Haverford, and Crane at Cornell—and maintained their professionalism in the exclusiveness of the nineteenth-century university rather than in the learned society. Another group outside of the learned society comprised popular writers who used folklore, such as Mark Twain, Joel Chandler Harris, Lafcadio Hearn, and Edward Eggleston. Tapping folkloric sources to satisfy the public thirst in America for medieval and oriental fantasies and native vernacular humor, they joined the American Folklore Society but were alienated from it because of their "unscientific" bent. Anthropologist Otis T. Mason called them "camp-followers" and urged the society, in his presidential address of 1891, to "part company" with them "at an early day." Literary interest in folklore ran high, but as a result of the American Folklore Society's original "scientific," professional orientation outside of academia and popular literature, the anthropological current gained strength. The anthropological emphasis that the American Folklore Society appeared to take was due largely to an emergent cultivation of professionalism.

Some dispute over folklore's dependence on scientific anthropology and over its exclusive cultural (rather than literary) connection came from a retired naval officer, Fletcher S. Bassett (1847–93) of Chicago, who in 1891 formed a rival organization to the American Folklore Society, the Chicago Folklore Society, which had its own local branches around the country. Apparently questioning Newell, Bassett wrote in 1893, "What, then, shall be said to those zealous scholars who claim that Folk-Lore is but a part of some other science—as only a proper dependency of some other kingdom of thought?" Bassett answered: "But if Folk-Lore, in its extent, embraces the matter of the sciences, by the quality and the degree of knowledge which it expresses, it differs from them all. One of the greatest authorities has said in advocating a Folk-Lore section of the British Association: 'I think the time has come for this. Anthropology has long since been recognized there; Folk-lore should also, now be recognized, and independently.'" To emphasize the new profession, he named the society's journal the *Folk-Lorist* (Newell preferred the title *Folklore Scholar,* which stressed the subject rather than the profession). The journal announced that the society was devoted to "collecting, preserving, studying and publishing traditional literature, especially, that of this country, west of the Alleghenies." The journal's editors treated the lore more as the product of literary art than as ethnological cultural evidence, and they extended the range of groups which held that lore: "Among the Indians, on plantation and cattle-range, in the factory and on the farm, in the crowded city and in the little village, among miners and sailors, professional men of attainments and uneducated laborers, in busy avocations of men and in the household life of women, among children and gray-hairs—everywhere, folklore is abundant, for it is the lore of the people, not of any class, and is to be sought everywhere."[25] In 1893, Bassett's society was briefly in the limelight as host of the Third International Folklore Congress at the World's Columbian Exposition in Chicago, but the society quickly faded from view after Bassett's death in 1893.

The formation of the folklore societies was part of a larger trend. During the 1870s and 1880s, over two hundred learned societies were formed. The rising middle-class professional sought distinction through membership in a "learned" society, especially those of a "scientific" nature. The subjects of the societies typically were not part of the classical university curriculum.[26] Folklore as a subject and an organization was not atypical in fitting this description. After its founding, the American Folklore Society had local branches which held meetings. The rationale for having branches was certainly because of the difficulty of traveling to a national meeting and because of the desire to build on local support, but branches also had the advantage of promoting a club atmosphere, familiar to the middle-class professionals who were apt to take part. They would typically gather monthly at a member's home and hear papers delivered, see objects displayed, or even witness performances. Indeed, the movement toward national professional associations grew out of earlier clubs. Most of the members of the Philadelphia Branch of the American Folklore Society had previously belonged to the Numismatic and Antiquarian Society of Philadelphia, and many of the same names appeared on the list of the University (of Pennsylvania) Archaeological Association, the Contemporary Club, and the Oriental Club of Philadelphia, all of which featured lectures and exhibits.

An episode that underscored the appeal to professionals of the "learned" associations was the Congress of American Scientists, held in Philadelphia in December 1895. This congress brought together the meetings of seven scientific associations, including the American Folklore Society, the Society of American Anatomists, the American Society of Naturalists, and the American Psychological Association, although most members held positions outside of the specialty. Newspapers gave front-page coverage to the proceedings and carried descriptions of the papers of prominent personalities such as Daniel Brinton, Franz Boas, and Heli Chatelain. Coverage of the first two days gave top billing to papers of the folklore society. On the last day, the *Philadelphia Inquirer* ran a four-column illustration of "A Group of Active Members of the Folk-Lore Society" below an article that editorialized: "The session of the Congress of American Scientists, which has been discussing important topics at the University of Pennsylvania closed yesterday. By far the most interesting feature of the day was a paper read by Dr. Daniel G. Brinton, before the Folk-Lore Society, entitled 'American Cuss Words.' After the weighty subjects previously discussed, Dr. Brinton's paper came with refreshing force to the tired minds of his listeners."[27]

The American Folklore Society was founded in the same period as the Modern Language Association (1883), the American Historical Association (1884), the American Economic Association (1885), the American Mathematical Society (1888), the American Physical Society (1889), and the American Dialect Society (1889). In keeping with the attitude toward learning then, the societies promoted devotion to, rather than the practice of, an esoteric, systematic body of knowledge. They called for an exclusive and independent circle of authorities, as a congress of "scientists," loosely defined, suggested. Nearly every group placed "American" in its title, and most used it as the first word. Placing American first emphasized the national scope of its membership but left coverage open to the world's topics. The choice and placement of words marked the societies in the United States as growing forces to be reckoned with. Their declaration of private national management, growing from a local club system, marked them as professional middle-class organizations.

To borrow from Erich Marcks's 1903 commentary, the organizations received impetus from "the free complement of rivalries." Commonly, members propagated polarities such as scientific/unscientific, anthropological/literary, and evolution/diffusion to create burning issues. Such polar rhetoric gave shape to a head-to-head competition in scholarship, which seemed to follow from the principles of evolutionary doctrine. The desired outcome was the dominance of one pole over the other; one direction was chosen. As professionals, they called for position taking on scholarly issues within the learned society, which related to the politics of the greater society. Such position taking polarized the learned society into factions and forces; it extended the naturalistic metaphor into scholarship; and it offered the learned society an intensity and exclusiveness to rival the university, as well as the body politic.

The career of Otis Mason (1838–1908) illustrates several concerns of the new professionals. Born in Maine and reared in Virginia, he went to Columbian College (now the George Washington University) in Washington, D.C., receiving, in the tradition of college education at the time, a general knowledge of biblical and classical studies, literature, and philosophy. After graduating in 1861, he stayed on to teach natural history, classics, history, English, mathematics, and geography. During the 1870s he championed the "general principles of Natural Science" at the school. By 1880 he was instructor of English and history; when he left in 1884 for the United States National Museum of the Smithsonian Institution, he was listed as a professor of anthropology. At the museum he took up the enormous task of sorting its cultural collections. Claiming fields of folklore and ethnology, Mason used the objects in the collections to establish a cultural history based on the evolutionary principles of natural science. As cultural history, Mason's studies were intimately connected to issues of the day, which were being hotly discussed in the nation's capital. Students of primitive and folk culture were naturally involved with such issues, he observed, because they participated in the search for the hidden "secrets of man's origin, progress, and destiny." In 1894 he published *Primitive Travel and Transportation,* a 350-page combination of a detailed catalogue of objects in the museum's collection and of the reconstruction of the development of modern transportation industries from "primitive" cultures, mostly American Indian. The study signaled his interest in the roots of industrialization; he argued that increased mobility, both physical and social, in a modernizing nation requires the charting of traditional, passing ways of life, which is best captured in the stable, classifiable item.

The theme of mobility underlay Mason's next work, *Woman's Share in Primitive Culture,* also published in 1894. The moving, socially aspiring "new woman" had by this time raised pressing political and cultural questions. What effect would changes in her traditional roles have on the family and society? Would she be industrious or leisurely, scientific or sentimental? Mason was led to write: "Of the billion and a half human beings on the earth, one half, or about seven hundred million are females. What this vast multitude are doing in the world's activities and what share their mothers and grandmothers, to the remotest generation backward, have had in originating and developing culture, is a question which concerns the whole race."[28] Mason followed in the next year with *The Origins of Invention.* Questions of women and industrialism were related, because women's roles in a nation of "mechanicalized" men became a topic of public debate, as did the "feminizing" consequences of genteel middle-class society on work and play. In educated Victorian America, folklore studies were part of a trend of meeting problems in the safety of the distant past or in removed place, rather than in the anxiety-ridden present. Victorians turned to what they valued (accumulable things and exclusive knowledge) in rising institutions which cherished the things and knowledge (museums and colleges) within rising social worlds which fostered their interests (professional societies).

From the earlier study of "popular antiquities," the study of "folk lore" had taken in two rhetorical changes that were important to the later Victorians. Dropping "antiquities" pointed out that lore was not always in relic form, but could still be found in the lives of people. Shifting from *popular* to *folk* changed the emphasis from the whole of a people to groups within industrialized society. Lee J. Vance, writing in 1887, noted that "there are few localities in the United States that do not have *some* peculiar item of superstition, or legendary lore. All these items of low civilization in the midst of our so-called 'high' civilization should be industriously gathered and preserved" (emphasis in original). He invited the reader to be a "folk-lorist," who could find that "the popular traditions or legends of Indians, Negroes, and Canadians alone form rich stores for the student of American Folk-Lore."[29]

The replacement of *popular* with *folk* showed that what were envisioned as "lower" and "backward" portions of the society were no longer thought of as prevailing either numerically or socially. Whereas the search for popular antiquities was thought of as an upper-class hobby, folklore study became a pursuit of middle-class professionals. Stressing their constant state of modernity and invoking the fear of slipping down the social scale, the new professionals, such as Otis Mason, stated that "the folk" are "old-fashioned people" and "all of us when we are old-fashioned."[30] Mason made the bourgeois case for folklore explicit in "The Natural History of Folklore," where he wrote: "Folk-lore is kept alive by public opinion, and is opposed to progress; invention and science are centrifugal, venturesome, individual. This ability to act in common has itself had a historical growth, beginning with such savage acts as beating time to a rude dance, and rising to a grand chorus, a great battle, or a modern industrial establishment employing thousands of men marking time to one master spirit."[31]

Mason's comment came two years after Mark Twain (1835–1910), another member of the American Folklore Society, published his elaboration on that theme in *A Connecticut Yankee at King Arthur's Court* (1889). In Twain, one can read a structure based on polarities between the nineteenth and the sixth centuries, between science and sentiment. Invoking evolutionary doctrine, Twain's preface announces that the customs touched on in "the tale" were "survivals" found at a later time, which can be assumed to have been practiced, befitting anthropological theory, during the sixth century. But Twain concludes, "One is quite justified in inferring that wherever one of these laws and customs was lacking in that remote time, its place was competently filled by a worse one." Practical and free of "sentiment," the central character, Hank Morgan, is the bourgeois Yankee, the chief superintendent in a Connecticut arms factory. One of Morgan's workers, who carries the mythical name Hercules, knocks Morgan unconscious in a factory squabble. Morgan wakes up in medieval England, but rather than becoming despondent over his fate, he decides to take advantage of the situation. Helping him is his antiquarian's knowledge of King Arthur's day. Remembering that the date of a medieval eclipse was imminent, he threatens the superstitious British with removing the sun if they do not give in to his demands. King Arthur's subjects become alarmed when the moon moves in front of the sun; after they give in to Morgan, the sun reappears from behind the moon. The result is that Morgan is given the title of Sir Boss and control of the British economy. He embarks on a campaign for industrial development, on the one hand, and for the destruction of traditional life on the other. At different times he calls King Arthur's

subjects "white Indians," "modified savages," "pigmies," "big children," and "great simple-hearted creatures." His plan to have a
modern industrial establishment mark time to a master spirit comes
finally head to head with the forces of tradition in a great nihilistic
battle. Morgan is knocked unconscious again, this time by the legendary figure Merlin, and when he awakens back in the nineteenth
century, he romantically yearns for his medieval bride. He smiles, "not
a modern smile, but one that must have gone out of general use many,
many centuries ago." As Morgan slips toward death, he mutters, "I
seemed to be a creature out of a remote unborn age, centuries hence,
and even *that* was as real as the rest!" With its finale of destruction, as
modernity confronts tradition in evolutionary fashion, it is no wonder
that the British literary critic and folklorist Andrew Lang (1844–1912)
preferred the relatively tame incorporation of folklore in *Huckleberry
Finn* to that in *A Connecticut Yankee,* despite Twain's appeal to Lang
not to judge the book according to the usual standards of the "cultured
classes." "Help me, Mr. Lang," Twain begged, "no voice can reach
further than yours in a case of this kind, or carry greater weight of
authority."[32]

Although members of the American Folklore Society celebrated
the rising "authority" of the modern middle-class professionals in the
late nineteenth century, they shared with middle-class Victorians
mixed feelings toward the cultural changes that they were helping to
propagate through their work. In their leisure, Victorians consumed
great numbers of books about medieval romances, fairy tales, magic
and superstition, and primitive handicrafts. Addressing the American
Folklore Society in 1891, then-president Otis Mason announced: "In
the last decade of the nineteenth century, when the world was looking
forward, it was a relief to vary this mental attitude by occasionally
glancing backward, and considering the past as it appeared by its
survival in the present."[33]

Three years earlier, Edward Bellamy had scored a success by
glancing backward from the vantage of a utopian technological
republic of the year 2000. Like Twain, Bellamy relied on dreams to
couch the confrontations between old and new versions of society.
More than that, old and new were vessels for feelings about the
longstanding reality of the traditional past and about the unreality of
the present, which was whirring toward the future. Like Twain,
Bellamy began with a preface that proposed to contrast centuries, in
Bellamy's case the nineteenth and twentieth. In the nineteenth the
protagonist is unable to sleep and therefore retreats to the isolation of
his subterranean chamber, disturbed by the unrest of resistant workers
whose strikes have delayed the progressive construction of his house

and the consummation of his marriage. Bellamy's novel reveals the idea of progress in its heightened form; his futuristic utopia was one relief from bourgeois ambivalence, although the view of militarism and regimentation of his future struck many as being unattractive. *Looking Backward* worked on the pleasing prospect that the past is set as if in a dream. The present is the location of reality, whereas the past and its workers always appear primitive. The past is thus interpreted in terms of the technological future.

Such a view of the past and the present helps to explain the "relief" that late Victorians obtained by looking backward into folklore. The *Nation* in 1905 found that a question posed by Andrew Lang resounded a common chord: "Why, as science becomes more cocksure, have men and women become more and more fond of old follies, and more pleased with the stirring of ancient dread within their veins?" Lang's answer was: "The exact sciences give us all headaches." He explained that "as the visible world is measured, mapped, tested, weighed, we seem to hope more and more that a world of invisible romance may not be far from us, or, at least, we came more and more to follow fancy into those airy regions, *et inania regna*."[34] Lang's answer was echoed far and wide in the popular press. In 1891, in the *Westminster Review,* William Schooling wrote on "Fairy Tales and Science." He opened by declaring: "For most of us there is a charm about the past that the present is unable to inspire; for most of us there is an attractiveness about fairy tales that some of us, at any rate, fail to find in science; the old-world myths and legends come to us across the ages with somewhat of the freshness of those early days, while science seems to many alike the cause and type of the dry prosaic temper of to-day."[35] Schooling's goal was to combine the romance of folklore with the banality of science. He proposed that folklore was the science of another age. Folklore differed in its level of organization and precision of measurement, but it provided the past with spiritual explanations. In that past age, folklore was the stuff of dreams—spirits, magic, and imagination. That stuff seemed to be absent from the cold, hard present. Folklore, with its reach for explanation and its grasp of imagination, could now fill the present with inspiration.

Studies of folklore brought out of the hidden past a relationship to the suppressed mental worries of the mechanical present. Bryan Hooker, an author of medieval romances, observed, for example: "The present day is exhibiting a curiously vivid interest in fairy tales; curious because that passionate self-consciousness which is always with us finds the foreground of its mirror filled with machinery, busy under a canopy of smoke; and it seems strange to discover the livid vapor shadowing forth the wings of dragons, or the faces of the little people glimmering between the wheels. Perhaps our very materialism is responsible for this new hunger after fantasy. Because the world, never so bluntly actual as now, is too much with us, we spend our vacations upon the foam of perilous seas." Reviewing Jeremiah Curtin's *Myths and Folklore of Ireland* for *Atlantic Monthly* in 1890, John Fiske, a staunch supporter of Spencer, ambivalently stated, "it is well that this work has been carried so far in our time, for modern habits of thought are fast exterminating the old world fancies." An editorial in the middle-class *Scribner's Magazine* (which advertised in the *Journal of American Folklore*) expanded on the theme in 1909. It told readers that "archaic man" was a "mere bundle of susceptibilities," dominated by "fear, passion, and the sense of mystery," whose sensitivity and world view were revealed through his folklore. Faced with cosmic events, primitive man was in a constant state of awareness, directly in touch with his world both spiritually and materially. To explore the folk mind of these ancestors of the "moderns," the editorial concluded, is to delve into "our own subconscious life."[36]

Folklore may have underscored the progress of the middle-class moderns above "primitive" life, but it also raised questions of lost fantasy, indeed, lost spirituality and intimacy with modern surroundings. The idea of progress was both mental and physical in the Victorian view. It was tied to spreading ideas on evolution, owing much of its popularity to Charles Darwin's *The Origin of Species* in 1859. In 1871, Darwin made the connection even more explicit in *The Descent of Man*. Referring to the anthropological adaptations during the 1860s of his work by Edward Tylor, John Lubbock, and John McLennan, Darwin weighed the arguments about whether man, as they claimed, rose culturally as well as naturally. Darwin commented: "To believe that man was aboriginally civilized and then suffered utter degradation in so many regions is to take a pitiably low view of human nature. It is apparently a truer and more cheerful view that progress has been much more general than retrogression; that man has risen, though by slow and interrupted steps, from a lowly condition to the highest standard as yet attained by him in knowledge, morals and religion." At the conclusion of the book, he endorsed the view of progress that was common to his age: "Man may be excused for feeling some pride at having risen, though not through his own exertions, to the very summit of the organic scale; and the fact of his having thus risen, instead of having been aboriginally placed there, may give him hope for a still higher destiny in the distant future."[37]

Darwin sided with the cheerier and more timely view. I say timely, because of the rapid industrialization and imperialism that claimed the

march of evolutionary progress as its justification. Welcoming participants to the Third International Folklore Congress, the president of
the Chicago Folklore Society, William Knapp, exclaimed: "We are
transforming, almost transformed. . . . Quaint faces, strange cos-
tumes, unintelligible tongues, have blended with the dominant civilizations of Western Europe and the New World beyond, while
venerable races have made obeisance to the material prosperity of
younger and novel institutions." In 1871, Tylor himself emphasized
that "not merely as a matter of curious research, but as an important
practical guide to the understanding of the present and the shaping of
the future, the investigation into the origin and early development of
civilization must be pushed on zealously."[38]

Tylor's "ethnography," describing a "natural history of civilization," greatly influenced ethnologists at the time with its definition of
culture—"Culture or Civilization, taken in its wide ethnographic sense,
is that complex whole which includes knowledge, belief, art, morals,
law, custom, and any other capabilities and habits acquired by man as
a member of society." Tylor's definition combined the whole and its
parts, and his comparison of sayings, tales, beliefs, artifacts, games,
and myths in different societies pointed to the great value of folklore
as cultural specimens. Although his ideas apparently derived from
Darwin, Tylor denied the debt. They seemed to owe more to a general
movement, since the late eighteenth century, toward a developmental
explanation of nature, and consequently progress, in the natural
sciences, a current that imbued laissez-faire economics of the period
as well as cultural studies. Thus Tylor, on the first page of *Primitive
Culture* (1871), stated his concern for "stages of development or
evolution," rather than for mechanisms that had been suggested
specifically by Darwin. Indeed, as historian of anthropology George W.
Stocking points out, "In a consideration of Tylor's alleged 'cultural
Darwinism,' the pertinent point is simply that Tylor's primary methodological tool depended, not on the 'survival of the fittest,' but on the
survival of the *un*fit—'processes, customs, opinions, and so forth,
which have been carried on by force of habit into a new state of society
different from that in which they had their original home.' "[39] Thus
Tylor introduced his doctrine of "survival in culture," which became a
basic idiom in late-nineteenth-century writing on folklore. He used it to
justify his claim that his work during the 1860s on *Primitive Culture* was
"arranged on its own lines, coming scarcely into contact of *detail*"
(emphasis added) with the work of Charles Darwin and Herbert
Spencer.[40]

In 1935, T. K. Penniman, although he began his history of
anthropology with 1835, the date of Darwin's visit to the Galapagos

Islands, noted that between 1835 and 1859 "the social scientists, the archaeologists and students of material cultures, and the ethnologists and biologists were all coming into relation with each other, and breaking down the compartments in which their sciences were imprisoned from each other. Further, all were trying to find principles of origin and development."[41] Darwin was an important symbol for evolutionary philosophy and for his age. His book gained renown for the heavy weight of its sifted evidence—a style that was repeated in anthropology studies—its appeal to the general educated public, its extension of man's way past beyond religious estimates, and its suggestion that "natural selection" is the mechanism for evolution. It was a symbol of a changing culture, much as was the naturalistic study of folklore that followed.

The Englishman Herbert Spencer, who made a case for industrial progress and laissez-faire economics on the grounds of Darwin's "survival of the fittest," found especially zealous followers in the United States. By 1903 more than 368,000 volumes of Spencer's works had been sold in the United States. The popular writings of folklore scholars John Fiske and William Graham Sumner applied Spencer liberally in their work. Preacher Henry Ward Beecher wrote Spencer with this observation: "The peculiar condition of American society has made your writings far more fruitful and quickening here than in Europe."[42] Although challenged by Lester Frank Ward and others, Spencer's ideas found a sympathetic audience in late-nineteenth-century United States, where industrialization and its social effects came later, but more quickly, once it did arrive, than in Europe.

Darwin's influence can be seen, too, in constant references during that period to folklore's connection with the anthropological "history and psychology of man." The "psychic unity of man" came to support the natural history of culture. Psychology was developmental and addressed the mental anguish of modern life. Sigmund Freud and his followers after the 1880s used folklore for much of their psychoanalytic evidence in discussing questions of dreams, fairy tales, and jokes. In "The Uncanny" (1919), Freud noted that the ambivalent reactions of moderns to folklore depended on the existence of "something familiar and old-established in the mind which has been estranged only by the process of repression."[43] The distant, hidden past, which is especially evident in primitive life and childhood, is the key to unraveling the present. To folklore-society organizers Newell and Mason, children and primitives were genuine "folk." Alexander Chamberlain (1865–1914), editor of the *Journal of American Folklore,* stressed the connection in *The Child and Childhood in Folk-Thought* (1896).

The psychology of the time used a concept similar to survivals: the traditions of the hidden past for the individual persist into the present as dreamlike impressions given to mythic interpretation. Although in altered form and with a meaning commonly outside of awareness, the impressions are made usable to the person by the therapeutic specialist. In addition, life is described in developmental stages through which a person naturally progresses. Even after the concept of a unified cultural past to the "varieties of man" had waned, the related concept of a personal past continued in folklore studies.

Adding to the interest in the "varieties of man" and their development was the increase in leisure travel by Victorians during the nineteenth century. Taking in a "pleasure trip" of weeks rather than days away from home, Victorians traveled further than people ever had, thanks to advances in transportation and the belief that "getting away from it all," especially to primitive surroundings, was therapy for the nervousness caused by modern life. In America, a trip west could include a visit to a ranch or a pueblo. On one such trip, J. B. Priestley recalled in *Midnight on the Desert* (1937), "Our guides, all smiles and enthusiasm explained how these Indians lived a happy communal life, almost entirely free from crime; and we representatives of the roaring, racketeering world outside stared at the plump mahogany women and children." Lewis Gannett added, in *Sweet Land* (1937): "The East is the new country; the West is old. In the East, history begins with Columbus. . . . In the West, time reaches back indefinitely and continuously." Later, the Amish received this treatment for their record of a past way of life: watching them engage in centuries-old customs, one advertisement read, would "carry worries off your shoulders."[44]

Some travelers began to collect folklore as part of the record of their trips. Most notable are Charles Fletcher Lummis's (1859–1928) accounts of his trek on foot across the United States in 1884. As a youth, Jeremiah Curtin (1835–1906) vowed to "see all countries," and he gained renown for a volume of folklore collected on a trip to Ireland. Others catered to the traveler's interest in native folklore. George Bird Grinnell (1849–1938), for example, published articles on western lore for magazines such as *Outing, Scribner's, Birdlore,* and his own *Forest and Stream* (later *Field and Stream*).[45] Headlines also came to collectors such as Stewart Culin (1858–1929) and Frank Hamilton Cushing (1857–1900) for "expeditions" into territories that had not yet been tamed by Victorians. Like the naturalist explorers, Culin and Cushing brought back cultural specimens for museums, which competed for the volume and antiquity of their holdings. Viewers read their often-sensationalized or sentimentalized accounts for their travel adventures.[46]

Related to the growth of travel attractions were "world's fairs," which began in the 1850s and were tremendously popular through the rest of the nineteenth century. After the 1851 London Crystal Palace Exhibition, which was devoted to industrial advancement, the honorary secretary of the Ethnological Society of London announced: "We may congratulate ourselves on the continued and increased interest which the educated classes of society are taking in ethnological knowledge. . . . Considerable attention was drawn to our science during the last year by the appearance of so many foreigners in London, who came to visit the Great Exhibition. And to witness the many varieties of man, assembled from every region of the earth, in the Crystal Palace, calmly studying the productions of each other, was not the least of the wonders of that fairy-like creation, whose physical existence is not about to pass away from us."[47] Other fairs, even grander, followed: New York in 1853, Paris in 1867, Vienna in 1873, Philadelphia in 1876.

Whether or not one visited the fairs, one often read about them in the metropolitan press or in countless souvenir books. These publications carried glimpses of exotic peoples and their strange customs, often found on the fair's midway. Every fair celebrated human progress, as seen in the advance of industry and science, and underscored that progress by exhibiting works of "primitive" societies. Later, representatives from such societies were brought to the expositions to perform. The "rude" and exotic songs, rituals, and dances created a stir in Victorian society, which was itself preoccupied with rituals and performances. As surviving, living expressions within a modernizing world, "folklore" took on more of a role at the world's fairs. International expositions at Paris in 1889, London in 1891, and Chicago in 1893 hosted world folklore congresses. In addition to showing the "advancement of learning," the London congress featured performances of "An English Mumming Play, Children's Games, Sword Dance, Savage Music, and Folk Songs. . . . It is further proposed to arrange a Loan Exhibition of objects . . . connected with and illustrative of Folk-lore."[48] The 1893 congress in Chicago had Indian villages set up right on the grounds, which regularly featured native performances. A photograph that appeared often in souvenir books showed a Dahomean native wrapped in an American flag in the fashion of his traditional costume.

The photograph was eye-catching, partly because Victorians found that the "many varieties of man" were coming to their homeland to stay and work. Attention to immigrant problems and race relations in America and Britain translated into ethnological studies of ethnic groups in the new land. Stewart Culin, for example, published *China in*

America (1887), which described Chinese immigrant folklore in Philadelphia and New York; and Jeremiah Curtin published "European Folk-Lore in the United States" (1889) in the *Journal of American Folklore.* The Victorians were meanwhile spreading their empire into "savage" lands, and many collections came from colonial officials, who wrote for a public back home that was eager to comprehend the exotic cultures now under their control. The Folk-Lore Society of England prepared *The Handbook of Folklore* (1890, revised in 1914) for public officials, missionaries, travelers, and settlers "whose lot is cast among uncivilized or halfcivilized populations abroad; to residents in country places at home; to medical men, philanthropic workers, and all educated persons whose lives and duties bring them into touch with the uneducated."[49]

Beyond such immediate influences, broader intellectual movements of nineteenth-century romanticism and nationalism encouraged the rise of interest in folklore and folklife. At a time of rising national republics, folklore provided romantic ethnic roots for emergent nations. Folklore could give a common heritage, a far-reaching past, to a splintered country. The brothers Jacob (1785–1863) and Wilhelm (1786–1859) Grimm in Germany and Giuseppe Pitrè (1843–1916) in Italy, for example, devoted collections to the poetic products of a national peasantry. A movement away from monarchism, especially after upheavals in Europe during the 1840s, encouraged an interest in the natural lore of the people, to offset the wide attention to the ostentatious extravagance of the elite.[50] Even in England, which already laid claim to a far-reaching past and appeared to be less influenced by romantic nationalism, another type of romanticism, a communal, ethnic romanticism, entered into the collection of folklore that was associated with rural remains. The place-name legend, the holiday celebration, the ruin—all conveyed a romanticized, "harmonious" Anglo-Saxon past in industrialized England.

From Charles Darwin, Herbert Spencer, and Sigmund Freud, Victorians learned that the past and its natural, primitive conditions were where one produced for oneself, where one expressed spontaneously and openly. It was, it appeared, where one was "really alive." In the past, in nature, in childhood, in folklore was where one revealed a true, deep self. The past was drawn in a single continuous line to the present, with sharp lines drawn between barbarian and civilized, medieval and modern, rural and urban. Unlike the present, the past is hidden and private. In private, one could engage in ritual and custom, utter old tales, and make things, out of the view of polite adults or the scope of conventionalized manner books. The past and private, the natural and exotic, are what came to be "folk" to the Victorians.

This view of folk is related to a Victorian concept of the body's being divided between private and public parts. In the rapidly growing Victorian cities, where residents faced more strangers than in the towns, material display became a way to communicate social status. Walking in this world of strangers, one moved in silence. Where was the oral tradition? Where was the connection to a community? In fashion, the body became a mannequin to dress and display. Shoes and corsets restricted movement, but layers of clothes moved the self outward. The overall surface appearance and decorative details were matters of importance, signals of one's class and decorum. One's approach was made more predictable by clear visual and oral signs. If fashion took on a greater public, ritualistic significance, then the layers that were out of view took on a private importance. The "privates" were where primitive impulses lay. Silk petticoats, other elaborate undergarments, and wearing jewelry, such as rings pierced through nipples, created a private tactile, sexual layer. Men's fashion especially stressed outward visual detail in accessories, such as the monocle, the walking stick, the pin, while swaddling the man in clothing.[51] In contrast, as the Victorians noted in their expositions, the primitive was scantily clad.

The apparent relevance of folklore to middle-class concerns over industry, mobility, display, women, and science helped to advance the folklore-studies movement at its Victorian height during the 1890s. In exposition, book, and magazine, the movement came to public attention as the eminent domain of folklorists, scholars of language and literature, and ethnologists.

Look more closely with me at the public roles of these professionals in discussions of industrialism and feminism. These two themes ran strongly in discussions of the era's tensions and consequently found their way into folklore studies. In George Miller Beard's widely circulated book *American Nervousness* (1881), for example, he invoked the traditional past to understand the present, for "the modern differ from the ancient civilizations mainly in these five elements—steam power, the periodical press, the telegraph, the sciences, and the mental activity of women. When civilization, plus these five factors, invades any nation, it must carry nervousness and nervous diseases along with it."[52] Claiming an expertise of the activities of ancient society and their changes in modern civilization, American folklorists provided briefs for a nation that was charged with nervous change.

The folklorists' labeling of primitive and folk activities commonly stressed modernist terms such as *industry* and *invention*. Besides Mason, who used the terms widely, Alexander Chamberlain wrote on

"Mythology and Folklore of Invention" for the *Journal of American Folklore* (1904); and Thomas Wilson published "Primitive Industry" for the *Smithsonian Institution Annual* (1893). They helped to fashion a distinctive social rhetoric. By connecting manual labor to "primitive industry," no conflict was implied. The development from handicrafts to industry seemed natural. The progressive present set the standard for the primitive past. The lack of conflict is noteworthy, since America during the 1890s was plagued by strikes from hand trades, which were protesting the "unnatural" industrialization of their work. A depression in 1893 brought criticisms that industries had over-produced and speculated. In that same year the anthropological building at the Chicago World's Fair held exhibits on labor-saving devices.

With museum exhibits emphasizing the preservation and display of valuable things of the past, often in arrangements that drew comparisons to the allure of department-store displays, many folklorists and ethnologists were able to find sympathetic and influential homes in museums—many dealing with natural history—for their work. The Museum of Natural History opened in 1869; the United States National Museum, in 1879; the University of Pennsylvania Museum, in 1887; and the Brooklyn Institute Museum and the Field Museum, in 1893. Each of these added ethnological sections to their collections. Often in their missions was a statement about aid to industry. Opening the Metropolitan Museum of Art, for example, Joseph C. Choate said in 1880 that the museum should "show . . . industry . . . what the past has accomplished for them to imitate and excel."[53]

From their museums, folklorists actively wrote and exhibited on divisions of culture: the past and the present, industry and craft, men and women. Between 1890 and 1903, ten presidents of the American Folklore Society, when they took office, held professional affiliations with ethnological museums. Joining Otis Mason, the president in 1891, at the Smithsonian Institution was Frank Hamilton Cushing, who wrote on Native-American folk crafts, tales, and "primitive motherhood." Cushing also did work for the University of Pennsylvania Museum, the home base of two more presidents of the American Folklore Society, Daniel Brinton and Stewart Culin. Culin regularly wrote in the "For Woman's Entertainment" section of the *Philadelphia Record* and contributed to the *Woman's Home Companion* and, later, to *Women's Wear Magazine,* with articles on folk toys and games, religion, tales, and decoration. "All the world," Culin satirically wrote, "is divided between virilists and feminists and the virilists are no more confined to men than the feminists to women. My theory affords a key to many mysteries. Virilists should marry virilists and feminists, feminists. I know of no better rule for compatability in married life. There is no more amusing game than picking people out and arranging them properly."[54] Indeed, picking people and objects and then arranging them properly, usually in an evolutionary scheme, are exactly what this connected group of men did.

Folklore studies helped to answer how civilization had progressed, measured in middle-class material and technical terms. It helped to answer how "mechanicalized" modern man came to be. One popular theory claimed that the control of arts and industries had switched from women to men. Whereas women manufactured the shelters, clothes, containers, and foods for domestic and community use, large-scale industries under the control of men had taken over these roles. Originally, society was matriarchal but had shifted over time to being patriarchal. Men were hunters and fighters; women were makers and providers. Mason stated: "In contact with the animal world, and ever taking lessons from them, men watched the tiger, the bear, the fox, the falcon—learned their language and imitated them in ceremonial dances. But women were instructed by the spiders, the nest builders, the storers of food and the workers in clay like the mud wasp and the termites." Reacting to Herbert Spencer's division of the history of civilization into, first, an age of militancy and, later, one of industrialism, Mason asked whether, "instead of an *age*, we should not rather say a *sex* of militancy and a *sex* of industrialism." If Victorian women now appeared to be idle and more concerned with leisure, it was no wonder, Mason thought, since they had earned that right from their taxing early industrial efforts. Nonetheless, "at the very beginning of human time she [woman] laid down the lines of her duties, and she has kept to them unremittingly."[55] In 1911, Anna Spencer followed Mason with an argument for women's adaptability to industrial work because women first "attained the discipline of a 'steady job.' The biologic hints of the busy bee, the industrious beaver, the ant, to whose example the human sluggard was long ago commended, all seem to have been taken lightly by the primitive man." She argued that women had the real character of labor, as the term came to be understood for the transforming industrial 1890s. To Anna Spencer, women embodied the character of modernity.[56]

Mason's ideas had precedents in Darwin's *The Descent of Man,* which posited the power of "sexual selection." As human beings developed, sexual differences increased, and heightened selection on the basis of beauty, rank, and possession occurred. The male became increasingly aggressive, while the female became increasingly domesticated. In 1861, J. J. Bachofen contributed another popular idea in

Das Mutterecht (The mother-right). On the basis of mythology and archaeological records, he asserted that the first period of human history was matriarchal. Although this notion was rejected in the twentieth century, it had wide-ranging uses for a society in the 1890s, which was concerned with the feminization of middle-class culture. In 1891, Elizabeth Cady Stanton used the theme in her speech "The Matriarchate, or Mother-Age" to the National Council of Women. Quoting Bachofen and Lewis Henry Morgan, she predicted a repetition of history, a return of female supremacy, or at least political equality. Susan B. Anthony followed by using Stanton's ethnological argument in support of woman suffrage.[57]

Suffrage played a lesser role in the "women's question," however, than did the suitability of women for a rising industrial order. Industrialism suggested that women could join the labor force in increasing numbers, but middle-class moralists usually called instead for the professionalism of women's "industry" in the home. If men had control of labor, women should control behavior. In the late nineteenth century, women had taken the lead in shaping the manners and recreations of middle-class life in this order—a life governed by rules of genteel tastes, feminine decency, and sentimental values, as dictated by manner books. The folklore collections that were compiled by members of this class consistently sported the word *manners* in their titles to describe cultures of "ruder ages" and "primitive peoples," many of which were right in their midst.[58] These collections, as well as the manner books to which they owed influence, separated the roles being played by the civilized and the uncivilized, men and women, and boys and girls.

Ambiguity remained, however, in the role of work for the sexes and for the age. For all the moralist literature about women's attachment to nature and home, women in larger numbers went out to work around the turn of the century. In 1901, *Cosmopolitan* reported that the modern woman suffered from "restlessness," "usefulness run riot." The section "Topics of the Time" in *Century* magazine asked in 1900, "Are we to see the complete passing away of women of leisure?" After all, the author claimed, "the women who work, in one way or another, because they must work to live, are joined in yearly greater numbers by women who work because they choose to work in order to be independent." Once again, ethnology was invoked: "It is . . . the instinct born of a profound need that leads all societies, once they have emerged from the primitive stage in which the labor of women cannot any more be dispensed with than the labor of men, to make, as it were, a kingdom apart for women of leisure." The conclusion?

Women should avoid overwork, and find serenity in a legacy of leisure, which followed an early ethnological stage of toil and struggle.[59]

Writers dwelled on the differences between men's work and women's work in primitive culture. George Wharton James (1858–1923) argued that if women were not active in invention for the industrial age, it was because their period of invention had passed. He had collected among Indians, and he credited basketry, weaving, pottery, house building, and food customs to woman's predominance in primitive culture, and hence to an earlier stage of modern civilization. His study, like so many others at the time, made a connection between the industrial order and folk-culture evidence in regard to men and women. Thorstein Veblen's "The Barbarian Status of Women" is probably best known. Others include "Women and the Occupations" and "Sex in Primitive Industry," by William Thomas, and Lester Frank Ward's "Our Better Halves." They argued that women, like their children, were treated like primitives. This kind of argument had its widest circulation with the publication of Olive Schreiner's *Woman and Labor* (1911), which in 1912 was one of the ten best sellers in America. In a "strange new world," such as moderns faced, she wrote, women had the choice of becoming a race of "laboring and virile" women, the equals of their ancient ancestors.[60]

The theme of work and primitivism appeared also in expositions. Grand displays at the World's Columbian Exposition and at the Pan-American Exposition featured Woman's Buildings to show the contribution of women to industry and arts, the hallmarks of civilization. At the World's Columbian Exposition the Woman's Building stood in contrast to the Anthropology Building, which bore the title "Man and His Works." The description of the Woman's Building pointed out, in contrast, that the building was unique for its "display of woman's work exclusively." Resenting the appointment of the Board of Lady Managers, as if women were not involved in industry, the description emphasized that "its membership comprises as many representative workers in the active industries of the country as if it were composed of men."[61]

The creation of special women's factions extended to the folklore congress at the exposition. A Women's Branch was set up, which included American folklore collectors such as Mary Alicia Owen, Annah Robinson Watson, and Mary Hemenway and foreign representatives such as the British Charlotte Burne and the Swedish Eva Wigstrom. Montreal established a Ladies Committee for its branch of the American Folklore Society; Mary Alicia Owen became president of the Missouri Branch; and women held executive positions in the Boston, Philadelphia, and Louisiana associations. Through the 1890s, however, women moved from factions into the mainstream of the folklore society. The percentage of women jumped from 10 percent in 1889 to 30 percent in 1900 to 37 percent in 1910. In 1910, women in the Boston Branch outnumbered men three to two. Historian of folklore studies Sue Samuelson points out that women were more involved and in greater numbers in the folklore society and its branches than in comparable learned societies of the time.[62] In 1899 the *Journal of American Folklore* featured Isabel Cushman Chamberlain's "Contributions toward a Bibliography of Folk-Lore Relating to Women." She listed eighty-one items from the important period of the previous ten years and remarked that "since the establishment of the Journal of American Folk-Lore, in 1888, the literature of the subject has vastly increased, but no more than the interest of women in this branch of science."[63]

It was not unusual, around the turn of the century, to comment on women's affinity for humanistic topics and the effect that this was having on men's scientific pursuits. The *New York Times,* for example, in July of 1905, devoted a special section to "The Rivalry of Sexes in Literature," used as a headline, and spread on the first page the question "Is Woman Crowding Out Man from the Field of Fiction?" For folklore studies, Stewart Culin remarked that subjects covered during the late 1890s increasingly became women's interests: animal and plant lore, children's folklore, folk tales, mythology, toys, and games. Also in 1905, *World Magazine* quoted him as having said that "the field is no place for a woman" and that in the field, folklore is rough-edged. His complaint was not against women such as Alice Fletcher and Fanny Bergen, he said, but against the sentimentalization of folklore studies, studies that he and the other founders had intended to be "scientific." His associations were common at the time: popularization meant sentimentalization, which meant feminization. Science was objective, rational, esoteric, lofty, and technical. In 1897, the year when Culin was president of the American Folklore Society, a reporter made a sketch of the annual meeting in Baltimore. Although most of the speakers were men, most of the spectators were women. A tally of articles in the *Journal of American Folklore* between 1888 and 1892 bears out the preponderance of articles by men but nonetheless supports Culin's contention. Of twenty-three entries by women, eleven were about beliefs that largely had to do with plant and animal lore; four were on tales; and three were on combinations of these genres. For the five years, the percentage of articles by women was greater than was their percentage of the total membership.[64]

Open to speculation is whether the men who formed the American Anthropological Association in 1902, most of whom had been president of the American Folklore Society during the 1890s (George Dorsey, Stewart Culin, Livingston Farrand, and Frank Russell) and most of whom were interested in material culture (which tended to stress masculine skills), were motivated by a reaction to the feminization of folk studies. They also may have been reacting to the control of the American Folklore Society by Franz Boas, who steered the *Journal of American Folklore* to stick to a small focus of oral tradition while leaving material and social culture to what Boas envisioned as the larger realm of anthropology. Of course there were crossovers, for figures such as Ruth Fulton Benedict, Elsie Clews Parsons, and Gladys Reichard (all Boas's students) were involved in both organizations. Yet to underscore the perception of masculinity in anthropology as opposed to the femininity of folklore, it could be pointed out that the women anthropologists primarily held positions in the American Folklore Society, and the *Journal of American Folklore* had women at the helm for most of the years between 1925 and 1946, while the *American Anthropologist* exclusively had men as editors during that time. Alice Fletcher became president of the American Folklore Society in 1905; three more women served as president during the 1920s and 1930s, while none ascended during that time to the presidency of the American Anthropological Association. Meanwhile, in England, Charlotte Burne boasted in 1912 of being the first woman to deliver a presidential address to a learned society in the Old World when she addressed the Folk-Lore Society. In the following year, the popular middle-class magazine *Woman's Home Companion* called for women's clubs to concentrate on folklore. It even outlined papers that should be read: "One paper should present the universality of myths, the curious resemblances found among them in races far apart in time and place. A second paper may give the ways in which they have been preserved to us. . . . Another paper might notice the growth in the spread of the study of myths and legends. Since Thoms in 1846 coined the phrase 'folk-lore,' societies have been formed in every civilized land to preserve the old stories, songs and traditions, and to study them scientifically. Immense value is placed to-day on their importance as throwing light on history, literature, religion, and language."[65]

Elsie Clews Parsons, president of the American Folklore Society in 1919 and 1920, was known as an ardent feminist, in addition to being the financier of the society during lean years. She signaled the end of feminist reliance on evolution and the idea of a primitive matriarchal age. In "Femininity and Conventionality," published in 1914, she argued that it is "apprehension of difference rather than actual difference which bulks so large now and always in the social regulation of sex. It is fear of the unlike rather than the fact of it." She argued that as the Victorian reliance on ceremony, convention, and segregation had waned and as the Victorian preoccupation with a usable past had subsided, so, too, would studies emphasizing evolution give way to the examination of social function.[66] But so, too, would studies of a distinctive women's sphere of labor decline as immediate political goals of the age—suffrage and employment opportunities—were met during the 1920s. Looking back on the briefs given earlier, Parsons realized the power of perception in shaping judgments.

The perception of industry could be seen changing too. By the 1920s, there was a sharp decline in folklore studies related to industrialism, as Americans appeared to accept their conversion. Symbolic of the triumph of American industrialism at the time was Henry Ford's Model T automobile. Cheap and efficient, more than 740,000 Model Ts were on the road in 1917. In 1920, one of every two cars in the world was a Model T. Ford had worked hard to ease the nervousness over industrialism. Steeped in country traditions, he refused to admit conflict in his transition to industrial mogul, and he tried to persuade the public to share his commitment to country values in an industrial age. In his industry, he raised wages, offered profit sharing, and emphasized country wholesomeness among workers. For the consumer he bragged about better quality at cheaper prices and improved responsiveness to consumer needs. By the 1920s his system was being hailed as the American System. It apparently needed no justification. The relation between Ford's promotion of folk dancing and of traditional string-band music received national attention, but not for its relation to industrialism. Rather, it was a sign of Ford's celebration of the "common man." Ford used living performers, and he obscured the chronology of the past. His nativist version of folklore was, rather, the moral fiber of the industrial present. In 1929 his large outdoor folk museum, Greenfield Village, opened in Dearborn, Michigan, with a combination of industrial and folk exhibits. Ford's industry was the American System, and folklife was a sign of its Americanism, at least until the disillusion of the 1930s tainted Ford's image and cast folklife, much of which was now stressing immigrant and occupational lore, in a less glowing light.[67]

I should not be misinterpreted to suggest that the character of folklore studies from the 1890s to the 1920s was somehow exclusively determined by feminism or by industrialization or by progressivism. Rather, I have brought out the connected influence arising then from needs of the present for perceptions of a usable hidden past. Discussion of perception is commonly absent in historiography because of the tendency to look inwardly into a subject, rather than outwardly to the society in which the subject grows in popularity and professionalism. To be sure, during the late nineteenth century, folklorists made links between their study and issues, then current, of progressivism, industrialization, and feminization. The folklore professionals brought such issues to bear on their studies because of their conviction that folklore, a product of the distant past, was inextricably tied to the progress of the present. This perception of a usable hidden past colored their study and their ideology.

Significant to that perception is that many who were writing about folklore during the late nineteenth century used folklore study as a spin-off from their other professions. Especially because they often were anchored to industrial politics and laissez-faire economy, their study held firm to Victorian ideology. Changes in events of the day and a shift among the professionals in folklore studies altered the perceptions of their subject. The founders of the American Folklore Society, who were already old when they established the society in the 1890s, began to die off in 1900. Franz Boas, who had different ideas from many of the founders, cast a large shadow on folklore studies after that time. More academicians and specialists in folklore appeared on the rolls of the American Folklore Society. As the American Anthropological Association and the Modern Language Association became more established, the subservient American Folklore Society became more narrowly responsible for the oral products of culture.

World War I and the events that followed it changed the way in which the educated middle class thought about the past and about culture. This changing perception becomes evident in the distinctions—the "apprehension of difference," to quote Elsie Clews Parsons—that arose among evolution, diffusion, and functionalism during this period of professional folklore studies. The photographic essay that follows illustrates several prominent figures and institutions during this period of transition at the end of the nineteenth century. In the third chapter, I discuss the distinctions among evolution, diffusion, and functionalism and their proponents separately, and I extend the intellectual criticism, begun here, from perceptions of the past to those of time and space.

2

People and Places in American
Folklore Studies, 1880–1900:
A Photographic Essay

In the late nineteenth century, the American popular press hailed the work of "scientific men and women" in the study of folklore. These men and women came mostly from the professional middle class in the eastern cities of the United States. They were doctors, lawyers, merchants, missionaries, government agents, and military officers. The public listened attentively to their pronouncements on the hidden roots of the industrial age and the shape of its growth. In their unveiling according to evolutionary doctrine of Victorian society's primitive past, these men and women addressed a tension in modern society between religion and science. As they saw it, religion guided the past; science would guide the future. They proposed that like the natural evolution of mankind from primitive animal forms, the cultural evolution of modern Western nations proceeded in a single line from races that had gone through barbaric and savage states of society. In these lower stages, superstition and ritual dominated society; in the advanced stages, rationalism and science guided life. The cultural specimens from those stages of tales, myths, customs, beliefs, games, and crafts that they examined were the evidence to speak about growing concomitant trends in their times of industrialism, materialism, feminism, and imperialism.

The scope of these scientific men and women was global. They mined manuscript sources and museum collections from all over the world to forge a unified natural history of civilization. Folklore was for them vivid evidence that forced them to reflect on the gulf between the present and the past, between the modern and the traditional. To advance folklore studies, these scientific men and women helped to establish lasting institutions of folkloristic investigation in museums, governmental agencies, and learned societies. These institutions, however, became instruments of change in folklore studies. Moving away from the dilettante interest of many of the scientific men and women in folklore, these institutions sponsored investigations that were geared toward the speciality of a cultural professional. Workers in these institutions commonly were expected to be experts on the traditions of a specific culture. They made intensive field observations of a specific group in one bounded place and time, and they associated this approach with "ethnography." They took a more heterogeneous view of culture. In this there was, not a successive line of culture from the past, but a diversity of cultures in the present. A shift was evident from a generalized account of cultural evolution to an empirical description of how cultures function. There were more questions of how cultures maintain themselves and how their folklore spreads. With these changes, folklore studies at the turn of the century made a transition from a century of history to a century of ethnography.

Acronyms used in this chapter to indicate photographic credits:

APS   American Philosophical Society, which has granted permission for the use of photographs

NAA   American Anthropological Archives, Smithsonian Institution, which has granted permission for the use of photographs

SB   Simon Bronner, Pennsylvania State University–Harrisburg Folklore Archives, which has granted permission for the use of photographs

UP   University of Pennsylvania Museum, which has granted permission for the use of photographs

American Folklore Society meetings in the late nineteenth century drew splashy coverage by the popular press. They drew leading "scientists of the day," the press reported. This drawing is taken from a section of the *Philadelphia Inquirer* for 29 December 1895, the day after the American Folklore Society's annual meeting. Entitled "Leaders of the American Folklore Society," the drawing capped several days of reporting the subject of papers delivered during the meeting. Daniel Brinton is the bearded man in the center with the top hat; up and to the right of him is Otis Mason; above Brinton is probably Alice Fletcher. To the right of Mason is Franz Boas; above him is Stewart Culin; to Culin's right is William Wells Newell (SB).

A rare look at the proceedings of a nineteenth-century meeting of the American Folklore Society is provided by an unidentified artist for the *Baltimore American*. Published on 29 December 1897, the drawing depicts the annual meeting in Baltimore held on 28–29 December 1897. The topics discussed by those pictured: W. W. Newell, "Opportunities for Collecting Folklore in America," A. S. Chessin, "Russian Folklore," C. C. Bombaugh, "Bibliography of Folklore," H. C. Bolton, "Relics of Astrology" (SB).

Lending his prestige to the founding of the American Folklore Society was Daniel Brinton, M.D. (1837–99), a member of the Philadelphia gentry. Brinton published widely on topics such as archaeology, religion, and linguistics. Brinton was the second president of the American Folklore Society, and he helped to organize its first annual meeting in Philadelphia in 1889. This portrait was painted shortly after Brinton's death in 1899 by the renowned artist Thomas Eakins of Philadelphia.

A center for folklore studies in the late nineteenth century was the University of Pennsylvania Museum. Folk religious symbols graced the façade of the building. In 1890, Stewart Culin established the Folklore Museum within the collection. Among the folklore authorities connected with the museum were Daniel Brinton, Stewart Culin, Henry Mercer, W. Max Müller, Frank Hamilton Cushing, Maxwell Sommerville, and Sarah Stevenson. After Daniel Brinton's death in 1899, Cushing's in 1900, and Stewart Culin's departure for the Brooklyn Institute Museum in 1903, folklore studies dwindled in importance at the museum (UP).

Another center for folklore studies during the late nineteenth century was the Smithsonian Institution. As assistant secretary of the Smithsonian, George Brown Goode (1851–96) encouraged ethnological and folklore collection as part of his goal of creating a museum of cultural history. The task of organizing the ethnological and folklore collection, estimated at 500,000 pieces, went to Otis Mason. Conducting field research and collecting for the Smithsonian was the Bureau of American Ethnology. Matters of concern in this early collecting period were techniques for gathering "specimens," as Goode called both natural-history and cultural-history materials, and ways to classify them. This photograph depicts workers at the United States National Museum sorting ethnological collections in the 1890s (NAA).

In 1884, Otis Mason (1838–1908) became curator of the Division of Ethnology in the United States National Museum. Mason became president of the American Folklore Society in 1891. His research concentrated on ethnological and folklore studies pertaining to issues of the day. He published books on the cultural origins of invention, transportation, women, and industry. From 1885 on, he was the frequent target of criticism from Franz Boas, who disapproved of Mason's use of a natural-science model for folklore. Mason used the occasion of his presidential address to deliver an impassioned defense of evolutionary theory, "The Natural History of Folklore." After Mason's death in 1908, Franz Boas wrote Mason's obituary for the *Journal of American Folklore* and warmly praised Mason for his achievements (NAA).

In 1868, Secretary Joseph Henry of the Smithsonian Institution suggested to John Wesley Powell (1834–1902; pictured here) that he take notes on the languages of the Indians while doing geologic research around the Colorado River. Powell documented language and myths told by Indians through the 1870s. In 1879, excited by living evidence of "pure" culture, Powell founded the Bureau of American Ethnology at the Smithsonian, to expand the collecting work. A strong believer in evolutionary theory, Powell encouraged field workers for the bureau to collect folklore to show that social development among aboriginal groups was similar to natural development. Reports that came out of the bureau dominated the pages of the *Journal of American Folklore* during its early years (NAA).

In 1905, Alice Fletcher (1838–1923) became the first woman to be president of the American Folklore Society. In addition to studying the folklore of Winnebago and Omaha Indians, she lobbied for the passage of federal legislation to give Indians more control over their lands. According to *Notable American Women,* Fletcher never drew "a sharp line between her scientific and humanitarian impulses." Fletcher was also outspoken in her criticism of the Bureau of American Ethnology for hoarding its data, but she supported the bureau's effort to promote professionalism (NAA).

Washington Matthews (1843–1905), president of the American Folklore Society in 1895, was an army surgeon who used his location in the Southwest to document Navajo rituals and crafts. For the International Folklore Congress of 1893 he brought a collection of Navajo artifacts and offered to read them in the way that folklorists read tales. In 1897 the American Folklore Society published his book on Navajo legends. In Matthews's obituary in 1905, James Mooney wrote: "By a faculty of mingled sympathy and command he won the confidence of the Indian and the knowledge of his secrets, while by virtue of that spiritual vision which was his Keltic inheritance, he was able to look into the soul of primitive things and interpret their meaning as few others have done" (NAA).

Frank Hamilton Cushing (1857–1900) was one of the founding officers of the American Folklore Society. He gained fame as "the man who lived with the Indians." Going to the Southwest for the Bureau of American Ethnology, Cushing joined the Zuñi and later became second chief of the tribe. His moving in with the Indians surprised his colleagues; yet the colleagues appreciated Cushing's intimate knowledge of Indian techniques. Here he is seen working on Southwest Indian pottery for the Smithsonian Institution (NAA).

Frederic Ward Putnam (1839–1915), fourth president of the American Folklore Society, organized the Boston branch of the American Folklore Society at the Peabody Museum. In addition, he helped to establish anthropology at the American Museum of Natural History in New York, where Franz Boas was employed. A zoologist by training, Putnam was known in anthropological and folkloristic studies for his organizational skills, including his service as permanent secretary of the American Association for the Advancement of Science. In 1893, Putnam was appointed head of the Anthropology Section of the World's Columbian Exposition in Chicago. He chose two specialists in folklore for his chief assistants—Stewart Culin and Franz Boas (NAA).

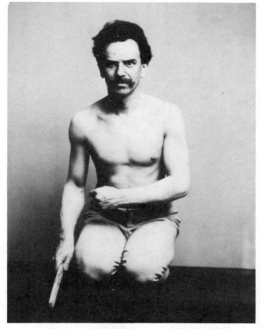

Franz Boas (1858–1942) is seen here demonstrating a Northwest Indian ritual for the Bureau of American Ethnology. Although he did not think of himself as a folklorist, he left his mark on folklore studies as editor of the *Journal of American Folklore* from 1908 to 1924. His students continued to control the journal until 1941. He left his mark, too, with extensive field collections of the folk tales, mythology, and art of American Indian groups. Trained in geography and physics, Boas helped turn folklore studies away from the natural-history model of evolutionary theory (NAA).

Stewart Culin (1858–1929) was curator of the American Folklore Society and in 1897 was its president. A rival to Boas, Culin chose a museum base rather than the academic route that Boas took. Culin made headlines with dramatic finds of artifacts in Asia, Europe, and the American Southwest for the University of Pennsylvania Museum and later for the Brooklyn Institute Museum, but he never established a power base from which to expand his influence. Culin also made headlines in the Philadelphia and New York society pages by putting his work above his marriage. Back in New York, his wife divorced him while he was doing field work in Arizona (NAA).

Folklore studies received public notice when the popular press gave attention in 1893 to the folklore exhibit in the Anthropology Building at the World's Columbian Exposition in Chicago. The exhibit featured religious and gaming objects, and it was organized to suggest that modern toys and games had evolved from uses in religious rituals. Some contents went to the Field Columbian Museum in Chicago, and the rest went back with Culin to the University of Pennsylvania Museum (UP).

Fletcher S. Bassett (1847–93), a retired naval officer, published a collection of naval folklore in 1885. In 1891 he founded the Chicago Folklore Society and served as its permanent secretary. His major achievement was organizing the International Folklore Congress at the World's Columbian Exposition in Chicago. Championing the literary value of folklore, Bassett's organization published the *Folk-Lorist* to rival the more anthropological *Journal of American Folklore.* A few years after Bassett's death in 1893, the Chicago Folklore Society (renamed the International Folklore Association) collapsed (SB).

Mary Alicia Owen (1850–1935) is described by historian of folklore studies Wayland Hand as the "most famous American woman folklorist of her time." She produced studies of black, Indian, and gypsy folklore from collections that she had made around her native St. Joseph, Missouri. Active in folklore societies on both sides of the Atlantic, Owen was covered in the *Times* (London) and created a "sensation," according to another report, for her address on voodoo at the International Folklore Congress of 1891 in London. She repeated this performance at the International Folklore Congress in Chicago in 1893. Her papers on voodoo led to *Old Rabbit the Voodoo and Other Sorcerers*, a book that rivaled Joel Chandler Harris's popular Uncle Remus books. She joined the executive committee of the "Woman's Branch" of the Congress, headed the Missouri Branch of the American Folklore Society, and served from 1908 to 1935 as president of the Missouri Folklore Society (SB).

James Owen Dorsey (1848–1895), a founder of the American Folklore Society, had been an Episcopalian missionary before he began working for the Bureau of American Ethnology in 1879. As a missionary he gained field-work experience among Indian tribes in Nebraska. Dorsey was an expert for the bureau in American Indian languages and was a careful collector of Indian myths and customs. For the American Folklore Society from 1888 until his premature death in 1895, Dorsey served on the first editorial committee of the journal, and he also joined the membership committee. To Boas, Dorsey's field work was a model of linguistically based ethnography; to Powell, Dorsey embodied a late-nineteenth-century conflict of science and religion, a conflict in which the empirical evidence of science would ultimately triumph over faith and belief. Dorsey himself did not voice any conflict and combined what historian of anthropology Curtis Hinsley refers to as "a deep human concern with stubborn attention to experienced truth. In sum, Dorsey brought forward the best of the American missionary tradition to the very edge of modern field ethnography" (NAA).

3

The Professionalization
of Time and Space

The late nineteenth century is significant for the standardization of time. Before then, travelers in the same area encountered different times depending on the town they were in. They would have to check with the local town clock for the time. For example, taking a trip between Washington, D.C., and San Francisco required resetting one's watch two hundred times. From 1870 on, American railroads called for a uniform time so as to simplify scheduling; army brass wanted it to help military planning; scientists wanted it to synchronize their observations. In 1884, twenty-five countries agreed to use Greenwich, England, as the zero meridian, to divide the earth into twenty-four time zones, one hour apart, and to fix a precise beginning of the universal day. During the late nineteenth century, work was more and more being measured by hours spent on the job, rather than by completion of the task. In 1900 the Sears Roebuck catalog carried a fourteen-page section on watches and clocks; only clothes and fire-arms consumed more pages. In 1895, H. G. Wells gained acclaim for *The Time Machine,* which imagined that time was a fourth dimension that one could travel through. Time became uniform and measured; it answered less to the forces of nature and more to those of man and machine. The exacting units of measurement fragmented a day into hours and minutes; life into months and years; and culture into stages and periods.

Spaces also had times, for to go to certain places, especially those away from cities, was to feel like stepping back in time. And distance across space was measured in decreasing time. Jules Verne brought the point home in *Around the World in Eighty Days* (1873); and in 1889/90 the trip took real-life journalist Elizabeth Cochrane Seaman (pseud., Nellie Bly) seventy-two days. Space, too, appeared to be more uniform; railroad transportation made the natural divisions of space less imposing. In an era of territorial expansion, landscapes were flattened into political spaces. During the late nineteenth century, the frontier in the American mind became an abstract idea of open space. Meanwhile, Jacob Riis pointed out the lack of space in city tenements. There were standards of adequate space, as well as time, he claimed.[1]

The professionalizing sciences of the 1890s tried to answer the call for absolute measurements of time and space. Geographers and naturalists offered more exact descriptions of space; historians and geologists gave them for time. Ethnological folklorists, such as Daniel Brinton and George Laurence Gomme, envied the ability of these specialists to date their materials exactly. To Gomme, "tradition" was vague; it needed precise references by folklorists working in a historical science to locations in what seemed to him to be a "longer past" and a "widening area." Juxtaposing time and space, Brinton suggested, in "The Aims of Anthropology" (1895): "Collecting and storing of facts about man from all quarters of the world and all epochs of his existence, is the first and indispensable aim of anthropologic science. It is pressing and urgent beyond all other aims at this period of its existence as a science; for here more than elsewhere we feel the force of the Hippocratic warning, that the time is short and the opportunity fleeting."[2]

The nineteenth century was a time of celebrating science, as well as science's promise of progress and rationality. Darwin and Spencer, among others, suggested social applications which would justify the uniform path of modernization as an evolution in stages from primitive, dark, or rural stock to modern, white, and urban civilization. Beyond *The Origin of Species* and Lubbock's *The Origin of Civilisation* (1870) are, to name some ethnological studies relating to folklore studies, Lewis Henry Morgan's *Ancient Society: Or Researches in the Lines of Human Progress* (1877), Sir James G. Frazer's *The Golden Bough: A Study in Magic and Religion* (1890), Otis Mason's *The Origins of Invention: A Study of Industry among Primitive Peoples* (1895), and Alfred Haddon's *Evolution in Art, as Illustrated by the Life-Histories of Designs* (1895). Ethnology was scientific; it applied natural history to culture. But ethnologist Richard Cull said as early as 1851: "When the Zoologist describes our study as the natural history of man, he only partially describes our pursuit. . . . The Ethnologist proceeds to investigate man in groups, a people, a nation, and variety; he proceeds to study the history of those peoples, nations, and varieties, tracing them as far back as history is able to conduct him; he endeavours to discover the sources of those peoples, nations, and varieties; he seeks out their affinities and connexions; and struggles after that dim and shadowy knowledge of man as he existed before the dawn of history."[3]

Despite the claims that rational science was making on the study of folklore, folklore had its sentimental side, which fantasized about time and space. The melodramatic tales were filled with supernatural events, violence, tragedy, and sex. Heroes defended some lands and conquered others. As folklorist Axel Olrik (1864–1917) insisted in 1909, actions were portrayed sequentially in episodes in a single strand. The characters represented extremes of good and evil; they were adorable children, suffering women, and struggling men. They seemed to hold popular appeal precisely because they transcended a specific time and space. They were constantly traveling, having adventures "once upon a time" in a "faraway land," and living happily "ever after." Within these frames, time and space are set in a human scale of "a distant valley" and "one day." Action is gauged by relative rapidity or slowness, however, rather than by standard units. As folklorist Wilhelm Nicolaisen has noted, "the centrality of . . . time," in many folk narrative genres, "speaks of our continued, demanding, vain, disappointing endeavour . . . to come to terms with time in our lives—to confront it, to understand it, to live with it, to mature in it, to wither in it, or more unreasonably to see it as a restrictive prison, escape from which brings ultimate freedom." As for space, he observes: "We find in the folktale, instead of flatness, an upper and a lower realm, as well as an inner and outer space. Home is not only nearby in a horizontal sense, but also above ground in vertical terms. It is to this home that one has to return, both from far away and from down below. Successfully conquered—that is, integrated and manipulated—space is therefore just as subjective and personal as conquered time. Ultimately one can only 'live happily ever after' in the acceptably structured space of a familiar habitat, in the landscape of home."[4]

In studies of folklife, the accounts described unusual "manners" of "ruder ages" and "removed lands," judged by the rigid middle-class standards of the day. The accounts dwelled on folk ingenuity and industry in "timeless" crafts and food customs or in medicine that has stood the "test of time." Folklife showed the closeness of man to nature and the glory of the toiling hand. Folklife and folklore were both parts of modernist science and antimodernist sentiment. They were both elitist and populist. They dramatized the dilemmas of a rising middle class, raising ambivalence about relations between passing tradition and whirring modernity as a difference between the fluidity and fragmentation of time, the rootedness and alienation of space, the continuity and splintering of society, and the spiritual compassion and rational impersonality of life. Coming from the professional middle class, folklorists were, not surprisingly, address-ing the ambivalence of the age in popular middle-class magazines such as *Harper's Monthly, Century, Nation,* and *Atlantic Monthly*—an outlet that they have not used, or have not been offered, in such frequency since that time.

As the century progressed, news seemed more immediate; the world, closer; the present, more important. Ethnology came to con-centrate less on the span of time and more on spheres of cultures. The turn of the century witnessed a growing diversity of theories to explain the similarity and difference in cultures across the world and within the nation. The spread of folklore seemed to be more the issue at hand than did its origin. As society modernized, so did the use of *folk* grow to describe, not the removed primitive, but the nearby man of tradition. With social changes accelerating during the late nineteenth century and with the increase in the professionalization of studies during that time, folklore and folklife were among the cultural studies to organize and prosper.

Although *folklore* was the popular term, *folk-life* cropped up within the American Folklore Society during this period as a term for the tradition of a particular area. In 1892, Walter Hough, an ethnologist at the United States National Museum, addressed the American Folklore Society on "Folk-life in and about the National Capital." In 1897 the *Journal of American Folklore* carried Heli Chatelain's "African Folk-life," and William Greenough published *Canadian Folk-Life and Folk-Lore.* In 1905 the first general book on American folklife appeared, written by a German, Karl Knortz (1841–1918), who was living in Evansville, Indiana. Entitled *Zur Amerikanischen Volkskunde,* the book covered beliefs, tales, rituals, and artifacts.

How had the American Folklore Society fared after its founding in 1888? Using measures of time and space, Lee J. Vance boasted, in 1893, of the spread of folklore branches to six cities. In the short span of time from 1888 to 1893, the society had attracted five hundred members, more than any comparable European organization. He wrote: "Prior to 1887, the study of popular tradition in America was unorganized. Since then the investigations of special students in different fields have been collated and systematized, and, above all, those interested in the subject have been brought together. Thus to-day there is a certain *esprit de corps* among American folk-lorists that was unknown some six or eight years ago." The society and its branches had, Vance said, a "social side and function," as well as its work; "already their influence has been felt in many quarters."[5]

Indeed it had been. John Fiske's *Myths and Myth-Makers* (1873) went through eleven editions in fifteen years. In 1890 the *Saturday*

Review noted the wide circulation of Francis James Child's volumes on ballads and Jeremiah Curtin's book *Myths and Folk-Lore of Ireland.* T. F. Crane, Lee Vance, and John Fiske regularly reported on new folklore books in popular magazines and discussed the folktale "vogue" stirred by Joel Chandler Harris's Uncle Remus books and Andrew Lang's books of fairy tales. The two main guides to popular periodicals at the time, *Poole's Index to Periodical Literature* and the *Reader's Guide,* indexed the *Journal of American Folklore.* The numbers of articles cited under "folklore" reveals a pattern from the founding of the American Folklore Society into the first decade of the twentieth century. *Poole's Index* listed 14 articles on folklore (folk song was listed separately) from 1887 to 1892; in 1892 to 1896, the number jumped to 77, but dropped down to 7 from 1902 to 1905, when *Poole's* ceased publication. The *Reader's Guide* (which indexed 56 periodicals, compared to *Poole's* 196) listed 117 articles for folklore between 1890 and 1909, not counting entries for the *Journal of American Folklore.* In 1905 the *Reader's Guide* ceased to index the journal. In the ensuing years, the *Reader's Guide* doubled the number of periodicals that it indexed, but between 1910 and 1924, only 58 articles on folklore appeared in it.

The "special students" of folklore had channeled their study to a wider audience during the 1890s but later made their studies and publications more specialized. In 1891 the society's council moved to "undertake the publication of a Library of American Folk-Lore." In 1894 the plan materialized as the "memoirs" series of the society. The first volume was *Folk-Tales of Angola,* by Heli Chatelain; it was followed by six books in the next five years. Together, the volumes had made a modest profit. But after 1910 the number of popular books generally on folklore, as well as the audience for them, dropped off. In 1909, Secretary Alfred Tozzer reported a drop in membership, and the society did not publish any monographs between 1904 and 1917. It was a time of change, a time of transition from the learned society, with ties to the public, to the scholarly organization attached to the university.[6] The theories that were prevalent in the society, too, moved from wide circles of evolutionary influence to new specialized theories of a shrinking time and space.

The organizational threads of folklore, folklife, and anthropology became more tangled. In 1897, William John McGee, of the Bureau of American Ethnology, wrote to Stewart Culin, then president of the American Folklore Society, about the relation of the American Folklore Society to the Association for the Advancement of Science, which had a section for anthropology: "There is no general society corresponding exactly to Section H (Anthropology); but it has come to be considered by Permanent Secretary Putnam and most of the officers and members that the Folk-Lore Society may be regarded as the cognate of the Section." McGee, following the lead of Frederic Putnam, who was president of the American Folklore Society in 1892, called for joint meetings. Just before New Year's Day of 1902, McGee went to Chicago to join Franz Boas, George Dorsey, Frank Russell, Stewart Culin, and Livingston Farrand, all of whom were former presidents of the American Folklore Society, to establish the American Anthropological Association.[7] In their studies of folklore and anthropology, they had pushed the professionalism of their organizations by presenting them as authorities on cultures in removed spaces and distant times.

The late-nineteenth-century professionalization of the study of folklore, folklife, and anthropology might seem removed from the currents of present scholarship. Study today appears to us to be more egalitarian, less historical and organic, and less willing to embrace universal claims. Study today tends toward the behavioral rather than the biological. Yet in the organizational schemes that were established, in the guiding principles of field work and comparison, and in the emphasis on the expressive products of behavior, folk and anthropological studies owe an intellectual debt. More than that, the growth of anthropological theory and its folkloristic relations during the late nineteenth and early twentieth century can be treated on its own terms for what it reveals of the social vision of that period. As Fletcher Bassett said to the Third International Folklore Congress, "Folklore has become a subject of the day." Marvin Harris, recounting that period in *The Rise of Anthropological Theory* (1968), explained its significance: "While ostensibly operating within a restricted theoretical frame, conclusions of the widest possible significance bearing on the nature of history and culture were formulated. These spread to adjacent disciplines and were incorporated into the intellectual prospectus of the public at large."[8]

In the changing views of folk society and in the shift of anthropological theory since the late nineteenth century, there is a legacy of modernist and antimodernist ideologies which called for mediation by the professional middle class. The study of traditional preindustrial societies during that time vacillated between a celebration of their romanticism and a recognition of their primitivism. The study of folklore and folklife drew popular interest, not just for what it uncovered about times past or peoples removed, but also for what it implied about the direction of the dominant modern culture. In the writings of the period's critics and reformers, such as Friedrich Engels, Thorstein Veblen, Lester Ward, Elizabeth Cady Stanton, and Jane

Addams, can be read the use of anthropological ideas to promote liberal social reform and egalitarianism, even as Otis Mason and Herbert Spencer had used them to defend industrial hegemony and social hierarchy. The study of folklife and folklore at that time typically dwelled in the "big house" of anthropology, and it, too, signified a search for the meaning of the past and of ways of life different from a world that Western "moderns" had wrought. It provided object lessons to help confront change and, often, the application of change.

Such are the themes in the following survey, which is divided into several approaches that were prevalent between, roughly, 1888 and 1942. The opening date marks the founding of the American Folklore Society, and the closing date marks the beginnings of a separate discipline, usually connected with the establishment of the first folklore institute at Indiana University. The dates also mark the height of approaches that attempted to systematize folklore in time and space.

EVOLUTION

Using hindsight, Stephen Toulmin and June Goodfield observed that the nineteenth century was "the Century of History." "Whether we consider geology, zoology, political philosophy or the study of ancient civilizations, the nineteenth century was in every case the Century of History—a period marked by the growth of a new, dynamic world-picture."[9] That century's version of history was evolutionary and owed its rhetoric to naturalists. It took charge when industrialism, Victorians felt, alienated them from nature, placing them too firmly in the present, whirring toward the future. In folklore studies, evolutionary doctrine was indeed a world picture, depicting universal laws for the development of civilization. Evolution intrigued Victorian thinkers, for it established their industrial civilization at the height of a cultural progression. Although evolutionary studies followed similar lines, they did not strictly form a unified theory. Proponents argued over the number of stages in cultural evolution, the origins of folklore in communal or individual authorship, the decay or improvement of various cultural institutions from earlier stages, and the role of mental similarity for explaining the resemblance of folklore items in far reaches of the globe.

Edward Tylor (1832–1917), as we have seen, provided the reference for many subsequent studies. In his library of works on the subject, he noticed similarities of customs among disparate societies and concluded that differing human beings possess a "psychic unity," a universally shared mental development. Because all human groups were mentally similar, he postulated a unilinear evolutionary model. The similarity of customs in different societies was therefore proof of the regular, uniform way in which culture progressed. The progression followed its own laws, similar to those of natural development. Following assumptions of natural development, Tylor assumed that nature and human beings who were close to it were simple and were related on a vertical scale to "higher" complex forms. Three stages— savagery at the bottom, then barbarism, and, ultimately, civilization— constitute the cultural ladder that all societies climb.

Societies differ, Tylor argued, because they progress at different speeds. Although falling back down the ladder is possible, it rarely occurs. Thus he explained the origins of beliefs and customs that were found in nineteenth-century Europe by drawing parallels with "savage" societies. Many of the customs that he found had lost their original meaning, he claimed, but still continued to be practiced, albeit in altered or decayed forms. Such items he termed *survivals.* By comparing survivals among different groups in the modern world with practices of "savage" societies, Tylor employed the basic method of the evolutionary approach, the "comparative method." Although following natural "history," the method was ahistorical. Customs that were recorded were not contemporaneous; Tylor assumed that survivals were not active in contemporary events but were frozen, irrationally, in later cultural stages. The ethnologist assigned time to the customs. Time therefore appeared to be absolute, assigned according to standards set by Western civilization.[10]

In America, Franz Boas claimed that Daniel Brinton was the "extremist" of evolutionary doctrine. Brinton made the announcement, for instance, that "a department of psychical anthropology, Folklore, is taken up with . . . survivals, and strange are its revelations. Our Christmas dinner is a reminiscence of a cannibal feast at the winter solstice. The dyed Easter egg is a relic of a myth of the dawn older than the Pyramids." Boas railed that Brinton had overlooked the possibility that similar customs could have come about as a result of transmission across cultures. Boas continued that there were those who, like Brinton, "believe it to be unlikely and deem the alleged proof irrelevant, and who ascribe sameness of cultural traits wholly to the psychic unity of mankind and to the uniform reaction of the human mind upon the same stimulus."[11]

Another lasting influence on the evolutionists in the American Folklore Society was Lewis Henry Morgan (1818–81). In *Ancient Society* (1877) he developed a detailed chart of the savagery/barbarism/civilization model, with additional categories of lower, middle, and later periods for each stage. This sequence, he observed, was "natural" and "necessary." He outlined the methods by which man had risen up the various levels by means of the invention of more efficient methods of production. He believed that "the great epochs of human progress have been identified, more or less directly, with the enlargement of the sources of subsistence." He also hypothesized that technological, governmental, kinship, and property systems travel together up the evolutionary scale, and he used the American Indians as evidence. In *League of the Ho-de-no-sau-nee, or Iroquois* (1851) he advanced the belief that the folklore of "legendary literature," because it instilled "superstitious beliefs," had retarded their progress up the cultural ladder. Although he did not rely as heavily on verbal folklore as other evolutionists had, Morgan brought attention to material folk culture in *Houses and House Life of the American Aborigine* (1881). Morgan's ideas were applied to folklore mostly through the work of John Wesley Powell (1834–1902), head of the Bureau of American Ethnology (BAE) from 1879 to 1902. Powell's staff at the BAE conducted much folklore-related research, and they dominated the pages of the *Journal of American Folklore* during the late nineteenth century. In 1902, Alexander Chamberlain, editor of the *Journal of American Folklore* from 1900 to 1907, estimated that of the forty articles that Powell had published in various fields, twenty-four had "a more or less folk-lore content." Two of these articles, "The Interpretation of Folk-Lore" and "The Lessons of Folk-Lore," carried Morgan's evolutionary ideas specifically into the study of folklore.[12] For Morgan, the evolution of folklore formed a line from the superstition and prejudice of the primitive to the desirable science and invention of a modern industrial state. In a twist of ideology, Morgan's work was also applied in orthodox Marxist interpretation, notably by Friedrich Engels in *The Origin of the Family, Private Property, and the State* (1884). Engels used Morgan's case that a communistic stage existed before industrial modes of production dominated society, and he also applied Morgan's historical argument that changing material conditions profoundly influence social relations. Engels then proposed ways in which the divisive conditions of modern industrial states could be changed to preserve a communistic society.[13]

Although William Wells Newell, editor of the *Journal of American Folklore* from 1888 to 1899, was a powerful ally to evolutionary doctrine, evolutionary theory was already on the defensive during the closing years of the nineteenth century. Folklorists found more cultures, and they showed more differences from one another. Their folklore did not always decay with time into survivals, but indeed, there were songs and myths that flowered and still held meanings for the group. With this evidence of added cultural diversity, the single family tree for culture that evolution theory suggested did not hold up as well. With field work among North American Indians, folklorists found individuals who innovated traditions for the group, rather than the evolution from a communal stage to the individualism of modern industrialism. Newell tried to revise evolutionary doctrine by taking into account the origins of folklore with individuals. He proposed more continuity among the processes of creativity found in the stages of culture.

Otis Mason also tried to undergird a revised evolutionary doctrine with his manifesto "The Natural History of Folk-Lore" (1891). He still believed in the natural-history model for folklore, but he lessened the emphasis on a single evolutionary line. With the awareness that folklore is not restricted to a savage state but can be found among educated groups as well, Mason allowed for the persistence of folk tradition in modern life, although he still drew sharp lines between the world of science and the world of folklife. Mason insisted that "the folk include all lettered people when they think and act like the folk rather than in accordance with the rules of science and culture. We all have traditions and manners that we cannot shake off, although we know them to be absurd." Mason announced that "we are concerned with the past of our race as well as with the present."[14]

The point about the present was further conceded by William Wells Newell in the same year, when he wrote a review of Alice Morse Earle's study of the Sabbath in Puritan New England. Newell wrote: "That definition of 'folk-lore' which restricts the use of the word to the survival of prehistoric practices and beliefs is deficient, in that it leaves out of account the considerable mass of custom and opinion which is emphatically folk-lore, but by no means of archaic origin or character. Modern manners and customs, such as those of the table and of society, ways of feeling, tastes and sentiments, habits of dress, and behavior, come under this head,—in short, all that body of traditional usage which a proper historical method takes into account as helping to give the color as well as the outline of history."[15]

Mason retreated from the grander claims of evolutionary doctrine for "the guessing of the riddle of existence"; rather, he said, "the folk-lorist hopes to restore much of the lost history of our race."[16] Although recognizing the upsurge of interest in the geography of folklore and its concern for transmission, he still insisted that natural history and its concern for origins was most productive, because it provided developmental laws that he assumed were integral to the building of a systematic science and an ordered, progressive society.

By the 1920s, evolutionary doctrine had mostly disappeared from American writings on folklore. A new generation, pursuing anthropology full-time and weary of the previous generation's dubious grand claims, took the place of the older scientific men and women who had touted evolution so highly. Newell recognized that evolutionary doctrine which was suited to his generation would not last. In 1901 he wrote in the *Journal of American Folklore:* "From the small body of anthropological students in America during the past decade have been removed many names, some of world-wide reputation, others beloved and admired within their own circle, and the places of these laborers have not as yet been filled."[17] Gone, for example, were Daniel Brinton, Horatio Hale, Frank Hamilton Cushing, J. Owen Dorsey, and John G. Bourke—evolutionists who used folklore for evidence. Nineteen hundred also marked Franz Boas's ascent, at the age of forty-two, to the presidency of the American Folklore Society. His presence as writer, editor, organizer, and teacher changed the direction of folklore scholarship during the next generation. In 1907, Newell died; he was followed a year later by Otis Mason.

Related to or reinforcing the wane of evolutionary doctrine were political and economic movements. Laissez-faire economics, which depended on evolutionary theory for justification, was under attack. Instead of encouraging progress and competition, laissez-faire economics encouraged the maintenance of the status quo and the rise of monopolies. During a giant depression in 1893, which was caused by overproduction and a lack of regulation because of the application of laissez-faire economics, William Dean Howells, in *A Traveler from Altruria,* satirized, for his economic views, the aloof, ethnocentric William Graham Sumner, who had already begun to work on the ideas that culminated in *Folkways* (1907). Sumner's rival Lester Frank Ward stressed the rationality of primitive culture and argued that uniform natural laws did not mysteriously arise to control social institutions; politically created laws are necessary in order to adapt to specific social conditions. Ward presaged the advance of government and planning. The economic argument followed from the anthropological one.

The continued flow of immigration reminded Americans of the influence that a movement of people could bring to another culture. "Our folk-lore is highly composite," Lee Vance acknowledged in 1896, "resulting from the great tides of immigration which have rolled over our shores and formed our present strange commingling of races." In 1921, over a million and a half visitors passed through the New York Armory and sites in other cities to view an exhibit of contemporary immigrant folk art.[18] Studies focused more on present social conditions and customs of Old World groups in the New World than on the past life of aborigines. Origins seemed less relevant; social conditions of the present appeared more pressing.

Another blow to the confidence in the inevitability of progress, as predicted by evolutionary doctrine, was dealt by World War I. Technological advance brought more destruction, rather than, as many evolutionary writers had predicted, the obsolescence of war. The world seemed more divided than united. A growing bookshelf of works such as *The Decline of the West* (1918) painted a gloomy picture, which was disturbing to Victorian scholars and the public alike. In France after the war, Arnold van Gennep (1873–1957) contrasted folklore according to natural history, which is the study of "dead facts," with biology, the study of living lore in a specific environment.[19] In Germany, Scandinavia, and America, geography and physical sciences offered new models for folklorists. Many wrote that perhaps, after all, the evolutionary scheme for culture was wrong; the admission was one way to ward off the predictions of gloom that had been brought by modern warfare and industrial capitalism.

To add to events that detracted from riding along with the evolutionary doctrine, one could point to the Russian Revolution. Russia had skipped a step, or moved back one, depending on the point of view, moving from a peasant economy to a communistic society. Around the same time, a new feeling of isolationism swept America. After seeking its place in a global community, America now was seeking exclusiveness, shunning the League of Nations, and stressing America's cultural distinctiveness. Accordingly, in 1893, Frederick Jackson Turner caused a stir with a paper about the influence that the settlement of the West had had on American culture.[20] More mobile, more aware of space, Americans brought attention, in their leisure and in their theories, to movement across the landscape.

DIFFUSION

In the year when the American Folklore Society was founded, T. F. Crane bucked the model of English studies that was common among his colleagues. He wrote in the society's journal in 1888: "While the scholars of England have directed their researches chiefly to the question of the origin of popular tales, German scholars have been more interested in the question of diffusion." Franz Boas, a German immigrant to America, continued the argument in the journal three years later with "Dissemination of Tales among the Natives of North America." Adding data from the field to Crane's literary evidence, Boas announced, "we may safely assume that, wherever a story which consists of the same combination of several elements is found in two regions, we must conclude that its occurrence in both is due to diffusion." Rejecting the possibility of the independent invention of tales, he made the claim that "whenever we find a tale spread over a continuous area, we must assume that it spread over this territory from a single centre." His explanation for the similarity of tales in far reaches of the globe was based on contact between geographically connected cultures. The task at hand was to know more of the "mode and psychology" of dissemination, the construction of texts, the history of individual societies, and the social role of lore within them.[21]

What were Crane and Boas referring to when they pointed to influential German geographic approaches? For one, the concept of *Kulturkreise* (culture clusters). In Germany and Austria, a group of ethnologists, including Fritz Graebner, Wilhelm Schmidt, and Wilhelm Koppers, reconstructed the movement of cultures by determining clusters of cultural traits that moved together. They took inspiration from Adolf Bastian's writings in the 1860s on *Völkergedanken* (folk ideas). Folk ideas are elementary ideas, common to humankind, that are modified by a particular environment. Folk ideas are embedded into a regional culture. Folk ideas travel and contribute to the civilizing process, Bastian thought, because among peoples, migrations and contacts occur that reduce the importance of the environment. Evidence of folk ideas and the effects of migrations on them will be manifested in traditional adaptations to the environment, namely, in cookery, shelter, and technology. To find the clusters of culture, the Germans began by collecting evidence of such adaptations, or traits, in a small area. Then, distribution maps were prepared, based on the frequency of traits, especially artifactual evidence, brought into an area by trade, war, travel, or geography. From such maps, the analyst came up with traits that originally belonged together. The analyst identified the resulting clusters as *Kulturkreise*. The addition of history for individual societies allowed for the determination of the *Kulturschichten* (cultural strata), which gave an outline of the civilizing process. Graebner's "Die melanesische Bogenkultur und iher verwandten," for instance, maps the spread of Melanesian "bow culture" outside of Melanesia. Graebner summed up a basic premise of his method: "It was not single dispersed elements, but a whole culture complex with its most characteristic traits which we have followed through all five continents."[22]

Criticisms of the *Kulturkreislehre* (culture-cluster school) centered on the school's generalized composites of traits, which give no indication of origin or variance, and the school's failure to deal with historical accidents, local or individual developments, and social change. Critics also objected to the school's overreliance on museum artifacts, which had been removed from their original contexts, and its acceptance of unrepresentative or exotic survivals. Still, the school was instrumental in revealing the advantages of studying individual societies.

Of the *Kulturkreislehre* writers, the one who was especially influential on Boas was Friedrich Ratzel (1844–1904). In 1882, Ratzel published *Anthropogeographie,* which gave a name to a brand of geographical determinism that was steeped in the expansionist politics of Germany. "The spatial unity of life" derives from the land, he declared; and it provides the material link among people which develops according to evolutionary laws. Supporting the civilizing imperative of imperialism, he asserted that the rise of a civilization is marked by its expansion of territory: "All people who remain at lower stages of cultural development are also spatially small. Their field of living is small, as is their field of action and their circle of vision. . . . All the qualities of a people that facilitate political expansion must always be of special value because of the abiding tendency toward the formation of bigger spaces."[23] As the civilizations expand, they are likely to affect simpler peoples. Culture becomes a matter of, first, a relation of people to their land and its subsequent manifestation in politics and, second, the contact of simpler peoples with one another and with the great civilizations. The expansion of the great civilizations into primitive areas thus is both natural and progressive.

Writing his ethnography *Baffin-Land* in 1885, Boas saved his longest discussion for "Anthropo-geographie." Later Boas came to see Ratzel's expansionist views as the other extreme from Brinton. The assumptions of geographic determinism and of the progressive evolutionary sequence from small to large spaces denied to Boas the integrity of cultural wholes and their inner dynamics. Boas leaned toward the study of the variety of cultures, rather than toward their inevitable unity. Ratzel's emphasis on historical ideas in a culture and on the influence of cultural contact nonetheless lingered on in Boas's ethnographies. The age's preoccupation with the geographic nature of cultural space was not limited to Germany, however. All at once, it seemed, periodicals arose which dealt with geography's relation to culture and politics: *National Geographic Magazine* (1889), *Annales de geographie* (1891), the *Geographic Journal* (1893), *Geographische Zeitschrift* (1895). Global in scope, they gave the charting and description of natural space more precision than it had ever had before. They also raised comparisons to the increasing contact of different peoples and to the shifts in control of their land and culture.

For the antiexpansionist Boas, field work among the Eskimo during the 1880s alerted him to the control that a people maintained over culture and over the integrity of a cultural whole. Educated in Germany, he followed some of the scientific spirit, if not the substance, of the *Kulturkreislehre*. Rather than being global in scope, Boas's ethnography stressed the necessity of observing and living in an alien culture over time. He attempted to mediate between the extremes that he saw in Brinton's evolutionary, comparative doctrine and Ratzel's geographic, diffusionist determinism. In 1896, Boas delivered an incisive paper on "The Limitations of the Comparative Method of Anthropology," which outlined his major criticisms of cultural evolution: (1) Universal ideas are not identical; rather, they vary, and the variance is caused by environmental and psychological conditions. (2) Cultural phenomena, without regard to chronology, cannot be compared, because they develop differently in different cultures. An ethnographer should therefore study the history of an individual society. (3) The focus of research should be, not on survivals, but on the processes by which culture has developed. (4) Similarities between discontinuous geographical areas are not satisfactory proof of a historical connection; rather, a continuity of distribution must be shown. Boas wanted more exacting description; such description would reveal social complexity, rather than the simplicity of historical evolution.[24]

Boas differed from German historical approaches by emphasizing individual cultures, rather than specific traits; by viewing variance, rather than stability resulting from diffusion; and by rejecting a progressive scheme for the development of a culture. He encouraged his students—who included notables in folklore research such as Melville Herskovits, Alfred L. Kroeber, Ruth Fulton Benedict, Ruth Bunzel, Margaret Mead, and Gladys Reichard—to undertake field research, which was atypical of the *Kulturkreislehre,* and to pay close attention to folklore. Indeed, the *Journal of American Folklore* was edited from 1908 to 1940 by Boas and his followers.

Boas's diffusionism brought a more relativistic world view to cultural scholarship. One culture was not qualitatively better than another, as the evolutionists would have it; rather, it was different. A culture and its art, lore, and technology should be appreciated on its own terms. If Boas's geographical training provided the model of diffusion and the importance of place, then his training in physics brought the growing relativistic trend in the physical sciences to the fore. Writing in *Science* in 1887, Boas noted, "The fact that the rapid disclosure of the most remote parts of the globe coincided with the no less rapid development of physical sciences has had a deep influence on the development of geography." Boas complained, however, that in "searching for similar phenomena," the physicist "loses sight altogether of the spot from which he started."[25]

Both Boas's anthropology and the physical sciences responded to the older absolutism of time and space. Building on the contributions of older scientists such as Hendrik Lorentz, Albert Einstein in 1905 answered with a theory of relativity which held that "every reference body has its own particular time," each correct on its own terms. Like Darwin, relativity had its social interpreters. In *The Elementary Forms of the Religious Life* (1912), Émile Durkheim observed that time is relative to a culture's social organization. In *Ulysses* (1922), James Joyce sets his central character in "the twelfth day of May of the bissextile year one thousand nine hundred and four of the christian era (jewish era five thousand six hundred and sixty-four, mohammedan era one thousand three hundred and twenty-two), golden number 5, epact 13, solar cycle 9, dominical letters C B, Roman indication 2, Julian period 6617, MXMIV."[26] Time, like culture, is relative to the system by which it is measured. In evolution, time is absolute and vertical; in relativity, time is referential and horizontal. In relativity, one's sense of place and motion from and to that place plays a much more important role. Thus the assumption that survivals found in a culture of the present could be connected to a different culture of another time did not hold up in a view of time and space that was heterogeneous rather than homogeneous. Boas's cultural relativism stressed the integrity of individual cultures and, often, the individual within the culture.

I dwell on Boas, not to deny the contribution of other folklore scholars, but because of his organizational influence. George Stocking acknowledged, for example, that "although German-born and deeply rooted in the intellectual traditions of his homeland, Franz Boas more than any other man defined the 'national character' of anthropology in the United States . . . there is no real question that he was the most important single force in shaping American anthropology in the first half of the twentieth century."[27] In addition to being German-born, Boas's Jewish heritage, which involved the Diaspora and being a member of a minority group, reminded him of the cultural influence of diffusion and the relativistic integrity of subcultures. Indeed, other prominent figures who were attracted to diffusion, such as Moses Gaster (1856–1939) and Joseph Jacobs (1854–1916), shared that heritage. In America, rising anti-Semitism (including restrictions on Jewish students at Boas's Columbia University and other colleges) and racial intolerance through the 1920s heightened Boas's insistence on cultural relativism.

Folklore was crucial to Boas's work, because it provided an excellent reflection of the culture from which it sprang. Folklore in the form of tales and myths was a culture's own measurement of time, motion, and social conditions. Still, as Gladys Reichard reflected in the forties, "Professor Boas did not study folklore because he was a 'folklorist' nor by studying it did he become one. He used it as an important part of the whole which he envisioned; a description of the tribes in which he was interested and an interpretation of their culture." His contribution to folklore, Melville Jacobs added, was "collecting and encouraging the gathering of folktales; in setting up rigorous criteria for the ways in which they should be obtained; in their use to show diffusion; and in noting the elements of social organization and culture they contained."[28]

As Boas examined the diffusion of folklore among North American Indians, his student Melville Herskovits (1895–1963) investigated American blacks and their relation to African roots. Like Boas, Herskovits wanted to crush racist notions of racial and ethnic inferiority that were attached to studies of minority or exotic cultures. Herskovits's major work, The Myth of the Negro Past (1941), made a case for a vital African-American culture. Herskovits denied that blacks had lost their African heritage when they entered the New World. Herskovits confirmed Boas's idea of variance in diffusion when he argued, "Turning now to consider the different degree to which differing elements in each of these cultures have responded to contact with non-African ways of life, we see that the carry-over of Africanisms is anything but uniform over individual cultures, being far greater in some aspects than in others."[29]

Unlike the Kulturkreislehre, who did not allow for individual control of culture, Herskovits claimed that culture "can be mastered by any individual without regard to race, or by any group that has the will and the opportunity to master it." He thus proposed the reinterpretation of retentions in new settings, an answer to Boas's call for understanding processes of enculturation. And unlike W. E. B. Du Bois in his evolutionary study of Afro-American houses and house life, Herskovits found that a unilinear development could not be supported by field evidence, which showed that various forms had developed differently.[30]

While Herskovits's writings reflected his preoccupation with interactive patterns of the individual in culture and the boundaries of cultures, another of Boas's students, Alfred L. Kroeber (1876–1960) parted company over the issue. Kroeber was especially active in folklore studies during the first decade of the twentieth century. In 1905 he helped to organize a California branch of the American

Folklore Society; in 1906 he was the society's president. From his study of California Indians, he plotted the distribution of various cultural traits, including folklore. Following Boas, Kroeber found that the clusterings of traits were nonrandom and could be attached to centers of dispersion. But he puzzled over the "distinctive character" of the California Indians while accounting for the historical spread of influence of southwest Pueblos. Kroeber questioned the boundaries that ethnographers had given to whole cultures and sought a view of a culture's self-identity from the inside of the culture, as evidenced through folklore. Folklore became a refraction of reality, rather than a reflection of it. In Kroeber's view during this period of his work with folklore, culture became less a matter of boundaries and more one of affect.[31]

Boas's interest in the diffusion of tales and myths is related to what has been dubbed the "historic-geographic" approach in folklore studies. It, too, tried to map dissemination and dispersion centers; but in the tradition of T. F. Crane and other literary scholars, it sought textual, rather than ethnographic, movements over the world. In America, the leading proponent of this approach, Stith Thompson (1885–1976), a professor of English at Indiana University who had been trained by George Lyman Kittredge at Harvard, looked for inspiration to Finnish folklorists from the late nineteenth and early twentieth centuries, such as Kaarle Krohn and Antti Aarne. Thompson was concerned with both variation and similarity caused by diffusion, but he tended to examine the life histories of specific folklore texts rather than societies. Of Boas, Thompson said: "Not only through his own labors but through that of his many distinguished disciples, Franz Boas made a colossal contribution to the study of every aspect of aboriginal American life. Not least important in these studies have been voluminous collections of folktales from every quarter of the continent. From him and his contemporaries . . . we now possess faithful recordings of native tales in such quantity that for a large number of representative tribes we can be reasonably sure that we now have something approaching the complete repertory of narrative material. Many of these collections are accompanied by linguistic texts, so that it is possible to use them for the study of narrative style. Both in respect to the faithfulness of recording and to the relative number of texts available to the student, we are better prepared for a study of the North American Indian tale than for even those of Europe and the Near East." Despite his debt to Finnish folklorists, Thompson said that he owed to Boas his attention to "folktale dissemination, of narrative style, of cultural adaptations, and of individual differences in narrators."[32]

While acknowledging the value of studying individual societies, Thompson called for a more comprehensive analysis of the tale and its forms. Thompson indexed motifs from reports of tales, and he mapped the distribution of sequentially related motifs or tale types. By noting the concentration of tale types in one area and its movement, Thompson identified paths of diffusion, for example, the "Star-Husband Tale" among North American Indian tribes.[33] The identity of the paths was supported by historical evidence, but through the tracing of items across space, rather than through a culture in time. Thompson looked to fully developed tales as signs of antiquity and to tale fragments as a sign of later circulation. Through the comparison of world-wide evidence he sought to find the tale's original form and home.

Boas and Thompson shared their age's attention to motion across cultural space and time, but differences mounted as their paths split between describing the whole of a culture and the material of folklore. While Boas was studying roles of individuals in the enculturative process, Thompson assumed the passivity of the bearers. Boas stressed ethnic connections to lore; Thompson stressed textual continuity across ethnic centers. Another difference between the historicalism of Boas and of Thompson lies in the purpose of study. Boas cautioned against using searches for the origins of specific traits as objects for study. The historic-geographic folklorists sought *ur*-forms and archetypes as their goals of research. While Boas revised and expanded German ethnography of individual cultures in *Ethnology of the Kwakiutl* (1921) and *Tsimshian Mythology* (1916), Thompson revised and expanded Finnish indexing work in *The Types of the Folktale* (1928) and *Motif-Index of Folk-Literature* (6 vols., 1932–36). In his own way, each established systematic approaches and outlined the character of his discipline in America.

Both Boas and Thompson had their detractors in their time, but they maintained their position of influence through the 1940s. Boas came under attack for overemphasizing empirical investigation at the expense of theory building. In 1956, Murray Wax complained that Boas had restricted the claims of anthropology to the point that creative research was virtually impossible.[34] The goals of accumulating data in huge volumes were ultimately unclear, and collection needed prior sifting. Even Boas's field work, for which he was celebrated, came under criticism, for critics revealed that he relied heavily on interpreters and selected aged informants. Many questioned Boas's claims to the objectivity of his ethnography.[35]

Thompson came under attack for not taking into account social conditions and the role of the individual teller in the transmission of folktales. The goals of his research appeared less relevant to folklorists who were interested in the social and psychological conditions that generate folklore. Thompson's devolutionary premise that fully developed texts decayed over time into tale fragments came into question. The selectivity of his evidence, which relied on haphazard collection, and its crude translation of an isolated telling, which may differ at other times, cast doubt on the true comparability of texts. Thompson minimized cultural differences among the texts to fit his classification, which may differ when viewed from within the culture.[36]

In the light of their time, Thompson and Boas moved their studies from the natural history of the nineteenth century to a physical science in the twentieth. During that time there was a nationally felt movement from the importance of environment to one of human artifice. Thompson and Boas gave folklore a "physical system." They emphasized the distinctive elements of folklore, its motifs, and its types. Like the standardization of time in the late nineteenth century, folklore in the early twentieth century took on standards of form, which were divided into associated zones of place.

Boas and Thompson had a lasting influence in reshaping their professional cultures—Boas for anthropology and Thompson for folklore. Boas, as Reichard noted, did not consider himself a folklorist. But he built the research of folklore into the anthropological repertoire; he helped to direct students to work and publish in folklore. Thompson, in his study of texts and his promotion of folklorists, helped to move folklore out on its own, for he drew attention to points of difference with the student of anthropology. Unlike the earlier generation, Boas and Thompson had students who had ties of loyalty to the academic institutions that trained them. For both Boas and Thompson, the student now had more to do and had to do it more systematically. The student was required to be isolated, in the field or in the library. The isolation and sense of mission that were thus instilled demanded loyalty to the profession, indeed, to the professors. The students relied on them for security and self-justification.

From the ethnographies and indexes that had been compiled by Boas and Thompson, students moved their discipline further by seeking more explanation. A world that realized its heterogeneousness also sought to explain its connectedness. What held the small worlds together? In the environment, biologists observed, organisms that are set in the specific time and space of nature hold roles that they are unaware of in the ecological order. Time and space also seemed to be increasingly divided at work. Labor was divided, tasks were assigned, and parts of a system contributed to the running of an organization. Was this true for culture? Does folklore, like a worker, have a role, a function, to play outside of one's awareness? In the anthropological current, folklore already provided evidence of the parts of culture; with descriptions of social life, more questions of function arose.

FUNCTION

Also calling for better description through the ethnography of individual cultures, Bronislaw Malinowski (1884–1942), between 1914 and 1918, studied the Trobriand Islanders of Melanesia. Unlike many previous students of primitive societies, he had the advantage of working through the native language over a prolonged period; he presented his ethnography as *Argonauts of the Western Pacific* (1922). He announced in the foreword that "the reader of this monograph will clearly see that though its main theme is economic—for it deals with commercial enterprise, exchange and trade—constant reference has to be made to social organization, the power of magic, to mythology and folklore, and indeed to all other aspects as well as the main one."[37] These different aspects operated as a structured system; the expression of one depended on the expression of the others. Malinowski considered the problem under study to be "sociological and geographical," thus corresponding to the basing of social conditions in space, which was common among Boas's ethnographies.

The economic theme that was the center of his study was the *Kula* (the Trobrianders' name for exchange and trade). Malinowski wrote that the *Kula,* "a half commercial, half ceremonial exchange . . . is carried out for its own sake, in fulfilment of a deep desire to possess. But here again, it is not ordinary possession, but a special type, in which a man owns for a short time, and in an alternating manner, individual specimens of two classes of objects." The exchange in the *Kula* differs from the exchange of currency, for the objects are not for individual consumption, but for a ritualistic, communal exchange. "Their behaviour at the transaction," Malinowski observed, "makes it clear that . . . it is treated also in a ritual manner, and arouses emotional reaction." Looked at as a structured system, the exchange forms a ring among the islanders. The result is that the bonds form among the often scattered islanders; their boundaries as a tribe are measured by participation in the *Kula.* The system of exchange had the function of maintaining the society. As Malinowski explains, "A big, inter-tribal relationship, uniting with definite social bonds a vast area and great numbers of people, binding them with definite ties of reciprocal obligations, making them follow minute rules and observations in a concerted manner—the Kula is a sociological mechanism of surpassing size and complexity."[38]

What set Malinowski's ethnography apart was its emphasis, not on origin and diffusion, but on the function of customs. To be sure, precedents were provided by the late-nineteenth-century views of Émile Durkheim and of William Robertson Smith. These writers had denied that Western religion was the culmination of many primitive religious systems. Religions are different and will remain diverse because they serve social functions for particular groups of people. Malinowski found, for example, that the islanders attached many beliefs of danger to apparently harmless trading trips to other tribes. These beliefs, which were part of their religious system, served to warn the islanders of their limits of safety and trust; the beliefs reinforced the islanders' social identity and self-reliance. These beliefs were not part of an irrational system bound to give way to Western religion; they deliberately served utilitarian purposes.[39]

Malinowski also built on the views of magic provided by Sir James George Frazer (1854–1941), author of *The Golden Bough* (1890). Frazer wrote the preface for *Argonauts,* but he makes it clear that Malinowski will depart from Frazer's own evolutionary doctrine. Frazer points out that Malinowski had singled out one system of exchange for special consideration, rather than looking at the world-wide comparison of "primitive economics." Malinowski had considered the culture of a single society on its own terms. Frazer also noted Malinowski's method, which takes "full account of the complexity of human nature." Indeed, Frazer admits that anthropologists had neglected the material and economic foundation of life, "because they were attracted to the higher side of man's nature." Also adding complexity was Malinowski's incorporation of geography, sociology, and psychology into his ethnography. As Frazer observed, Malinowski had brought together views from "a number of sciences, each of which considers a single part of man's complex organism."[40] Frazer wrote his preface in the hope that Malinowski would either continue to study "primitive economics" generally or add the comparison of "savage and barbarous peoples"; but Malinowski, exploring the motives for perpetuating customs and the mechanisms by which a society is maintained, emphasized the observation of a specific culture as it was set in time and space. Like Boas, Malinowski concentrated on the variation, rather than the unity, in culture.

Malinowski, like Boas, was born in Europe and finished his career in the United States. Malinowski, however, spent fewer years in America than Boas did, and Malinowski's main organizational influence was on British anthropology. Still, I spend time here on him and his British colleague A. R. Radcliffe-Brown, because their writings were the immediate influences on applications of functionalism by American folklorists. Malinowski was born and raised in Poland. His graduate education was in physics and mathematics, but while recuperating from a bout of tuberculosis, he read Frazer's *Golden Bough,* which inspired him to take up anthropology and folklore studies. He sought out prominent anthropologists in London, including Folk-Lore Society president Robert R. Marett, author of *Psychology and Folk-Lore* (1920). Between 1924 and 1930, Edward Evans-Pritchard recalls, Malinowski taught most of the social anthropologists who subsequently held chairs in Great Britain and the Dominions.[41] But his influence was also felt in the United States. He died in 1942, shortly after his appointment as professor of anthropology at Yale University.

In his teaching and writing, Malinowski described an equilibrium model of culture—society as an integrated, homeostatic organism. The *Kula,* for example, forms a system of mutual interrelationships in an area that was known for its exclusiveness and war. The function of an institution, or an organized system of activity, like the function of an organism, is the role that it plays within the interrelated whole in fulfilling universal human needs. He divided needs into three categories: (1) primary or biological, such as procreation, nutrition, or protection; (2) derived or instrumental, such as economics or education; and (3) integrative or synthetic, such as magic, religion, play, and art. Magic, Malinowski argued, is a reaction to man's knowledge of his impotence. Malinowski wrote that man's "anxiety, his fears and hopes, induce a tension in his organism which drives him to some sort of activity."[42] Every cultural form rested on some individual need.

In *Argonauts,* Malinowski called for the ethnographer to study a society as a closed structure to determine the functions of its parts. He concluded by asserting that "there is room for a new type of theory," in contrast to evolutionary doctrine (citing Tylor and Frazer), diffusion (citing Ratzel and Graebner), and "anthropo-geography" (citing Ratzel). "The influence on one another of the various aspects of an institution, the study of the social and psychological mechanism on which the institution is based, are a type of theoretical studies which has been practised up till now in a tentative way only, but I venture to foretell will come into their own sooner or later. This kind of research will pave the way and provide the material for the others."[43] In contrast to the hidden past of origin and the great extent of diffusion, Malinowski's "institution" moved ethnography to its modern meaning of the immediate present. In his functionalism was the direct observation of how a specific culture operates in a present time and over a limited space.

In 1926, however, Malinowski touted "functionalism" as the "right method" in social anthropology. Functionalism is, he wrote, the "explanation of . . . facts . . . by the part they play within the integral system of culture, by the manner in which they are related to each other within the system, and by the manner in which this system is related to the physical surroundings. The functional view . . . insists therefore upon the principle that in every type of civilization, every custom, material object, idea and belief fulfils some vital function, has some task to accomplish, represents an indispensable part within a working whole." Magic, for instance, now was "a remedy for specific maladjustments and mental conflicts, which culture creates in allowing man to transcend his biological equipment."[44] He implied that every cultural item was indispensable to the working of a social system as a whole.

Malinowski's functionalism was environmental, because he integrally connected material conditions to social life. Frazer observed that for Malinowski, "that material foundation, consisting in the necessity of food and of a certain degree of warmth and shelter from the elements, forms the economic or industrial basis and prime condition of human life." Using the organismic model further, Malinowski wrote: "Culture is nothing but the organized behavior of man. Man differs from the animals in that he has to rely on an artificially fashioned environment: on implements, weapons, dwellings, and man-made means of transport." Customs exist, Malinowski argued, as "a blend of utilitarian anxiety about the most necessary objects of his surroundings, with some preoccupation in those which strike his imagination and attract his attention."[45]

Malinowski's use of such terms as "organized behavior" and "institutions" echoes the spreading rhetoric of bureaucracies in Western society at the turn of the century. Incorporation had been the answer to manage the growing extent of industrial capitalism in the early twentieth century. By 1904, for example, about three hundred industrial corporations had won control over more than two-fifths of all manufacturing in the United States; by 1929, the two hundred largest corporations held 48 percent of all corporate assets.[46] The corporations appeared to be their own societies, indeed cultures, with their chiefs, myths, and rituals; their social structure was bureaucratic. In 1925, Sinclair Lewis used the theme in *Arrowsmith,* which won the Pulitzer Prize. The protagonist enters a building in New York and contrasts the older horizontal landscape of the prairies with the dominant vertical landscape of the cities: "Born to the prairies, never far from the sight of the cornfields, Martin was conveyed to blazing lands and portentous enterprises. One of the row of bronze-barred elevators was labeled 'Express to McGurk Institute.' He entered it proudly, feeling himself already a part of the godly association. They rose swiftly, and he had but half-second glimpses of ground glass doors with the signs of mining companies, lumber companies, Central American railroad companies."[47] In the vertical bureaucracy, time and space had shrunk, but the effect was to reveal the diversity within the smaller boundaries of time and space.

Bureaucracy, as Henry Jacoby points out in *The Bureaucratization of the World* (1973), "refers to the fact that man's existence is directed and controlled by central agencies; not only is he unable to escape from the regulation and manipulation, he seems to depend on it."[48] In Malinowski's attempt to trace structural relations in a society is a bureaucratic imagery; in the abstract, his ethnography dealt with the social regulation and manipulation of an economic system.

The image of many large organizations in a society, instead of an overarching cultural unity, can also be seen in the replacement of the ideas of natural history with those of biology among intellectuals. The organismic model of biology and physiology, for example, understood life to be the function and development of a dynamic organism within a closed environment. The living body assumed an organic unity in a unique time and space. Activities of the body assumed invisible functions that were crucial to its existence. Biology stressed the observable variation of forms and environments. Following the organismic model, the later psychology of Freud treated the psyche as a balanced system. When motivated by drives, behavior becomes a goal-directed action to reduce anxieties and to maintain the system. Combining psychology and philosophy, the pragmatist William James described the function of thought as helping to sustain "satisfactory relations with our surroundings." In 1929 the structuralist Roman Jakobson declared: "Any set of phenomena examined by contemporary science is treated not as a mechanical agglomeration but as a structural whole, and the basic task is to reveal the inner . . . laws of this system. What appears to be the focus . . . is no longer the outer stimulus, but the internal premises of the development; now the mechanical concept of processes yield to the question of their function." For polity, Max Weber presented a model of the individual in a bureaucratic organization in terms of an actor's motives in typical situations; these motives are judged by intended and unintended consequences.[49]

The connection between this biological functionalism and the bureaucratic management of the period becomes explicit in the popular writing of Henry Ford and Bruce Barton in the 1920s. In Henry Ford's *My Life and Work* (1923), Ford said that his model for success was to follow a "natural code." He explained: "The primary functions are agriculture, manufacture, and transportation. Community life is impossible without them. They hold the world together. Raising things, making things, and carrying things are as primitive as human need and yet as modern as anything can be." His goal was to create an economic system wherein each of the different roles—those of manager, worker, purchaser—would serve to gain from interrelated needs and the elimination of waste. In 1925, advertising executive Bruce Barton used this bureaucratic view of functionalism to fashion a reinterpretation of the life of Jesus Christ. The result was *The Man Nobody Knows* (1925), a best seller that sold 250,000 copies in only eighteen months after its publication. Referring first to needs, Barton states that "the race must be fed and clothed and housed and transported, as well as preached to, and taught and healed." The resulting religious structure is bureaucratic: "Thus *all* business is his Father's business. All work is worship; all useful service prayer. And whoever works wholeheartedly at any worthy calling is a co-worker with the Almighty in the great enterprise which He has initiated but which he can never finish without the help of men."[50]

Around the same time that Malinowski, Ford, and Barton were publishing, British anthropologist A. R. Radcliffe-Brown (1881–1955) was writing his ethnography *The Andaman Islanders* (1922), in which a bound cultural group set in a specific space and time was again examined. But Radcliffe-Brown carried even further than Malinowski the analysis of the role that customs play in the maintenance of an organization. Radcliffe-Brown espoused a different brand of functionalism, often referred to as structural functionalism.

Radcliffe-Brown drew his inspiration from Émile Durkheim's study of the worship of a totem god among Australian aborigines. In Durkheim's view, the worship reinforced the society's identity and continuity. Function, for Durkheim, revolved around the role that social solidarity plays in shaping a culture.[51] Following Durkheim, Radcliffe-Brown played down Malinowski's biological and psychological motives and emphasized instead the social functions of status and cohesion as they operate in an integrative social whole.

In his study of Andamanese customs and beliefs, Radcliffe-Brown denied Tylor's and Müller's view that myths arise out of native explanations of natural phenomena. The Andaman Islander, he asserted, "has no interest in nature save in so far it directly affects the social life." The motives that Radcliffe-Brown inferred also ran toward utilitarian needs but were social rather than material in their characteristics. A social structure, Radcliffe-Brown wrote, is "an arrangement of persons in institutionally controlled and defined relations." "As the word function is being used," Radcliffe-Brown explained in "On the Concept of Function in Social Science" (1935), "the life of an organism is conceived as the *functioning* of its structure. It is through and by the continuity of the functioning that the continuity of the structure is preserved. If we consider any recurrent part of the life-process, such as respiration, digestion, etc., its *function* is the part it plays in, the contribution it makes to, the life of the organism as a whole. As the terms are here being used a cell or an organ has an *activity* and that activity has a *function*" (emphasis in original). Cultural activities therefore contribute functionally to the maintenance of the social structure: "The Andaman Islander finds himself in an ordered world, a world subject to law, controlled by unseen forces." Customs, rather than functions of materialism or anxiety, "are simply means by which certain ways of feeling about the different aspects of social life are regularly expressed, and through expression, kept alive and passed on from one generation to another."[52]

Other structural/functional analyses carried further the causal relationship between customs and social life. Meyer Fortes, in his study of the Tallensi in West Africa, claimed that "the Tallensi have an ancestor cult not because they fear the dead—for they do not—or believe in the immortality of the soul—for they have no such notion—but because their social structure *demands it*" (emphasis added). Edmund Leach, however, criticized the assumption of unity in the social structure and claimed that any social system contains opposing factions. Using the example of myth, he found that different myths validate rights of different groups of people within the same society. He concluded that myth is a "language of argument, not a chorus of harmony."[53]

Difficulties arose when function was used as an explanation, because a function could be construed as a consequence rather than as a cause. For example, do couples go through marriage ceremonies because the custom preserves the social structure? The institution of marriage may have the effect of encouraging social harmony, but that does not explain why couples enter into matrimony and participate in its ceremonies. Malinowski himself recognized the problem of causation in *A Scientific Theory of Culture and Other Essays* (1944). He wrote: "This type of functional analysis is easily exposed to the accusation of tautology and platitude, as well as to the criticism that it implies a logical circle, for, obviously, if we define function as the satisfaction of a need, it is easy to suspect that the need to be satisfied has been introduced in order to satisfy the need of satisfying function. Thus, for instance, clans are obviously an additional . . . type of internal differentiation. Can we speak of a legitimate need for such differentiation, especially when the need is not ever present; for not all communities have clans, and yet they go on very well without them."[54]

Moreover, why do activities occur that are, in Malinowski's terms, nonfunctional? Malinowski was at a loss to explain why world wars occurred when in his view they served no utilitarian purpose for modern Europe. Addressing the American Sociological Association in 1959, its president, Kingsley Davis, warned that functionalism as a special movement had better be dropped, for the terms that it provides are ambiguous and, after all, not explanatory. For example, Marvin Harris later declared that social structures are created abstractions. Turning Radcliffe-Brown's analogy around, Harris warned, "It is as if in attempting to discover the functions of the spinal columns of amphibia, we ran the risk of examining a series of headless frogs."[55]

The historian of anthropology Fred Voget speculated that Americans, working in an open society, had become skeptical of the closed system that the European anthropologists had drawn. Americans tended to view cultures through the careers of typical individuals, while Europeans described a social life that was dominated by an orderly arrangement of statuses.[56] Yet an American that offered a powerful hybrid form of functionalism was William Bascom (1912–1981). Born in Illinois, Bascom, like Malinowski, began his studies in physics. He went to Northwestern University, where he received his Ph.D. in 1939 under Melville Herskovits. Bascom's areas of interest lay in the tribal cultures of Africa and Micronesia. He took a special interest, he wrote, in the folklore of these areas, because folklore is an excellent mirror of culture and, furthermore, because it serves to perpetuate culture.[57] Through the war years he worked as an economist until he rejoined the Northwestern faculty in 1947. In 1957 he left for the University of California at Berkeley, where he taught folk narrative, directed the Lowie Museum, and helped to establish a Master's-degree program in folklore. His research in African folklore, art, and religion resulted in several books, including *Ifa Divination: Communication between Gods and Men in West Africa* (1969), which won the Pitrè International Folklore Prize. His influence on folklore studies was especially noteworthy in the 1950s as he brought out a series of articles in the *Journal of American Folklore,* laying out his functional approach.

The most important of these articles was "Four Functions of Folklore" (1954), which was the presidential address to the American Folklore Society in 1953. Attempting to reconcile humanistic and anthropological perspectives prevalent in the society, Bascom proposed that traditional functionalism, as introduced by Malinowski and Radcliffe-Brown, provided a framework for interpreting folklore in

both culture and literature. He said: "To fully understand folklore and
its role in man's life, we must have more knowledge of the specific
functions of each of these forms in various societies, literate and
nonliterate, and more of the tedious but extremely rewarding comparisons of the details of folklore texts with those of culture and actual
behavior." Assuming that folklore maintains the stability of a culture,
he presented four ways in which folklore fulfills this role. Through the
first function of amusement, a person finds escape from the repressions imposed by the society. Thus the system continues by means of
the built-in safety valve of folklore. Second, folklore validates cultural
activities such as rituals and institutions for those who perform and
observe them. Third, folklore educates persons in the values of the
society. Fourth, folklore maintains conformity to accepted patterns of
behavior. More than education, folklore can apply social pressure and
even social control, in forms such as lullabies or proverbs. A fifth
function overarches the others. Folklore, Bascom summarized, integrates society and makes it cohere.[58]

With his fifth, and most basic, function, Bascom took into account
Leach's postulation of disharmony as well as harmony, which are
evident in the social effects of folklore. Bascom argued that folklore
integrates society by giving expression to the values of factions in a
society, but by offering the safety valve of this expression, the larger
society reduces sources of open conflict and it therefore coheres. As a
result of the cohesion of the society, culture remains stable. Perhaps
as a result of the special American concern in the 1950s for the
dissenting individual's role in a conformable society, Bascom's functionalism postulated that individuals in society have more of a
purposeful role in shaping their culture than Radcliffe-Brown had
seemed to imply. Bascom concluded "Four Functions of Folklore" by
asserting that folklore "is used to inculcate the customs and ethical
standards in the young, and as an adult to reward him with praise when
he conforms, to punish him with ridicule or criticism when he deviates,
to provide him with rationalizations when the institutions and conventions are challenged or questioned, to suggest that he be content with
things as they are, and to provide him with a compensatory escape
from 'the hardships, the inequalities, the injustices' of everyday life.
Here indeed, is the basic paradox of folklore, that while it plays a vital
role in transmitting and maintaining the institutions of a culture and in
forcing the individual to conform to them, at the same time it provides
socially approved outlets for the repressions which these same institutions impose upon him."[59]

Bascom's brand of functionalism tried to mediate other apparent
intellectual divisions. There was, for example, the split between

humanities and anthropology in the special attention, on the one hand, to the texts of folklore and, on the other, to the customs of culture. Analysis of texts and the consideration of the context of the culture are necessary, Bascom argued, to attack a common problem of the camps of folklore studies—what folklore does for the people who tell it. One had to look within the text of folklore, as well as the social context, to find reasons that certain functions are needed. To answer this question, Bascom's functionalism integrated Malinowski's biological motives and Radcliffe-Brown's social-structural motives. The result, an inventory of different types of functions that folklore plays, was an eclectic analysis. Some functions were more important in some instances of folklore than in others.

Yet because Bascom's functionalism stressed, even more than had Malinowski's and Radcliffe-Brown's, the immediate social conditions of customs and the purposes of the participants in those customs, his functionalism stressed the psychological functions of folklore. To Bascom, folklore is especially essential to the maintenance of society because it is a mechanism for dealing with anxieties. In "Four Functions of Folklore," Bascom argued that "folklore reveals man's frustrations and attempts to escape in fantasy from repressions imposed upon him by society, whether these repressions be sexual or otherwise and whether they result from taboos on incest or polygamy, or from a taboo on laughing at a person afflicted by yaws. The concepts of compensation and the escape mechanism are fully as suggestive when applied to the familiar theme of rags to riches, or to the Cinderella and Frau Holle tales, as when they are applied to the Oedipus myth. But folklore also reveals man's attempts to escape in fantasy form the conditions of his geographical environment and from his own biological limitations as a member of the genus and species *Homo sapiens.*"[60] Most of Bascom's examples were taken from African and American Indian tribes, but he left the door open for functional analyses of folklore in modern American culture.

Following Bascom, folklorist Frank Hoffman explained the persistence of Anglo-American erotica by positing the social functions that such material played within the culture. Sex is one of the strongest human drives, he argued, and society sublimates that drive through institutions such as marriage. Hoffman wrote: "It is as a resolution to this conflict that erotica perhaps serves its most important function in society. Indeed, I believe that one might make a strong circumstantial case for the origin and preservation of erotic folklore as a kind of universal safety valve or release from sexual tension and frustration." In another functional analysis, Evon Z. Vogt proposed that water witching in America constituted a ritual response to situations of technological uncertainty. "The *certain* answers provided by the dowser relieve the farmer's anxiety about ground-water resources and inspire confidence to go ahead with the hard work of developing farms" (emphasis in original).[61]

But while most American psychological approaches judge motivation from the individual's standpoint, functionalism deduces such information from the culture. For example, Roger Abrahams and Alan Dundes have proposed that in elephant jokes, which were popular in the 1960s, the elephant was a symbol for blacks. Both elephants and blacks were hard to miss, yet they appeared awkward with newly found power. By directing attention to a symbolic form at a time of racial tension, the elephant joke served the function of reducing anxiety and helping to stabilize American culture. In a study about the stability of an occupational group, Patrick Mullen, following Malinowski, concluded that risk situations effected magical beliefs among Texas Gulf Coast fishermen. He found that as the risk of danger increased, so did the number of magical beliefs surrounding a fishing situation. But one must ask, Did risk cause the rise of beliefs, or did beliefs engender the risk?[62]

Following Radcliffe-Brown, Henry Glassie in *All Silver and No Brass* (1975) observed that Christmas mumming in an Irish village had held a fragmented community together. He asserted that mumming reflected a period when "community was still a concern of its members," and he attributed the demise of both mumming and the community to the changing social needs of more recent generations.[63] Folklorists have tended to shy away from structural functional approaches, partly because they omit kinship and polity from their scope. When these approaches are used, they serve to explain the persistence of conservative communities that are attached to isolated geographic areas or religious sects. Malinowski's frame of social context and literary content is typically the source of the "traditional functionalism" that was used for many years by folklorists, although they commonly replaced the assumptions of a closed society with a looser definition of community or a focus on the individual.

Joining the chorus of criticism against traditional functionalism, folklorist Elliott Oring attacked functionalism's explanation of origin. While he accepted some functional explanations for the existence of folklore, he insisted that origins must be found in historical antecedents. Unintended effects of a cultural item cannot account for its origin. Further, functions that allegedly generate effects may be falsely generalized as causing all instances in which certain conditions are present. Function, however, can vary according to the conditions of a specific situation. Oring hurled his sharpest barbs at William

Bascom's four functions of folklore. As Bascom implied, can functional statements, in situations in which conscious purpose is presumably absent, be considered explanations? Oring argued that a function is logically a consequence, not a cause. Oring countered the functional explanation of the elephant joke by pointing out that the structure of the joke is the vehicle for the humor, not its function. For example, consider this joke: "How do you hide an elephant in a strawberry patch? By painting its toes red." The essential ingredient here is the mixing of categories in a social context wherein the categories, which are incongruous, are understood.[64]

Ideological conservatism was another disturbing feature of functionalism during the postwar period. Functionalism raised assumptions of a stable social system as an ideal; cultural expressions validated the establishment. Functionalism had precedents in bureaucratic management, but further, it appeared to underlie Nazi Germany's use of folklore to promote national solidarity and loyalty to the head of state.[65] In a functional analysis, the role of folklore in raising tensions and sparking actions seemed minimal. The contact and conflict between opposing classes, technologies, and world views were typically absent. Yet folklore as a pronounced possession of disenfranchised groups could appear to be less accepting and less collective than functionalism implied.[66]

With the passage of time, functionalism became less an explanation for origin, which its original practitioners claimed, and more an accounting for the persistence of a cultural item. By the 1940s, functionalist Robert Merton was referring to a less sweeping role for functionalism as "a type of interpretation," and later he offered it as an "exercise in analysis." Indeed, through the 1970s, introductory guides to folklore presented functionalism as a way for the student to get beyond description, although they rarely discussed any theoretical significance.[67]

Possibly the harshest criticism of functionalism came from British anthropologist Edward Evans-Pritchard (1902–73), who claimed that functionalism mostly served the ethnographer's sense of professionalism. Evans-Pritchard wrote that "what Malinowski calls a theory is not really a theory at all but is a guide to the collection and setting forth of data, a fieldworker's *vade mecum*, a wordy *Notes and Queries*. It never rises above the descriptive and operational level of analysis; and it is for the most part a verbose elaboration of the obvious and the erection of commonplaces into scientific concepts."[68] Evans-Pritchard's criticism suggests that functionalism remained in name, if not in theory, because of its contribution to the cultivation of an objective analysis associated with professionalism. By analyzing abstracted functions, the professional furnished, as Alan Dundes stated in his introduction to functionalism in *The Study of Folklore* (1965), "answers to questions that if asked directly would probably not be answered."[69] The professional took on the role of a therapist reporting the hidden motives and unforeseen effects of expressions that are used in a group.

After the universals of natural history no longer seemed appropriate to the situations of modern life, functionalism underscored the exclusiveness and authority of the professional who was studying other people and arriving at generalizations. Functionalism faltered, however, when it went beyond describing the relation of culture to a specific time and place in a closed society. Malinowski himself pointed out that functionalism "is meant primarily to equip the field-worker with a clear perspective and full instructions regarding what to observe and how to record." It seemed to offer a focus lacking in the "get everything" approach that Boas's ethnography sometimes took. But to a functionalist such as Meyer Fortes, functionalism "tries to establish generalizations that hold *irrespective* of period and place and to test them by empirical study in living communities; whereas history is the description of past social life in its local and chronological setting" (emphasis in original). Kingsley Davis observed the implication of this view for the profession when he said: "The early rise of functionalism helped to make a place in sociology and anthropology for those wishing to explain social phenomena in terms of social systems, as against those who wished to make no explanation at all, to explain things in terms of some *other* system, or to plead a cause" (emphasis in original).[70] The perception of science had changed from natural history to biology and, finally, Fortes pointed out, to behavioral science.

Although there was a departure from using function as explanation, raising questions of function provided a transition from Boas's extreme of relative time and place to the postwar concern, in cultural studies, for mind and behavior. Together, these two concerns made the twentieth century, in contrast to the nineteenth, the century of ethnography. The world picture of the nineteenth century—the century of history—transformed into smaller and smaller frames of action during the century of ethnography. Structure and experience became more frequent organizing principles as society appeared to be more fluid and more abstract. Marshall McLuhan's postwar studies of the electronic media had mass appeal because they touched on basic changes in the perception of what was important. The industrialism that contributed to the rise of evolutionary and geographic doctrines in turn gave society a postwar technological transformation, especially in visual communication, which signaled the turn from felt time and space to observable mind and behavior. As McLuhan wrote, "During the mechanical ages we had extended our bodies in space. Today, after more than a century of electronic technology, we have extended our central nervous system itself in a global embrace, abolishing both space and time as far as our planet is concerned."[71]

In Malinowski's posthumously published *A Scientific Theory of Culture* (1944), he set "functional analysis" within a broad "behavioristic approach." To answer how this would be scientific, he described the view of a field worker: "When he first takes his residence among people whose culture he wishes to understand, to record, and to present to the world at large, he obviously is faced with the question of what it means to identify a cultural fact. For clearly, to identify is the same as to understand. We understand the behavior of another person when we can account for his motives, his drives, his customs, that is, his total reaction to the conditions in which he finds himself."[72] Nonetheless, many did not equate understanding with identification, and approaches grew out of a search for explaining the complexity of the kinds of behaviors and ideas that are expressed by folklore.

Function provided a point of departure for the preoccupation about mind and behavior, for it implied that behind forms of social activities there are persons and groups who are capable of holding a variety of values and interests. Cultural items may not be as pragmatic as Malinowski assumed, but they are commonly goal oriented; they are used rhetorically in social situations. From function came attention to context and observable behavior; from function came the admission that social life was complex. Folklore studies received the opportunity to analyze function, symbolism, transmission, and motivation, in terms of a specific body of material and its socially situated performance.

Before that occurred, however, folklore studies needed to mediate the poles of culture and of text. Often that mediation was drawn as an opposition between anthropology and literature. It was less a disciplinary clash, however, than an intellectual transition from time and place to mind and behavior, for many integrated disciplines were involved. That anthropology and humanities were singled out indicates a self-conscious organization of the varied currents that were running through the scholarly interest in folklore. Folklore studies appeared to be a post–World War II offspring that would grow on its own. And as it grew, this organization suggested, it would establish its own ground and its own views. With the efforts to mediate culture and text, folklorists—like other students of integrated studies, which were emerging at the time from ethnic studies to American Studies—developed approaches that gave them a sense of discipline.

TOWARD A FOLKLORISTIC APPROACH

As late as 1936, Stith Thompson reported that he was the "only non-anthropologist" at the American Folklore Society meeting, which usually was held in conjunction with the meeting of the American Anthropological Association. "The major difficulty facing the society," the Committee on Policy of the American Folklore Society declared in 1941, was "a failure to assess the importance of the fact that, by its very nature the Society and its *Journal* are peripheral to two major concerns—those of anthropologists and those of persons in the humanities."[73] During the 1920s and the 1930s, "non-anthropologists," such as Stith Thompson, Archer Taylor, and Louise Pound, became president of the society. They published major works on, respectively, folktales, proverbs, and ballads. By the late 1940s the presidency of the society alternated between anthropologists and literary scholars. The annual meeting also alternated, between an anthropological organization, usually the American Anthropological Association, and the Modern Language Association. That lasted until 1967, when the society began to meet on its own.

Writing in *Anthropology Today* (1953), Thompson noted: "Recently we have been hearing reports of a considerable withdrawal of American anthropologists from the American Folklore Society. There may, of course, be many reasons for this defection, but it would be a heavy blow for folklore as well as for ethnology if scholars in these fields should cease to support one another. The ethnologist can hardly hope to have an understanding of a people if he disregards so important a part of their lives as their tales and myths, their songs and dances, and their chants and ceremonies. Folklorists likewise frequently need the experience and skill of the trained ethnologist to set a model for their own work."[74] The dichotomy was a false one to a large extent, for ethnologists did indeed work with the materials of folklore, and they represented many models, outlined in this chapter, not just one. The purpose of establishing the opposition was to justify a mediation by an independent, textually oriented discipline of folklore. The same year that Thompson published his comment, Warren Roberts received the first American Ph.D. degree in folklore at Indiana University under the direction of Stith Thompson. Roberts's dissertation was on the distribution and origin of "The Tale of the Kind and Unkind Girls."[75] For his degree, Roberts was required to take separate examinations from the Departments of English and Anthropology.

Meanwhile, anthropologists after 1940 began to experience fragmentation into specialties of economic, political, social, and psychological studies. Surveying ethnology in 1968, Fred Eggan pointed to the Wenner-Gren symposium on "Anthropology Today" in 1952 as a turning point. "It was apparent that ethnology in its traditional sense was rapidly losing ground." Archaeology took over historical interests, and ethnohistory dominated documentary data. The cultural materials collected by Boas and his students were superseded by classification, kinship, polity, economics. "We are taught to worship Abstraction," Kroeber remarked in 1959. The former domains of anthropology have been taken up by others who had an attachment to the materials of culture. "European folk ethnography is closest to what we in England and America call folklore, and in folkloristic activity the students of English and other current languages of civilization are more numerous than we." In 1964, Melville Jacobs, in his cultural-anthropology textbook, placed the period of "anthropological folklore" between 1860 and 1940. Although he did not explicitly give the reasons for the terminus of 1940, he cited Boas's passing leadership in folklore research and the inappropriateness of folkloric data to "hard" and "behavioral sciences." Old hands such as Kroeber complained: "As our daily bread, we invent hypotheses in order to test them as we are told is the constant practice of the high tribe of physicists. If at times some of you, like myself, feel somewhat ill at ease in the house of social science, do not wonder: we are changelings therein; our true paternity lies elsewhere." Anthropologists who remained close to folklore during this period, such as Bascom and Herskovits, announced their connection to the common problems of the humanities. To Bascom, the common problems were the social context of folklore, the relations of folklore to culture, which might be phrased as the cultural context of folklore, and the functions of folklore. Yet Bascom also complained that "his colleagues in folklore are often so preoccupied with the problem of origins and historical reconstruction that they overlook problems of equal or even greater significance, for which one can hope to find satisfactory solutions."[76]

Stith Thompson gave impetus to the independence of folklore studies with the establishment of summer "folklore institutes," held at Indiana University beginning in 1942. Although teachers were drawn from the disciplines of anthropology and literature, they were brought in to train, in large part, specialists in folklore. Louis C. Jones, an English professor who wrote on the folklore of New York State, was one who participated. He recalled finding, to his surprise, not English teachers or anthropologists in the audience, but "people wanting to pursue folk tales, folk songs, folk things. It was not yet a career, but it

Folklore Institute at Indiana University, Bloomington, Indiana, Summer 1946. Standing from left to right (as identified on original)—1st row: Wayland D. Hand, Erminie W. Voegelin, Samuel P. Bayard, Thelma James, John Jacob Niles, Sven Liljeblad, Svatava Jakobson, John A. Lomax; 2d row: Richard M. Dorson, Paul G. Brewster, Alan Lomax, Roman Jakobson, Stith Thompson, Ernest W. Baughman, Vicente T. Mendoza; 3d row: Suzie Hoozasian, Hallie Craytor, Mrs. Goodwyn, Mrs. Mendoza, Ruth Ann Musick, Mrs. Green; 4th row: Ariane de Felice, J. Mason Brewer, Mrs. Plummaus, Frances Gillmor (photo courtesy of Louis C. Jones).

was a passion not, as it was before, tied to something else."[77] With the advent of the Ph.D. degree in folklore, the independent discipline mixed ethnology, in the traditional sense, and literature; but a difference was that the topics in folklore study were closer to home than were those in ethnology. For Thompson at Indiana University during the late 1940s and 1950s, for example, William Hugh Jansen wrote his dissertation on an Indiana teller of tall tales named Abraham ("Oregon") Smith; John Mason Brewer wrote on preacher tales told by blacks in Texas; and Marie Campbell wrote on European folktales that she collected from eastern-Kentucky narrators.[78]

Herbert Halpert, one of the new breed who called themselves folklorists, illustrates the independent discipline's odyssey and its return home. Studying from 1936 to 1940 in anthropology at Columbia University under Ruth Benedict and George Herzog, Halpert was preoccupied with folklore and decided not to pursue a Ph.D. in anthropology, which called for areas of archaeology and physiology.

Halpert switched to Indiana University to study folklore with Stith Thompson in the English Department. Soon afterwards, Halpert began the *Hoosier Folklore Bulletin,* which contained modern collections of tales, proverbs, legends, and riddles from around the state. In 1947, Halpert completed his doctoral dissertation, "Folktales and Legends from the New Jersey Pines: A Collection and Study." In 1956, Halpert told the American Folklore Society, "It still amazes me that there was so little crossfertilization between anthropology and literary scholarship, in spite of the fact that Boas, as well as Child, was a founder of the American Folklore Society." In 1980, Neil Rosenberg said of Halpert: "He spoke as one of the first folklorists to embody these two strains. Equally at ease in the field and the library, he has stressed in his teaching and writing both the 'functional' and the 'comparative' approaches."[79] In 1968, Halpert established the Department of Folklore at Memorial University in Newfoundland, Canada.

Distinguishing the folklore of the folklorist from that of the anthropologist in the 1950s was more who and what was being studied than how it was being studied. Francis Lee Utley, a professor of English, pointed out in 1952 that folklorists, broadly speaking, stressed "the folklore of the native White and the Southern Negro (with a brief glance at the immigrant White) as opposed to the folklore of the aboriginal Indians." The chapter headings of Richard Dorson's sweeping *American Folklore* (1959) underscored the "folklorist's" interests: "Native Folk Humor," "Regional Folk Cultures," "Immigrant Folklore," "The Negro," "A Gallery of Folk Heroes," "Modern Folklore." The materials of folklore to the folklorist were aesthetic products with appreciable forms—tales, legends, songs, baskets, proverbs, games, and festivals—rather than social organizations of kinship, economy, and polity. Reporting to the American Council of Learned Societies in 1963, Thompson's successor at Indiana, Richard Dorson (1916–81), who was trained in history and literature at Harvard but who studied anthropology with Herskovits at Northwestern, declared that "folklore differs . . . in being a distinct and independent discipline, and that it embraces so vast a field of cultural behavior, of learning and scholarship, that an academically qualified folklorist can be trained only through a separate graduate curriculum."[80] In that same year, the University of Pennsylvania added a Ph.D. program in folklore and folklife.

The independence of folklore from anthropology took its impetus from the resistance of the new breed to being relegated to a subfield of anthropology. Richard Dorson railed against William Bascom's separation of folklore—to Bascom, "verbal art"—from ethnography. Dorson also complained about Melville Herskovits's having assigned the study of folk literature to the folklorist and the larger realm of custom to the anthropologist. For Dorson, folklore was tradition, "a vast area of human culture and behavior."[81]

Concern for behavior was related to postwar America's questioning of the individual's role in what appeared to the middle-class professions to be an impersonal mass culture. Persons were known less by their background than by their behavior. That behavior was highly variable; one person could take on various identities. Time and space hardly seemed to define culture. Culture, like suburbia, sprawled. In the service-and-information economy that was replacing the dominance of manufacturing, one assumed roles and put on "fronts." Identifying personality in this impersonal economy became more elusive; indeed, the presence of "personality" implied a celebrity or an eccentric. Culture seemed to have more actors with parts to play, or a microphone to speak into.

The proliferation of electronic forms of communication led to questions about the varieties of cultural communication. Study of culture gave way to study of situations, what political scientist H. L. Nieburg called "milieu therapy." Culture needed more specialized adjectives—sub, ethnic, folk, regional, age, occupational—to describe it. In a mass culture that seemed to become more and more insincere, the study of man was giving way to the study of communication.[82] An important index of sincere communication was its manifestation in material surroundings, rituals, gestures, and narratives. In a society that was saturated with messages and strangers, communication seemed to be more encoded. Its cultural translation became more important; maybe, then, one could get beyond the speakers' words and read their minds.

To this mass society, a realm of sincerity lay in subcultures and traditional activities. There, the intimacy and intensity that were associated with "culture" seemed to lie. Folklore and folklife studies reminded the public and the professions of still-vital subcultures, active traditions, meaningful expressions, and alternative ways of life. With the concern for their roles in modern life and for their explanations in sociology and psychology, there was a need for new integrative approaches, which would take into account the variability of cultural communication. The theories of the early professional movements worked with static biological and rooted social terms, which hardly seemed relevant to a technological society on the move. Yet the influences of the early movements ran deep and affected the shape of theories to come in anthropology and in folklore studies.

Even more than *communication*, the word *behavior* came often from the lips of cultural scientists during the 1960s, an age that was indeed preoccupied with action and change. Many disciplines made expansive claims into the realm of everyday behavior that was not class bound. The vocabulary took a turn to the objectivity of behavioral science and a turn away from ideology. Rhetorical moves were made from *group* to *network,* from *culture* to *interaction,* from *tradition bearer* to *performer,* from *folklore studies* to *folkloristics.* Modern man and modern woman appeared to be less followers of polity and culture and more choosers of varied identities and expressions.

The many chronicles of the state of humanistic disciplines at that time attested to a state of confusion over the borders of cultural studies. American Studies, ethnic studies, Women's Studies, popular-culture studies, and regional studies took on folkloristic and anthropological components. *Interdisciplinary* characterized almost every discipline. Yet these specialties focused on a slice of culture, instead of on the total study of humankind. Once called tradition, folklore could become an approach. The "folklore of" an item could mean its analysis, rather than merely its oral tradition. In the next chapter, I survey the folkloristic theory that came into its own after World War II. Drawing largely on its anthropological and humanistic legacy, folklore and folklife studies would contribute in their own way to the realignment of the academic professions.

4

Folklore in an Era
of Communication

Among the phrases used to describe the twentieth century is Samuel
Eliot Morison's "The Great Change." Rapid technological advances
had made life seem drastically different—immediate, simultaneous.
Broadcasting brought speakers' voices into your living room just as
they spoke; the telephone covered thousands of miles in an instant;
cars and planes pushed passengers toward the same goal. To be sure,
changes in communications brought by printing had had strong
effects on eighteenth- and nineteenth-century life, but in the twentieth
century the effects of the rapid, widespread advance of electronic
communications appeared ever more immediate, indeed sensational.
The new communications changed society and scholarship as well.
Morison defends his case by citing that "broadcasting music by radio
began in 1920; forty years later there were 200 million radio and
television sets in America." Then he writes: "American scholarship
and science now came of age."[1]

Talking of change can sound exclusive. If collecting folklore from
living persons teaches us anything, it is that old ways do not simply
disappear once new technology comes in. *Old* is a relative term,
geared to the youthful perception of the present. Mostly it comes to
mean *other*—other than what is dominant. Old, or other, ways and
theories are not moths, never again to witness the caterpillars whence
they sprang. An amount of integration and simultaneousness commonly occurs. Diffusion, for example, was commonly discussed in
evolutionary doctrine, but diffusion came into its own as its students
fashioned a new heterogeneous perception of space while "older"
evolutionary doctrine remained stuck on viewing progress from a

single perspective. In an era of communication, radio and telegraphy provided diffusion with a more active association—transmission.

Still, Boas's and Malinowski's ethnographies were both progressive, speaking often in evolutionary terms. Moreover, in anthropological scholarship, evolution continued to describe the influence that technology and ecology had on cultural change. The sweep of perception arranged theory into trends, and the trends were promoted in the dialectic of theory by a claim to the main and contemporary currents of scholarship. Daniel Brinton, for instance, in 1895 contrasted his evolutionary methods to those of the "folk-lorist of the old school." He claimed that "until the folklorist understands independent invention, he has not caught up with the progress of ethnologic science."[2]

Independent invention presupposed the isolation of the world's peoples; it stressed the historical development of invention. After the great communications inventions of the late nineteenth century had been put in place, attention turned to what the inventions did— processes and consequences resulting from transmission. In addition to transmission, for example, the "form" of the transmission came into the spotlight of scholarship. Taken together, the apotheosis was in "transformation." Historian Warren Susman argues: "*Transformation* was a key word in the late nineteenth and early twentieth centuries, becoming significant not only in the world of science and magic but in the world of history and social science as well. History increasingly had to confront the changing of forms in which experience was expressed—often rapid change because of technological innovation. Such transformations created the need for still others."[3]

If you replace history with folklore, you have a basis for many changes to occur in the currents of American folklore scholarship during the twentieth century. To Henry Belden, writing in 1905 on "The Study of Folk-Song in America," for instance, the priority was "not only what ballads have survived in America, but how they have survived—what changes they have undergone, how widely they are known, and what the course and manner of their transmission have been." Two years before he wrote this, the first International Wireless Conference was held to draw up regulations for wireless transmission. Among the disputes was a common form for a distress signal, as different countries held out for their own forms. Later the issue of form and transmission was given ample publicity with the sinking of the Titanic in 1912.[4]

It was with great excitement that another folklorist who was concerned with transmission, T. F. Crane, welcomed the formation of "FF Communications" (Folklore Fellows) in an article for the *Nation* in 1916. Crane marveled at the rapid spread of that loose organization, which had been founded in 1907, to nineteen cities around the world. The organization appeared to Crane to be rather simple: it had a managing committee and a bureau of information. He called for American participation in it. The volumes that attracted his attention emphasized forms and their means of transmission: they concerned a "story, widely spread in literature and oral tradition."[5]

At the time when Crane was writing, Americans heard about the power of communications in the war across the sea. To be sure, it is easy to overstate the influence of war on intellectual currents, but the fact remains that World War I provided a turning point in the use of electronic communications and the perception of events. Diplomats issued ultimatums over the telephone and demanded immediate answers. More than ever before, the spread of news made more nations more active and more quickly. "All the world's telecommunications facilities," wrote one historian, "which should have been turned to peaceful uses, were set to the frantic uses of war." In 1917 the diplomatic observer Sir Ernest Mason Satow remarked that war came because statesmen had not been able to keep pace with the "rapidity of communication by telegraph and telephone." With its several fronts, rapid communications, mass movements of people, and visible powers of destruction, the war provided lessons of simultaneousness and immediacy that seemed abruptly to end the passive evolutionary metaphor in cultural discourse.[6] Other metaphors that emphasized the active simultaneousness and immediacy of time and place took the place of evolution, and instead of a one-dimensional perspective to culture, a multiple perspective of society took hold.

Evolutionary studies had stressed the forms of language. The mechanisms for transmission either were not considered or were reduced to the single channel of talk. Reported only as words, lore was therefore viewed from a single perspective. The word *communication,* which is now more in vogue to describe everything from publication to education, conveyed a multiple perspective because it emphasized the various and simultaneous ways that messages are sent and received. Appearance, setting, and gesture relay information simultaneously in different ways; and they are often just as important, if not more so, than verbal forms. The meanings of information can change, depending on how and through what medium the message is relayed.

Descriptions of scholarship took on a multiple perspective beginning in the early twentieth century. To replace Brinton's perception of theories succeeding one another in a progressive line, Boas used the metaphor of different simultaneous camps, which was reminiscent of the rhetoric during the years before World War I. In "The History of Anthropology" (1904), Boas wrote: "Beginning with records of curious superstitions and customs and of popular tales, folklore has become the science of all the manifestations of popular life. Folklorists occupy themselves primarily with the folklore of Europe and thus supplement the material collected by anthropologists in foreign lands. The theorists of folklore also divided into the two camps of the adherents of the psychological theory and those of the historical theory." Historian of folklore studies D. K. Wilgus reported that in Anglo-American folksong scholarship, collectors had engaged in the "Ballad War" between a communal or individual origin for ballads. Then a "broadening of approach occurred," which resulted in looking at "various aspects of the problem concurrently."[7] "Schools" described how scholars divided less than did "perspectives."

In America, a multiple perspective took hold, too, in the conversion of the university to a multidepartmental structure. The subjects of the late-nineteenth-century learned society selectively became departments in the university. Anthropology is a prime example. Its intellectual perception was altered by the establishment of the institutional base in the university. Boas, especially, came to wield influence from his position at Columbia University after 1899. Historian of anthropology Regna Darnell notes that "Boas' students . . . came to constitute the major power bloc in American anthropology early in the century, headed academic departments which looked to Columbia and to Boas for access to publication outlets and money for fieldwork."[8]

That folklore was not given a departmental foothold was significant for its development. Dan Ben-Amos has remarked about the American Folklore Society, for example: "Boas and Newell controlled the Society, but their ambition, particularly that of Boas, was to establish authority over university research and teaching. Indeed, in due time Boas achieved his goal in anthropology, but folklore lagged behind and only many years later gained a stronghold at the university."[9] To arise separately, folklore studies had to come from a coalition and a transformation of departmental forces. That occurred with a coalition of language, literature, and music interests that helped forge the early folklore curricula at Indiana, North Carolina, and Pennsylvania universities.

Folklorist Louis C. Jones had recounted that a contributing factor in the rise of folklore studies in the university was that "the decade from 1931 to 1940 was, of course, the period during which America suddenly became aware of the fact that it had a folk tradition. President and Mrs. Roosevelt, the Federal Writers' Project, the Index of American Design, the Federal Arts Project, and scores of other New Deal forces brought to the attention of a confused and struggling people an awareness of their native culture."[10] The literature of the

1930s was devoted to the common man, the heroic figure of the Great Depression. Folklore, brought out in books, photographs, and painted murals by federally sponsored projects of the Works Progress Administration (WPA), showed the vitality of the nation by celebrating other common-man heroes such as Davy Crockett, Sam Patch, and Mike Fink. Folk songs and folk arts no longer were a sign of backwardness, but were a source of pride in a forbearing American spirit.[11] The nation saw in its native folklore a longstanding tradition that had carried on before the depression and would carry the country through it. Articles and books on American folklore appeared in the popular press with a frequency that had not been matched since the late nineteenth century.

Much of the interest in American folklore followed the upsurge in studies of American literature and arts in the 1920s. One of the cultural consequences of World War I and America's "coming of age," as critic Van Wyck Brooks called it in 1915, was that the United States declared itself a civilization that was distinct from Europe. A new generation of intellectuals, trained in America, supported the claim by means of studies of American literature, arts, and folklore. In 1926 and 1927, three monuments to this effort appeared: *Main Currents in American Thought,* by Vernon Louis Parrington (which won the Pulitzer Prize), *The Rise of American Civilization,* by Charles and Mary Beard, and *The Pageant of America,* edited by Ralph Henry Gabriel. In 1931, Constance Rourke, in her book *American Humor,* used the evidence of folklore and a lively subliterature of nineteenth-century newspaper and magazine stories to point out another lively American tradition. Twelve years later, in *The Roots of American Culture,* Rourke expanded her argument and ranked folklore as an important source of an imaginative American spirit.

The university curriculum responded to this upsurge of inquiry into the American experience. The curriculum eased its reliance on European history and culture as the core of learning and added an American component for a liberal-arts education. Yale University offered the first Ph.D. in American civilization in 1933, and Harvard followed with an American civilization program in 1937. This unveiling of American civilization brought together the fields of history and literature to form an integrated study. Out of this multiple perspective came several theses and dissertations in the 1940s that used folklore as evidence of the American historical experience, including Richard M. Dorson's studies of Davy Crockett and New England subliterature.[12]

Anthropology lagged behind in the trend; anthropology in the universities stressed primitve cultures in Africa and Asia or among

American Indians. But many English Departments, taking on the study of American literature, added American folklore to their offerings. The content of these courses tended to stress the influence of immigrant and regional groups on the creation of a heterogeneous American folklore. Adding to the attention being given to a non-aboriginal study of folklore were colorful American folklore teachers such as Harold Thompson at Cornell University, Benjamin Botkin at the University of Oklahoma, and Mody Boatright at the University of Texas, who achieved something of a celebrity status at their institutions. Recalling English professor Harold Thompson's first American folklore course at the State Teachers College at Albany (now the State University of New York at Albany) in 1934, Louis Jones recalled how this course was different from courses in anthropology or primitive poetry: "This was the first time a course covering a large segment of our folk culture was offered to undergraduates, and it became the model for many to follow in later years. . . . One of the ironies and great innovations of this course in American folklore was that he insisted that his students go into their own families and their own communities and collect the oral tradition that was there. . . . He encouraged them to think of folklore in America rather than American folklore; thus the student of middle or southern European background sought to discover what traditions his people had brought here and to learn that these traditions had come to him from another land but were indeed universal."[13] Conceiving of a composite folklore *in* America, Thompson offered a multiple perspective, a heterogeneous view of the American experience. Folklore was close at hand, he affirmed, and it appeared in various, simultaneous forms. Jones took over the course in 1940 and, like his contemporary Herbert Halpert, eventually established a folklore-studies department at Cooperstown (State University of New York) in 1964.

The growth of a multiple perspective in academia can be traced to a variety of influences. The growth of bureaucracy in American society, a multilevel structure that plays simultaneous roles, helped introduce concerns of function, networking, and maintenance into scholarly discourse. In communications, the linearity of print became less dominant. Telephones, movies, illustrations, and photographs joined print as being equally, if not more, important in the transmission of images. They were simultaneous forms, each giving a different and dramatic perspective to absorb and transform knowledge. Gertrude Stein thought that for the youthful generation of 1905 to 1920, cubist painting anticipated this new way of seeing, which was influenced by communications. The depiction of three-dimensional space on a two-dimensional canvas and the movement of the eye to take in many distinctive details from one corner of the painting to the other underscored a multiple perspective. The reporting of World War I reinforced the new way of seeing. She wrote: "Really the composition of this war, 1914–1918, was not the composition of all previous wars, the composition was not a composition in which there was one man in the center surrounded by a lot of other men but a composition that had neither a beginning nor an end, a composition of which one corner was an important as another corner, in fact the composition of cubism."[14]

Another war metaphor underscored the power that broadcasting had in shaping the way people hear. On 31 October 1938, Orson Welles's radio adaptation of H. G. Wells's *The War of the Worlds* seemed so immediate, so true to life, that many listeners went into a panic. In the weeks preceding the broadcast, the bombardment of crisis reports from Europe had set a fearful mood in the nation. Throughout the thirties, President Roosevelt had used "fireside chats" over the radio to calm the nation. In 1939, when Gallup poll takers asked what problem was most on their minds, the majority of Americans answered, "Staying out of the war." President Roosevelt's fireside radio chats and Welles's broadcast showed that electronic communications were more than tools; they were themselves actions, presences evoking responses.

That the immediacy of communications brought more uneasiness about domestic and foreign problems is brought out by the transformation of the 1939/40 World's Fair in New York City. The 1939 Fair opened with the theme of "The World of Tomorrow." Emanating from the Court of Power, major attractions were provided by General Electric, American Telephone and Telegraph, General Motors' Futurama, and Eastman Kodak. Because the attendance was too small for the fair's organizers to make a profit in 1939, they switched successfully to the theme of a super country fair in 1940. In place of the Soviet Pavilion, a bandstand went up in an area that was renamed the American Common. Folk performers and a folk spirit filled both the stage and the fair.[15]

World War II provided more indications of transition. In *The Big Change: America Transforms Itself, 1900–1950* (1952) Frederick Lewis Allen described a cubist canvas of a new technological civilization, marked by a simultaneous self-consciousness and awareness of others. Mobilization for the war brought together soldiers from different regional, racial, and ethnic cultures. This was no "European" war, as World War I was sometimes described. Fighting seemed to occur everywhere at once. Cultural forms, too, jumped outside their lines. "Hillbilly" music spread; writers such as William Faulkner used "streams of consciousness." Invoking T. S. Eliot, Ralph Waldo Ellison, in the best seller *Invisible Man* (1952), defied linearity by writing, "The end is in the beginning and lies far ahead." The switches to folklore that Ellison and Faulkner used liberally in their narratives succeeded in completing the effect of simultaneousness and three dimensionality, because folklore appeared to be an expressive side beneath and beyond modern situations.

Folklore took on the rhetoric of communicative art. The path had been paved by the broadening of art during the 1920s to include photography and craft and the work of "untrained" artists. Communication appeared to be the way to mediate the old polarity between culture and text. *Process, experience,* and *art* became keywords in a language of immediacy. The rising power of communication called on art to convey experience. Philosopher John Dewey, in *Art as Experience* (1934), worried that art had been separated from the actor. The medium of building, book, painting, or statue, he argued, increasingly obscured the experience. "The task," he wrote, "is to restore continuity between the refined and intensified forms of experience that are works of art and the everyday events, doings, and sufferings that are universally recognized to constitute experience." In 1935, Joseph Freeman, in his introduction to *Proletarian Literature in the United States,* announced that art "has its own special function, the grasp and transmission of experience. The catch lies in the word 'experience.' " In events such as the 1939 World's Fair and WPA projects, *folk* translated into a nontechnological notion of *the people* and their potential for intense experience. Ben Botkin, on a federal folklore project in New York City, wrote, for example: "And what makes a thing folklore is this tellable, listenable, and repeatable quality, close to mother wit and common experience, heightened by popular fantasy. The folklore of modern life, especially in the big city, is buried under the complicated overlay of modern industrial society (folklore itself being 'extra-technological' and 'extra-institutional'), its voice drowned out by louder and more urgent traffic and trade." Botkin's *Treasury of American Folklore* (1944) and its many sequels, much as they were later maligned, drew popular appeal then because, as their titles implied, they offered a wealth of nontechnological experience through the common artistry of folklore. Botkin had created a cubist canvas of folklore, in which everything, arranged as simultaneous bits of information, occurred everywhere at the same time.[16]

The resurgence of folklore during the 1940s was an extension of the search for experience in an era of communication. Defining folklore in 1949, William Bascom wrote, "the term folklore has come to mean myths, legends, folktales, proverbs, riddles, verse, and a variety of other forms of artistic expression whose medium is the

spoken word." Ernest Sutherland Bates, writing on "American Folklore," could comment, in the *Saturday Review of Literature,* that a
result of "our recent patriotic movement" has been an increased
attention to American folklore. "We have begun to realize that we are
just emerging from a most romantic and picturesque phase, rich in
many of the raw materials of art. . . . There has been a most determined effort to recover it in some measure and at least get it safely
recorded before its memory has grown too dim." Answering the call,
Allen Eaton's popular exhibits on rural folk arts for the Russell Sage
Foundation and for the United States Department of Agriculture drew
attention to the effects of rural electrification and urbanization on
America's native artistry.[17]

Although the influence of spreading communication technology
can be seen before the war, postwar prosperity brought a revolution in
consumption and communication. Americans per capita had more
telephones, radios, and, later, television sets than any other nation.
The economy depended more on communication as it made the
transition from depending primarily on manufacturing to depending
predominantly on service and information.

Folklore came once again to the fore as a cultural palliative. In
1950, Stith Thompson observed: "We have all seen folklore become a
very popular subject of discussion and comment. It has invaded the
radio programs of every section of the country. . . . We have seen the
vogue for hillbilly songs carried to an extreme, and the cowboy has
become a cult, especially with youngsters. Folk dancing, real and
modified, has flourished and there has also grown up a great demand
for professional folksingers." He immediately followed by touting the
autonomy of folklore study, in universities, societies, and even in the
Library of Congress.[18]

During the 1950s, which were marked by a perception of conformity in American society, folklore gave many, as it did for writers, an
expressive side to a conforming society. Thompson's 1950s underscored a search for identity. The titles of popular books then underscored the banality of postwar life: *The Man in the Gray Flannel Suit,
The Status Seekers, The Organization Man,* and *The Lonely Crowd.* In
1957, Richard Dorson saw the connection with folklore and announced to the American Folklore Society, "There is much for the
American folklorist to ponder over in David Riesman's *The Lonely
Crowd.*" He assured "the other-directed groups that dominate American life, particularly the teenage advance guard," that they had an
identity after all. They had a distinctive folklore: jive talk, droodles,
parodies, and parlor puzzles. And they could look to the traditional life
of Appalachia, the passionate messages of ballads and legends, for

vicarious intensity. During the 1950s and early 1960s, colorful folklore titles answered the demand for identity and intensity: *Blood-stoppers and Bearwalkers, South from Hell-fer-Sartin, Deep Down in the Jungle, Black Rock,* and *Saints of Sage and Saddle.*[19]

Thompson's speech, given to the Modern Language Association and published as the inaugural piece in *Midwest Folklore* (1951), was significant for its turning-point rhetoric, as seen in the title "Folklore at Midcentury." Thompson contrasted his piece with Boas's speech in 1937 to the American Folklore Society, which capped fifty years of anthropological achievement. Thompson announced: "It seems to me only the wildest type of nervousness that would fear the domination of folklore here by the anthropological group. They are so far outnumbered by the many literary and amateur folklorists in the country that I am certain they would never make folklore study go in a direction that it did not wish to."[20]

Who, then, is in this autonomous "new generation," as Thompson called it, of folklorists? Speaking as folklore's elder statesman, he answered: "A different motive actuates the man or woman who is primarily a student of folklore. He is not a reformer, either of artistic taste or the amusement habits of his generation. He recognizes folklore for what it is, that part of the culture which is handed down by tradition from one generation to another. Living in a world of books, concerts, phonographs, radio, and international contacts, he sees all this body of traditional material as something immensely interesting in itself." In this world of immediate communication and formal contact, in this separated realm of listener and performer, the study of folklore—"that part of the culture handed down"—offered to bring closer to the present the lessons of tactile compassion and informal learning. Moving from his generation's preoccupation with time and space, Thompson recognized that in this world, the "next years may well bring first rate studies on the relation of folklore to . . . history, sociology, and psychology."[21] Thompson foresaw that, for the study of cultural communication, a shift in perception would be brought by electronic communication. Although this did not fully take hold until the 1960s, it brought with it new keywords. Less did time and space constitute the matter at hand; more were mind and behavior put into perspective.

Like other currents, this one runs through many of the arts and sciences. A book on "the varieties of communication," Edward Hall's *The Silent Language* (1959), went through ten editions in nine years. Proceeding from the observation that "in recent years the physicist, the mathematician, and the engineer have accustomed themselves to looking at a wide range of events as aspects of communication," he

Fellows of the American Folklore Society, Bloomington, Indiana, 28 July 1962. From left to right—1st row: Benjamin Botkin, MacEdward Leach, Erminie Wheeler Voegelin, Catherine Luomala, Thelma James, Wayland Hand, Francis Lee Utley; 2d row: Charles Seeger, Warren E. Roberts, Newbell Niles Puckett, Mody P. Boatright, Louis C. Jones, Stith Thompson, Archer Taylor, Arthur Palmer Hudson, Richard M. Dorson; 3d row: Morris E. Opler, Samuel P. Bayard, D. K. Wilgus, Edson Richmond, George Korson, Sol Tax (photo courtesy of Louis C. Jones).

declared that "culture is communication and communication is culture." The renowned literary critic Kenneth Burke also used communication as an essential part of his cultural analysis during the 1950s, but he emphasized the role of a linguistic system. If technology depends on electrical signals, then culture, by analogy, depends on linguistic symbols. But the voice has to be elevated to a level of performance if it is to be heard in an electronic world. Louder and more theatrical, set on stages, captured in frames, communication became hieroglyphic. Language, with its "grammar of behavior" and its "vocabulary of motives" in a system of communication, can then become a basic metaphor for cultural analysis. Such analysis worked on the deciphering of symbols into "meaning."[22]

For philosopher Ralph Ross in *Symbols and Civilization* (1962), communication is "meaning." Language becomes essential to survival, but other "forms of communication . . . store and transmit knowledge, hold a society together, and direct conduct." In 1964, Marshall McLuhan, in *Understanding Media: The Extensions of Man,* scored a success by offering an explanation of ways in which television, the most powerful form of communication, directs modern conduct. In 1967, Marshall McLuhan gave youth, a rebellious and theatrical generation, a catchphrase when he published *The Medium Is the Message*. An influential book for a quieter decade, David Riesman's *The Lonely Crowd* (1950, thirteen editions in sixteen years), used direction—other and inner—to characterize Americans and, in an era of conformity and communication, predicted a move to the "other." The concern of the other-directed person is to conform—not to "relate" to others, but to "impress them," to be "emotionally in tune with them." Much of his discussion centered on changes that mass media had brought to life. To analyze folklore, Riesman saw the problem as "how the situation in which the transmission of the story takes place affects the listener (or reader) and how this situation in turn alters the content of the media."[23]

In these studies, authors drew conclusions from the observation of behavior, which they hoped might lead to more knowledge of mind. For B. F. Skinner, whose books circulated widely during the 1950s, behavior had the appeal of being a "process, rather than a thing. . . . It is changing, fluid, and evanescent." Behavior reflected the variability and immediacy of life; segmented, too, like life, its study would be built up from the examination of specific events. Although many rejected his analogy between humans and machines, the appeal of behavior for analysis remained. In *A Behavioral Approach to Historical Analysis* (1969), Robert F. Berkhofer, Jr., pointed out, in multiperspectival fashion, that "there is no *one* behavioral approach, only approaches, because of the many arguments over the fundamental interpretations of human behavior."[24]

The Self-Conscious Society, as Eric Larrabee called America in 1960, had by then a bookshelf full of works to describe its mind and its states of consciousness. In 1939 and 1953, Perry Miller published volumes on *The New England Mind*. In 1941, Wilbur J. Cash came out with *The Mind of the South;* in 1950, Henry Steele Commager offered *The American Mind;* in 1957, Arthur K. Moore published *The Frontier Mind*. Not strictly psychological studies, these books were more historical studies of perception, based on records of behavior. Henry D. Shapiro, in his preface to *Appalachia on Our Mind: The Southern Mountains and Mountaineers in the American Consciousness* (1978), demonstrates the heightened attention that this scholarship devotes to behavior, process, and experience: "The concern of this book is with the taxonomy of reality, the process by which experience is defined, ordered, organized into coherent and actionable schemes, the process by which a new reality or reality newly perceived is integrated into existing knowledge, the process by which taxonomic schemes are rearranged to make space for new knowledge, the process by which knowledge becomes the basis for public action."[25]

As American voices were raised and as communications became more theatrical, public action came to command the attention of analysts who were looking for cultural symbols. Commonly that action was arranged into the communications metaphor of frames. In 1948, political scientist Harold Lasswell described diplomacy in terms of "attention frames." He defined them as "the rate at which comparable content is brought to the notice of individuals and groups." In contrast to the frame of folk cultures, he said, the frame of modern urban life is "variable, refined, and interactive."[26] Similarly, Skinner divided events into "frames of behavior." Especially lasting in influence was sociologist Erving Goffman's "frame analysis" in *The Presentation of Self in Everyday Life* (1956) and *Behavior in Public Places* (1963). Using the theatrical metaphor of performances, Goffman described framed events that serve the symbolic function of "impression management," which is demanded by a service-and-information economy.

This influence that communications had on postwar scholarship can be seen in folklore studies. Folklore was viewed as a complex frame of mind and behavior; it was a form of communication that demanded separate study, much as other forms such as literature, art, and film had developed into distinct specialties. The field of folklore studies became significant in the understanding of communication during this postwar era, because it provided a multiple perspective to gauge traditional expression and impression in the modern world— and in those simultaneous "other" or "older" worlds. To bring this viewpoint out, I offer a discussion of four organizing concerns in folklore studies: community, structure, symbol, and performance.

COMMUNITY

As electronic communications spanned the landscape and defied time, the cultural barriers of nature declined in importance. Boundaries were more abstract, consisting of invisible connections among subgroups of a massive whole. The connections could overlap, and they could vary in the time they took up: they could be ethnic, religious, regional, and occupational. *Community,* with its connotation of flexibility and its association with communication and the concept of communality in an individualistic modern life, became a keyword of scholarship.

The eminent sociologist Howard W. Odum had emphasized the keyword as early as the 1920s. He claimed that "folk regional sociology" responded to his conviction that "perhaps no greater advance has been made in the after-war period than the increased recognition of the institution of community, whether it be community of organization, of fellowship, of industry, of arts and letters, of learning, of religion, or of citizenship." This was not to say that community had become stronger. Cultural scholarship, especially folklore studies, commonly increases the recognition of items that are threatened with replacement, as I pointed out earlier for traditional technology and oral tradition. The sensational sociological study *Middletown* (1929), by Robert S. Lynd and Helen Merrell Lynd, warned the nation that even in the heartland of traditional values, "living moves along . . . at a bewildering variety of gaits." Subtitled, with an eye toward generalization, *A Study in Modern American Culture*, *Middletown* was the study of a community, showing how traditional notions of community had fallen into a bureaucratic model of making money and managing problems.[27]

To replace the studies of primitive cultures that were tied to space, there were studies of communities closer to home, marked by social connections. In 1931, Stuart Chase had a best seller on that theme. In *Mexico: A Study of Two Americas*, Chase found benefits in the folkways of Tepoztlan. Free of the business cycle and the machine civilization, Tepoztlan is a place where "community spirit is strong— as in old New England barn raisings." Also finding the essence of community in peasant Mexico, anthropologist Robert Redfield called it a "folk society." Marked by isolation and "intimate communication," it is "an organization of people doing many different things successively as well as simultaneously." The many things are functionally interrelated; activities are "interdependent and consistent." To Redfield, the contrast of this society was the modern urban society.[28]

Studies of the types of communities that are represented by Mexican peasants extended into the American setting. In this setting were tight-knit, separatist communities that were not swept up by modern bourgeois culture. Researchers sought out the distinctive communities of Amish, Cajuns, Hasidic Jews, Appalachians, Sea Islanders, and fishermen, to name a few. In Pennsylvania, especially, "new folklife" researchers stressed the community in their studies. There, since the nineteenth century, scholars had stressed the distinctiveness of the area's German folkways in contrast to the dominant Anglo-American way of life elsewhere. They had a Pennsylvania-German Folklore Society, a Pennsylvania Folklife Society since 1951, a lineage of university teaching across southeastern Pennsylvania, and some of America's first folk museums. After World War II the Pennsylvania-German folklorists found a wider audience for their models of community study.

Don Yoder, a long-term editor of *Pennsylvania Folklife* and a teacher at Franklin and Marshall College and the University of Pennsylvania, described the move toward folklife studies as a "20th Century re-discovery of the total range of the folk-culture (folklife)." Folklife stressed the interdependence and isolation of communities. From Yoder's vantage point in Pennsylvania, the primary concern was a preindustrial, rural community that was tethered to regional and ethnic traditions, although later he came to recognize "contemporary folklife"—alterations of older forms—in urban and industrial settings.[29]

The new folklife influenced a new generation of students, who were looking for the intimate communication of tradition among ethnic and regional groups. These students went beyond isolated groups, for tradition-bound communities could be discerned among family, occupational, and neighborhood groups, within a city or mass culture. Living next to one another in an era of communications, residents did not need to feel that they were part of a community. Although the idea of community became more fluid and more abstract, it was still important for setting boundaries on tradition. Community became so entwined with folklife study that John Michael Vlach, one of the new generation, would declare in 1985: "It is a truism, or at least it ought to be, that folklife study involves close consideration of the concept of community. Originally conceived as an adjunct subfield of ethnology, folklife research needs its communal constraints to distinguish its objectives from the broader, more inclusive mandate of anthropology. Instead of studying all of culture, folklife scholars concentrate on the particular ideas and behaviors that demonstrate localized social patterns which are connected to family, neighborhood, town, or region."[30]

Traditions of family, neighborhood, town, or region can simultaneously be communities. These "communities" typically are abstract, not material. By 1982, Henry Glassie, in *Passing the Time in Ballymenone,* who had earlier influenced regional study with his *Pattern in the Material Folk Culture of the Eastern United States* (1968), had come to a fluid notion of community. In *Pattern* he had used the distribution of similar folk-house types on the landscape to chart separate American regions. But in *Passing the Time,* the landscape no longer told him as much about community. As an American studying an Irish countryside, he wrote: "Our society, shifting (its critics say) from rugged individualism to frightened selfishness, needs information on how people form voluntary associations. . . . To help my profession and by extension my society, I wanted to study people as they grouped themselves through action, but I was not worried that I did not know where I was. Had there been a village with a name, I could have been misled, for I wanted to construct a community as the people who lived in it did, and there was no reason to assume their arena of action would match a territory on a map." Community had been viewed as units of time and place, but more works like Glassie's revealed that the sense of community was a state of mind, a feeling of people about themselves. The classification of communities into bounded units, which the ethnography of time and space had earlier sought, seemed like an artificial and limited view, because individuals in America and elsewhere defined their communities so variously. To get at the culture of communities meant recording more of the perceptions of residents. Howard Marshall, who had studied with Glassie, found, for example, that residents variously described Little Dixie in Missouri—"the world with your county in the middle." After realizing this internal view, Marshall then recorded the overlapping communities revealed in shared external patterns of housing, cookery, and political allegiance. For both Glassie and Marshall, the community as a source of culture had to be abstracted from evidence of perceptions found in what people said, made, and did.[31]

Related to the rage for abstracted communities were the social touchstone of *group* and its communicative extension, *network*. The group and the network suggested less of a connection to space and time than did folklife's community; the group and the network offered even more simultaneousness and immediacy to description. Folklore in mobile, complex cultures could work wherever people met. A person on the telephone could work many "networks," could take on different traditions of speaking, without even moving.

If such communications suggested simultaneousness and immediacy in society, then the shift in scholarship to a model of simultaneousness and immediacy can be dramatically seen in the changing folkloristic usage of the words *esoteric* and *exoteric* during the twentieth century. As early as 1902, Franz Boas introduced *esoteric* to describe the specialized knowledge of culture within a community. Such knowledge is often kept by "guardians," who influence the wider exoteric knowledge. Later, Boas saw folklore as the key to this process, for the teaching of culture was made effective through rituals, myths, and folk tales. In 1938 he tied folklore directly to esoteric and exoteric processes in a community. Boas viewed folklore as the vehicle for maintaining tradition and for making adjustments in the social structure. He explained: "The esoteric expresses the reaction of selected minds of the community to their general cultural environment. It is their attempt to systematize the ideas that underlie the culture of the community. The more or less strictly esoteric doctrine exerts its influence upon popular belief so that there is a mutual and inextricable interrelation between the two." This can occur in modern culture, because "the resurgence of palmistry, spiritualism, and astrology at times of particular social stress shows also how readily folk beliefs are taken up by the educated and how they may be organized into systems." William Hugh Jansen (1914–79), writing in 1959 on "The Esoteric-Exoteric Factor in Folklore," shifted the usage of esoteric and exoteric to mean, with *esoteric*, a group's folklore about itself, and, with *exoteric*, a group's folklore about other groups. One's traditional knowledge of one's own ethnic group would be esoteric; a slur on another group would be exoteric. Citing overreliance on geographic isolation to categorize in-group and out-group differences in lore, Jansen thought that "failure in or an incapacity for communication" was a contributing factor to the creation of esoteric and exoteric lore. With the group being defined by communication, more types of groups, beyond occupational and geographic ones, opened for the folklorist's investigation. The group could be defined simply by the perceptions of its participants and the situation that they were in. Jansen's usage implied that the direction of lore was across or in groups in a channel of communication. Esoteric and exoteric appeared to be equivalent directional signals. Rather than Boas's tiered model, Jansen's model implied that society consisted of fluid, competitive groups. Fluid and functional, Jansen's esoteric/exoteric factor offered a pluralistic view of society based on the multiple perspective of postwar communications.[32]

Alan Dundes extended the emphasis on group in his influential definition of *folk*: "Folk can refer to *any group of people whatsoever* who share at least one common factor. It does not matter what the linking factor is—it could be a common occupation, language, or religion—but what is important is that a group formed for whatever reason will have some traditions which it calls its own. In theory a group must consist of at least two persons, but generally most groups consist of many individuals. A member of the group may not know all other members, but he will probably know the common core of traditions belonging to the group, traditions which help the group have a sense of group identity" (emphasis in original). Almost twenty years later, in the *Handbook of American Folklore* (1983), Roger Abrahams would still assert that "the term *folklore* has come to mean the accumulated traditions, the inherited products and practices of a specifiable group, a social unit which has some notion of its own groupness." Ironically, defining the folk group in this way negates the need for *folk,* since no social units exist that are not groups. Abrahams admits to the circular reasoning that folk groups are groups that have a folklore; but this idea of the folk group points out the simultaneousness of folklore and the small group. Folklore is an essential form of communication in a group, and one's sense of a group is communicated by its folklore. The group and the even less bounded "network" act to stress the limited collectivity in which folklore works, in contrast to the homogeneity of mass culture or the "frightened selfishness" of modernity. That the latter two can exist simultaneously, however, casts doubt on the exclusiveness of folklore, or the *sine qua non* of the group. Ultimately, the need for a group is perceptual, a matter of communicating what Dundes called "identity" and what Abrahams referred to as "a sense of social solidarity."[33]

The move from community to network is a move toward more communicative immediacy. Although fluid, community still implied some historical precedent; the network is pressed into the present, subject to an immediate situation. Too, it stations folklore permanently in the modern world. For Michael Owen Jones, for example, "people possess multiple identities, of which one or more dominates at any particular moment and in any particular situation, for which a certain behavior may be appropriate." The minimal units of analysis would be the "individual" and "interactional and communicative networks," which are manifested in unique "events" (rather than group or culture).[34]

Many folklorists would retain the concept of group, since it gives the basis of shared tradition. Dan Ben-Amos used it in his oft-cited definition of folklore: "artistic communication in small groups." Barre Toelken, in his textbook *The Dynamics of Folklore* (1979), expanded on the theme by pointing out the group as "people who share informal communal contacts that become the basis for expressive, culture-based communications." The dominance of communications in these definitions meant that the environment would appear to be simultaneous and immediate. Toelken, like Ben-Amos, tied studies of such groups in "context." With context, Toelken explained, "several kinds of simultaneous surroundings may affect the interactions among the members of a folk group: a particular place, a particular time (of day, month, year), a certain group of people present, an esoteric language being used, a particular shared culture or tradition, a particular activity taking place, and so on."[35]

Having encouraged the consciousness of community, many folklorists during the 1970s moved community toward a situated network of simultaneousness and immediacy. This made community so fleeting as to need constant recommunication. To give some solidity to community and the communication among its members, many folklorists had tempered such extreme dynamics, by scooping structure from the mercury of modern life and scholarship.

STRUCTURE

The entrance of community into scholarly discourse resembles that of "structure." From roots in work done during the 1920s, structure shot up during the 1950s and bloomed through the 1970s. In 1974, Alan Dundes boasted that "in the past several decades, there is no theoretical trend which has had more impact upon both the humanities and the social sciences than structuralism."[36]

Structure reacted to communications in two ways. First, seeking structure entailed the investigation of relationships among expressive forms. Robert Scholes, writing on structuralism in literature, for example, emphasized that "structuralism is a way of looking for reality not in individual things but in the relationships among them." Second, structuralism restored divisions that had been broken down by communications. The telephone and television did not stop at the door; categories of public/private, outside/inside, and silence/noise flowed into one another. One could not easily sense a message's direction or shape.[37]

Generally, the invoking of structure implied an antimodernist ideology: it searched for "base concepts," a limited number of traditional structures underlying the apparent fluidity of cultural expression. If meaning in the nineteenth century was contained in a hidden past, structural meaning now lies hidden beneath expression. In such a view, content is alienated from form; feeling is distanced from expression. For Scholes and others, structuralism is an intellectual way in which to restore wholeness, to break down and then build up and, in the process, to derive meaning.

Yet structuralism appeared to be modernist, too, because it was connected to communications: it was time-free, relational, and multiperspectival. In their introduction to *Structural Analysis of Oral Tradition* (1971), for example, Pierre Maranda and Elli-Kaija Köngäs Maranda wrote: "Instances of narrative communication—which can be captured and archived as texts—then are on the level of performance and can be called surface structures; under every performance there is a process in which some materials, such as inherited or international tale plots or actual experiences, are transformed to fit the deep ('timeless') structures of the culture." Dundes meanwhile identifies a multiple perspective when he asserts that structural analysis "can facilitate all kinds of different modes of interpretation." Commenting on Dundes, Ulf Drobin adds: "A structural description of a genre is not absolute, but is a generalization of various degrees of abstraction, which mirrors the common features in the material investigated."[38]

Of the material that had been investigated by structuralists, most of it has turned out to be folklore. Structural analysis has been especially applied to folklore, Svatava Pirkova-Jakobson explains, because of its "features as a collective product."[39] Traditional expressions emphasized the possibility for coherence of forms in a system of communication. Although many theories are termed "structural," following from the general use of structure that I described, the structuralist currents of folklore scholarship usually followed from the methods used by Vladimir Propp and Claude Lévi-Strauss.

In 1928, the Russian Vladimir Propp (1895–1970) published *Morfologija skazki* (Morphology of the folktale), in which he arranged the actions of fairy tales in a linear sequence. Although Propp is usually singled out as the originator of "morphological study," others approached the subject around the same time. In "Towards a Morphological Study of the Folktale," also published in 1928, for example, A. I. Nikiforov asserted: "Ideas about a new methodological approach to the folktale, which may be termed morphological, have appeared both in foreign and in Russian scholarly literature. They can be found in certain sections in the books of K. Spess, W. A. Berendsohn, A. van Gennep, and of our own V. Skovskij and R. Volkov." Nikiforov envisioned structuralism as a way to get beyond diffusion as explanation; structuralism would reveal "laws of plot formation" and "the schematic structure of folktale action."[40]

Propp's move to structure came out of a multiperspectival view of classification. He complained that the arrangement of tales according to theme was misleadingly narrow. Tales about animals were separated from tales of magic, for example. But a tale could have elements of both, he argued. Themes and actors change in the tales, but the actions tend to be constant. Symbols are assigned to the actions, and the actions are arranged in sequence to offer a linear representation of structure. A tale, he wrote, "may be termed any development proceeding from villainy (A) or a lack (a), through intermediary functions to marriage (W*), or to other functions employed as a denouement." He found the sequence of "functions"—the act of a character to advance the plot—to be identical. Having described the structure, explanation still had to come from the comparison with "cultural, religious, daily, or other reality."[41] Structure was a means of unveiling reality.

Although Propp's structuralism was suppressed in the Soviet Union, it led an influential second life when *Morphology of the Folktale* was translated into English in 1958. In its fullest application, Propp's method was applied by Alan Dundes in *The Morphology of North American Indian Folktales* (1964). Propp's linear-structure model worked to unveil the composition of the narrative as an observable structure.

In contrast, another type of structuralism, associated with Lévi-Strauss, uncovers the structure of the world through the composition of the narrative. Rather than finding a sequence, the analyst takes key concepts out of order and regroups them to reveal basic relations, usually expressed in binary oppositions. Lévi-Strauss described the procedure as a multiperspectival, simultaneous "orchestra score." All the notes that are written vertically constitute "one gross constituent unit, i.e. one bundle of relations." If Propp found structural continuities, Lévi-Strauss stressed structural discontinuities. As Dundes explains: "Since Lévi-Strauss is trying to identify oppositional paradigms in the world described in myth, he does not choose to be limited by the chronological order in which elements of the paradigm occur in a given narrative. If high/low, night/day, male/female, etc. instances occur anywhere in the narrative, Lévi-Strauss feels free to extrapolate them and re-order them in his delineations of the paradigm."[42]

Lévi-Strauss emphasized myths as the most effective entrances to describe the world that is revealed in expressions translated from thoughts. Henry Glassie extended the range of expressions to old houses. When examined free of their contexts, houses offer a mediation between nature and culture; they reveal, as myths did, concepts of order. Glassie wrote: "Structuralism is social scientific modernism. It is modernist in its concern with principled abstraction rather than particularistic realism. The structuralist's interest is in process more than product, in hidden law more than manifest shape, in relations more than entities, in the universal, the unconscious, the simultaneous, the systematic. Thus structuralism provides the social scientist with an entree into his own times, a period pioneered by physicists and artists." Glassie refers to the current "fashion" of structure: "Its method enables the analyst to locate an unexpected abundance of information in discrete things—things floating free of the their contexts—and it enables him to relate apparently unconnected phenomena into systems."[43] But despite the search for meaning in the systems themselves, as if outsiders could get into the heads of insiders, cultural and historical relations ultimately came from outside.

As the structure of oppositions underlies expression, the opposition *outside/inside* undergirds structuralism. I showed that the blurring of this opposition through communications was what gave rise to a need for clearer structures. In addition, the multiple perspective of

Lévi-Strauss's structure forced the issue of the standpoint from which structures are ordered—inside or outside. For both Dundes and Glassie, for example, structures were keys to realistic classifications. Dundes used structuralism to derive structural definitions of genres, while Glassie used it to obtain a geometric system of arranging house types. The dilemma of structural standpoints to judge such classifications came out in the oft-cited *emics/etics* opposition.

The *emics/etics* concern arose out of the work of Kenneth Pike, who drew an ethnographic tie with linguistics by pulling *emic* from *phonemic* and *etic* from *phonetic*. In use, emic approaches are usually construed to be actor oriented. Emics describes patterns of culture with reference to close observation of the culture itself. Etics is thought of as entailing analytical approaches imposed on a culture. What Pike stated, however, was that "an emic approach must deal with particular events as parts of larger wholes to which they are related and from which they obtain their ultimate significance, whereas an etic approach may abstract events, for particular purposes, from their context or local system of events, in order to group them on a world-wide scale without essential reference to the structure of any one language or culture."[44]

Pike's distinction involved more than just pointing out the neglect by scholarship of the native point of view in favor of categories imposed by an educated class; Pike's distinction had to do with the nature of the unit derived. Emic units are structural in that they relate to a cultural system; etic units are nonstructural in that they are comparative and culture free. Etic units are more communicative; emic units are perceptual. Both units, however, can be subjective, despite claims to the contrary, because views of natives typically represent a diversity of opinion which the analyst must interpret. Etic units, although based on observable characteristics, are open to individual perceptions.

Structuralism, as I have noted, takes apart and then builds up. It is at bottom a mediation of emics and etics, for it attempts to structure native perceptions; it takes apart heard (or seen) expressions to describe their wholeness. When brought back together, structure could not stand as an end in itself. As Glassie states, "the tracing of structure begins rather than exhausts scholarly possibilities." In making the next step, Glassie, like Dundes and others, calls for the drawing of meaning from structures, whether on the surface of expression or in the depths of a world view, as signs. They acknowledge the hiero-glyphics of modern communications, and indeed, Glassie notes that "the usefulness of the object-sign distinction requires knowledge as to whether the artifact is a sign to the sender or the receiver or both."[45]

Having shown boundaries, signs would, Dundes and Glassie hope, reveal the possibilities of meaning. Structures are our modernist versions of boundaries, which are still open to dispute; and the very process of structuring skews the results toward a modernist stand-point. Having established structure itself as a basic concept, symbols had to be discerned and deciphered to bring meaning to the analysis.

SYMBOL

The promise of the word *symbol* to deliver meaning to twentieth-century scholarship can be traced to the changing view of messages that people send. Modern communication appeared to reinforce a "hieroglyphic civilization." It became more visual, for one thing, relying increasingly on images. As it did so, different levels of meaning could be discerned. The scientific Rorschach test, which requires subjects to read abstract designs, entered popular culture because a public saw it as a way of telescoping modern imagery. The public believed that a reading of a literal image—the butterfly, for example—had "deeper" meanings for the psyche. Analogously, the popular press reported the deeper meanings of advertising, pop art, and fashion.[46]

Second, as communication multiplied messages without face-to-face contact, people believed that others did not mean what they said. Woody Allen played on this tendency with great effect in his movie *Annie Hall* (1977). As Allen talks to Hall, subtitles flash on the screen to tell what they are really thinking. Speakers could be actors, taking on roles without letting their faces give away their feelings. A public encountered diverse systems of speech; language could simultane-ously appear to be specialized, as in scientific jargon, and uniform, as television suggested. Books by William Safire and Edwin Newman hit the best-seller lists in the 1970s with commentaries on the multiple uses and abuses of language. Popular parodies of "bureaucratic double-talk" and "valley talk" conveyed the idea that language didn't just have to be heard; it also had to be deciphered.[47]

Third, communication, especially radio, television, and theater, made it more difficult for the audience to get involved. Unlike audiences in the nineteenth-century theater, modern audiences could not interrupt; they had to listen and watch in silence. Less aware of a specific audience and left alone to become more ritualized, perfor-mance dealt more in symbols for its effect. At the same time, public life in a world of strangers seemed artificial and external. The assump-tion that with the breakdown of community, an audience consisted of strangers also meant that symbols replaced familiarity and action to denote status, knowledge, and feeling. The ordinary, the "slice of life," became subjects for theater and film. In public, the ordinary was heightened, by rituals of communication, to provide necessary symbols for living.[48]

Victor Turner, in *The Forest of Symbols* (1967), described the alienation of inside/outside, private/public, and surface/depth in laying out his symbolic analysis, which was based on the structure of traditional rituals. To Turner, the rituals became "systems of meaning . . . interpreted by informants and as observed in action." He continued: "We also become aware that a complex relationship exists between the overt and the submerged, and the manifest and latent patterns of meaning."[49] His underlying assumption is that people master their world by manipulating symbols.

Clifford Geertz is another writer who relies on structures that lead to symbolic analysis. Geertz offers Balinese cockfights as an example. Geertz viewed the cockfight as a performed text, an "imaginative work built out of social materials." Values of the society are articulated through symbols of the text. Participants learn and reflect a Balinese cultural "ethos" and "private sensibility." In other words, the cockfight reinforces social reality and acts out the potential extremes of that reality. Geertz compares this reading of cockfights with other events in Bali to underscore the point that symbols will occur in systems. He finds similar meanings—that is, reflections of reality—in festivals at village temples and in consecrations of Brahman priests.[50]

Geertz and Turner have influenced many studies from folklore to literature. In one folklore study, Thomas A. Burns and J. Stephen Smith, for example, looked at Sunday-morning services of an urban black Holiness church, and concluded that such regular events constituted rituals that had symbolic components. They claimed that the service revealed the social hierarchy of the sect, what they identified as a confirmative symbol. The service also encouraged a more advanced status within the sect, a transformative symbol. Burns and Smith conclude that the Sunday service as a "symbolic statement 'about' being and becoming is actually concerned with expressive behaviors as symbols *of* (being) and *for* (becoming) reality." Still another study, by Gerald Pocius, of Newfoundland hooked rugs views the opposition of egalitarianism and hierarchical social relations in the maintenance of symmetrical and asymmetrical designs. He writes: "If we look at the organization of the outport, we see that basically it was egalitarian in terms of the vast majority of residents, the fishermen. At the same time, however, it was hierarchical in terms of a tiny minority, the merchant and the clergyman." Discussing the use of rugs, Pocius notices: "The symmetrical, geometrically repetitious rugs—those with community design antecedents—are used almost exclusively in the kitchen. These 'egalitarian' designs are displayed in the context where equals would meet. On the other hand, those rugs with individual antecedents are used in the front room where hierarchical interaction takes place."[51]

If such a symbolic scheme stresses structures in texts—whether material or literary—as being social in meaning, Alan Dundes has argued for psychoanalytical meaning in their structures. In the structure of American weddings, for instance, he notes the binary oppositions between bride and groom, married and unmarried. Dundes infers from this structure that "through the ritual act of throwing away her floral bouquet [the bride signifies] her willingness to be, or intention of being, *deflowered*" (emphasis in original). Other texts are not so literal; they require connections to the culture. Dead-baby jokes, for example, he ties to public awareness of the abortion issue during the 1970s. Through redirecting the disturbing issue to symbolic humor, the jokes unconsciously relieved anxiety.[52]

Going beyond applying psychoanalysis, folklorists have mined behavioral and cognitive interpretations of symbols. In his *Folk Housing in Middle Virginia,* Glassie tied the transformation of houses toward symmetry and enclosure as a psychic need for order during the late eighteenth century at a time—around the American Revolution—when possible disorder was perceived. Drawn to the structure of an individual's work, Michael Owen Jones, in *The Hand Made Object and Its Maker* (1975), discerned an imposing sense of enclosure when the maker was near crowded spaces. Drawing back into the countryside, his chairs opened up. Jones read into the forms a structure of psychic states.

Of course, the reading of symbols is often external, brought to the maker or society by the analyst. I. C. Jarvie complains, for example, that "to seek the meaning of symbolic interpretation of an utterance or ceremony presupposes that a determinate meaning exists." For Jarvie, "a bystander's explanation of what is going on is quite enough." Dundes admits that "a given item of folklore may mean different things to different tale tellers or to different audiences"; but he insists that an important meaning to be inferred is unconscious. Dundes argues that "among its functions, folklore provides a socially sanctioned outlet for the expression of what cannot be articulated in the more usual, direct way." Folklore exists because it offers symbolic mechanisms at different, simultaneous levels. And meaning needs to be drawn because of the saturation of messages, what Dundes refers to as "the assiduous collection of scores and scores of folklore texts."[53]

Even if one does not accept Dundes's interpretations, his premise is true for most symbolic interpretations. One answer to substantiate the decoding of folklore as part of a hieroglyphic civilization is to describe folklore more in terms of a performance in a system of communications. Roger Abrahams explains: "Every agency, artifact, and entity within a culture is potentially capable of reflecting the whole of the constructs of that group. But in order to so reflect, it must be presented within some context of the culture from which it emerged."[54] In what came to be called "the ethnography of communication," the effect of the "big change" had come full circle, from society to scholarship and back to society.

PERFORMANCE

If speaking needed to become performance in order to be heard in an electronic world, then speaking would also gain meaning as the medium of staged sincerity. In the shift, too, from a manufacturing economy to one based on service and information, "performing" services and speaking in routines became a greater part of daily life. Process and product became more distant from each other. It is not surprising, then, that folklore—with its intimate connection of speaker and listener, as well as process and product, and its connotation of sincerity—should have drawn the attention of scholarship that was seeking meaning from communication in society.

Dell Hymes's "The Ethnography of Speaking" marked an influential formation of performance analysis. In Hymes's view, both ethnography and linguistics used speech for cultural patterns and grammar and therefore could be combined. Speaking, he claimed, "is patterned within each society in culture-specific, cross-culturally variable ways." He called for ethnographers to uncover patterns that control speech, functions that are served by speech in specific situations, effects that situational context has on speech, and dynamics of performance. People didn't merely speak; they "interacted." The constant usage of *interact* (and later *enactment*) implied the alternating roles of performance and audience among people. With the recognition that communication among people involved more than speech—gestures, dress, setting, for instance—Hymes later changed the label to the "ethnography of communication."[55]

Methods that are involved in the ethnography of communication included close scrutiny of specific situations as they naturally developed. Texts were still essential to the ethnography, but additional information concerning surroundings, actions, and biographies was collected. Hymes suggested structuring the situation into components of a sender (addresser), a receiver (addressee), a message form, a channel, a code, a topic, and a setting. Communicating behaves as a cultural system; the goal of analysis is to come up with theories to describe the operation of the cultural system. That system varies, however, and indeed can be described as a multiple perspective. Richard Bauman and Joel Sherzer say in their preface to *Explorations in the Ethnography of Speaking* (1974): "Differences in the purposes to which speech is put and the ways it is organized for these purposes are observed, whereas the scholarly literature seems to consider only that languages and their uses are fundamentally the same. In recent years, work to remedy this situation has come to be known as the ethnography of speaking."[56]

Dell Hymes gave folklore its due for helping to remedy the situation in *Toward New Perspectives in Folklore* (1972), which by its very title referred to the multiple perspective of the new ethnography. In his chapter "The Contribution of Folklore to Sociolinguistic Research," Hymes categorized folklore "in terms of the study of communicative behavior with an esthetic, expressive, or stylistic dimension." Thus it is appropriate to have folklorists take up the ethnography of speaking, with "its goal a view of the speech of a community as ways of speaking."[57]

The editors of *Toward New Perspectives,* Richard Bauman and Américo Paredes, cautioned that no single consensus existed among the contributors but that general trends did emerge, one of which was the movement from the consideration of folklore as an item to the consideration of folklore as an event, described in specific situations. Second was a concern for "artistic act, expressive form, and esthetic response" in emic terms. Third was "a concern for the achievement of greater formal precision in the description and analysis of folklore, not as an end in itself but with a strong commitment towards the integration of form, function, and performance."[58]

What were the differences? Dan Ben-Amos thought that folklore emerged from confrontations within small groups; he questioned the old criterion of tradition for folklore. Following an emic argument, he pointed out that people may themselves not use tradition to categorize folklore. Roger Abrahams, however, retained the concept of tradition as an integral process of folklore, a kind of minimal unit, in structural terms. Although he recognized Ben-Amos's group setting for transmission, he added that folklore also occurred between groups and within a broader idea of community. Richard Bauman rejected the group basis of folklore by arguing that individuals interact even though they do not share membership in a similar group. Rather, they possess "differential" identities. His criterion for folklore is "artistic verbal performance," which is based on a shared aesthetic of spoken language. Still another segment of performance analysis is presented by Kenneth S. Goldstein, who emphasized the history of individuals as a factor in evaluating performance.[59]

An extension of the movement toward performance appeared in 1975 as *Folklore: Performance and Communication*, edited by Dan Ben-Amos and Kenneth S. Goldstein. The introduction asserted that the contributors viewed folklore as "human verbal symbolic interaction of a performing kind." One purpose was again to make precise descriptions, but now they concentrated more on uncovering rules for social behavior as implied by a linguistic model. Using the precedent of Albert B. Lord's *The Singer of Tales* (1960), Bruce Rosenberg, for example, found that American preachers, like Lord's Yugoslavian epic singers, performed sermons according to oral formulas and stylistic conventions. Each performance of the sermon was a unique event, which was influenced by audience, actor, and stage.[60]

Again, disagreements arose. Abrahams considered the cognition of folklore to consist "of a store of traditional items which can be retrieved from memory whenever a situation calls for them." Ben-Amos and Goldstein thought folklore was a more spontaneous, emergent reaction to "a set of rules, a system of communication, a grammar, in which the relationships between the attributes of verbal messages and the social-cultural reality are in constant interplay." The editors criticized the use of *rhetorical*, which Abrahams suggested to describe the new ethnography. They preferred *performance* and *communication*, because they were more inclusive terms for the symbolic qualities of "face-to-face interaction." The qualifier *face-to-face* stressed the standard of electronic communication, while *interaction* implied an impersonality of public action.[61]

Whether in *interface, interaction, interdisciplinary, transaction,* or *transformation,* the new lexicon's emphasis on the prefixes *inter* and *trans* invoked the electronic crossing of barriers of time and space. The terms that were in vogue stressed the confusion of categories, a blurring and shifting of items and institutions that had formerly been thought to be stable and rooted. *Performance* seemed most appealing, because of its application to the era's increased emphasis on showmanship and "impression management," as perceptions of social mobility and change increased in the society. To Richard Bauman, for example, "performance thus calls forth special attention to and heightened awareness of the act of expression, and gives license to the audience to regard the act of expression and the performer *with special intensity*" (italics added). Roger Abrahams elaborated: "Reality itself . . . appears to be layered, made up of different levels of intensity and focus of interaction and participation. A very precious commodity is being negotiated, after all, one which is remarkably vital and which, in fact, we might call our socio-cultural vitality. For it is in these states of ritual or performance, festive or play enactments that in many ways we are most fully ourselves, both as individuals and as members of our communities."[62]

The "young Turks," as Dorson called the performance-oriented folklorists, further emphasized their cybernetic precision by referring to their study as "folkloristics." Like other precedents for this current of folklore studies, folkloristics has connections to European movements of the 1920s. Eugen Kagarow, writing on "Folkloristik und Volkskunde" in 1929, showed the simultaneous use of different terms for folklore and its study across Europe. *Folkloristik* provided a scientific term to differentiate between the materials and their study. It was an umbrella term for the study of folklore. Kagarow drew a geometric structure for study, with *Folkloristik* at the center, flanked by cultural history, folklife, literature, folk psychology, art theory and history, and dialectology. For the young Turks of the 1970s, *folkloristics* emphasized that folklore is behavioral and measurable and its study precise.[63]

The 1970s was a time of renewed concern for structure and formula, as changes in the society seemed to obscure or threaten underlying structures. Referring to the contributors in *Toward New Perspectives*, for example, Américo Paredes quipped: "Their scholarly careers are scarcely older than our military involvement in Southeast Asia. That is to say, they are men and women representing the scholarship of the present times." Life seemed more uncertain and fluid. Performance analysis offered to unveil some predictability to today's minimal units—its situations. By isolating stages where boundaries could not be easily discerned, performance analysis offered to reunite actors with their art.

BEYOND COMMUNICATION

Folklore studies now commands an area between the simultaneousness of America as an impersonal mass society and a *self*-conscious society of specialized individuals. The station of folklore studies in the area, however, has not been consistent. After beginning in the nineteenth century as a broad inquiry covering lower-class tradition, folklore studies in America narrowed to cover oral traditions of isolated regions. Since World War II, folklore studies has broadened once again, this time to take in all "artistic communication in small groups." In the changes, folklore studies has responded to, and has acted on, intellectual needs in the society. As folklore studies has taken in more of the public as its object, it has become more public. Although folklore studies today is more secure in the professional landscape, it is once again remapping its place.[64]

In the 1970s the keyword of performance synthesized many concerns of community, structure, and symbol for folklorists and other intellectuals who were commenting on a mass society that called for its members to act so as to be able to impress one another. In 1974, however, Richard Sennett, in *The Fall of Public Man,* reported the decline of the other-directed, public man. Donald M. Lowe, in 1982, added that as a result of "urbanization, mechanization, rationalization transportation, communication, visualization," the experience of the present was "much more mechanical, discontinuous, and external than before." Sennett complained that a preoccupation with personality and narcisissism was the result of actors who were increasingly being deprived of their art—that is, acting without feeling—in the daily life of modern culture.[65] Although difficult to prove statistically, the transition in the nature of modern experience received humanistic critiques.[66] The synthesis of performance, they pointed out, missed a cultural and historical context outside of communication channels. More of the culture that was meaningful and genuine seemed private. In 1974, geographer Wilbur Zelinsky commented, after making a study of the public life styles of Americans, that "expanding our zone of scientific attentiveness in matters human and geographic beyond the familiar chambers of the economic, demographic, social, and cultural into the deep corridors of personal perception and the appetite for self-creation is one way to enrich our understanding of the former." Sennett reflected that "society and social relations may continue to be abstractly imagined in dramatic terms, but men have ceased themselves to perform." Sennett observed, rather, that "one's energies are directed toward finding out what it is one feels, rather than making the feeling clear and manifest to others."[67]

To many critics of culture, folklore was a still-active medium of identity and feeling, of genuine artistic performance. W. Edson Richmond, in his introduction to the *Handbook of American Folklore* (1983), for example, contrasted the expressions of folklore tellers and politicians: "Though an oft-repressed and subliminal aspect of our culture, its repertoire of 'dirty' jokes, of racist jokes, is certainly far more revealing of popular attitudes than are the pronouncements of politicians. Moreover, since to be called a part of folklore these jokes must be recurrent forms, an analysis of their evolution often discloses the shifting attitudes of a group far more vividly than do studies of political action." Henry Glassie, in the same volume, compared the assembly-line manufacture of automobiles with folk construction of objects and concluded that the former "seems more the product of circumstance than of culture." In folklore is contained a human involvement and genuineness, Richmond and Glassie suggested, that is not found in the public expressions of national life.[68]

But in the rush to identify this genuineness, the privacy of expression and the artifice of tradition are often given short shrift. Wilhelm Nicolaisen drew attention to the problem in his presidential address to the American Folklore Society in 1983, where he said: "The intellectual dilemma that we have inherited has its roots in two fundamentally very different views of craft and folk culture, for while the idea of artisanship or craftsmanship has always implied individual skills and one person's pair of hands, the notion of 'folk' has conjured up almost invariably an image of community, of group, of lack of individuality, ever since it was first introduced into the English language almost a century and a half ago. Tradition, that key ingredient in so much folk cultural activity, has been equated with communal creation and re-creation in an atmosphere of anonymity, and the emphasis has been on the transmission of knowledge, customs, and beliefs through such anonymous channels in an almost mystical fashion."[69] Fewer than 5 percent of the papers at the annual meeting, he pointed out, dealt with individual folk performers. Nicolaisen's plaint contains the portent of a movement beyond performance and communication to the introspection of Sennett's other man—the private man—lurking in the shadowy substrata of culture.

Although performance is commonly acknowledged as the cynosure of the 1970s, it, like structure and function before them, came to search for its explanation during the 1980s. In 1984, Dundes quipped that performance is just "glorified description." Ironically supporting his case was Elizabeth Fine's application of performance theory, *The Folklore Text: From Performance to Print* (1984). After a long exposition, she arrived at the realization that performance analysis gave a more accurate rendering of the conditions of folklore performance but that proper interpretation was still unclear. Nonetheless, intellectually, performance analysis allowed "persons who might not otherwise be able to experience the verbal art of a culture to more fully appreciate its integral, aesthetic presence." In the end, it failed to overarch as explanatory theory; it moved next to function and structure as methods of analysis.[70] After making an argument in 1972 that with communication as a defining characteristic, tradition is not necessary to the definition of folklore, Dan Ben-Amos, in 1984, noted that tradition is ultimately paired with performance. Performance is one of many orientations toward tradition. Tradition, he argued, is what has "remained a symbol of and for folklore." In 1985, Gary Alan Fine made the case that performance, no longer an intellectual rebellion, had been rapidly incorporated as a descriptive criterion. Speaking of the groundbreaking *Toward New Perspectives in Folklore* (1972), Fine remarked, "When read today the early papers of this approach seemed filled with obvious truisms; performance theory had been well-integrated into the discipline." No longer a keyword, performance fell from the attention of generalized theory. Rather, it became a take-off point for new movements that are being aimed at analyzing cultural expressiveness.[71]

One direction was the realization of Sennett's private man or Nicolaisen's individual artisan. This was a person who responded to surrounding conditions and an inner disposition through the creation of a tradition. This was "Charley," a Kentucky chair maker in Michael Owen Jones's *The Hand Made Object and Its Maker* (1975) or Philip Simmons in John Michael Vlach's *Charleston Blacksmith* (1981). Still, these artisans engaged in crafts that had a long historical association with folklife study. But then folklorists introduced other artisans who created forms that were not immediately recognized as a collective folklife. There was Sandra Stahl's mother, spinning stories from personal experiences; there was Tressa Prisbrey, creating shelters and designs from recycled bottles.[72] Moving in this direction meant, as Nicolaisen stated, that "the reasons for the continued choice of such responses are at least partially embedded in what the choice speaks to: the need for self-expression within a predictable and comfortable context; the desire for acceptability without slavish, imitative conformity; the creative urge that is satisfied to be fulfilled within the patterns and demands of tradition; the provision of identity in the present through conscious links with the past; the orientation through folk cultural symbols below and beyond the level of daily experience." Folklore is not faceless and interchangeable; nor is it reducible to "dynamic human expression." It is, in Nicolaisen's view, "the expressions of the tension and interplay between individual and society, between variation and repetition, between isolated self and communal other."[73]

If one direction is inward to the isolated self, then another direction is outward to the communal other. More than entailing a concern for groups—ethnic, occupational, or regional—the communal other is organizational. It exists in different organizations of social structure. During the 1980s, the public has become more accustomed to hearing about the worlds of power, organized worlds that were creating cultures of their own. The public has heard about the corporate world and, later, corporate cultures, about the fashion

world, and, later, about the culture of consumption.[74] The organizational model of business seemed more prevalent in society. A biography of Chrysler's chief, Lee Iacocca, and a survey of corporate
successes, *In Search of Excellence,* remained on top of the best-seller
list for most of 1984. Alan Trachtenberg gave a historical account of
the rise of an organizational society in *The Incorporation of America*
(1982); an ethnographic account was given in *Organizational Culture*
(1985), edited by Peter J. Frost and others; and a political account was
given by Walter F. Baber in *Organizing the Future* (1983). A page from
a booklet, *Folklore/Folklife,* put out by the American Folklore Society,
was devoted to the subject "Folklore and Organizational Life." "The
stories that people tell, the ways they decorate their work space,
ceremonies in which they take part, and ritualistic interaction provide
data essential to understanding human concerns and the culture of an
organization," the page concluded. The wording was later subjected to
vigorous debate by the membership, for it seemed to eclipse the older
group model of occupational folklore. Political undertones surfaced.
In the use of the heading "Organizational Life," some people sensed a
conservative acceptance of corporate hegemony, and others read into
it the liberal doctrine of class conflict. The page was the only one in the
booklet that was challenged by the membership. It was a sign that the
keyword *organization,* no matter what the political interpretation of it,
portended a change of folkloristic approach.[75]

The broader implication of *organization* was its vision of society,
much as performance and function provided their own. It implied a
breakdown of community, region, and nation as the dominant social
worlds of people. In a modern society that was noted for its increasing
individualism, institutional settings define more identities: the office,
the military, the city, the media, the school, the profession, the
government. More cultural associations are voluntary and overlapping. Richard Dorson noted the shift in his keynote address for the
pivotal conference Folklore in the Modern World at Indiana University
in 1973: "The unofficial culture can be contrasted with the high, the
visible, the institutional culture of church, state, the universities, the
professions, the corporations, the fine arts, the sciences. This unofficial culture finds its own modes of expression in folk religion, folk
medicine, folk literature, the folk arts, and folk philosophy. Yet the
unofficial culture reflects the mood of its times fully as much as does
the official culture, for both are anchored in the same historical
period." In proposing the "contemporaneity, as opposed to the antiquity, of folklore," Dorson contributed to an organizational concept of
culture.[76] Yet he underestimated the intimate connections of the
official with the unofficial; he did not chart the complexity of organiza-

tional models in both cultures and its influence on the circulation of folklore.

Where the organizational concept had gone was indicated by the proceedings of a conference, Myth, Symbols and Folklore: Expanding the Analysis of Organizations, held in California in 1983. A summary reported that "papers concerned ceremonials and rituals in corporations, the effects of folklore on organization and performance, leadership needs of the 1980s, the symbolic management of organizational life, quality-of-work issues approached through expressive needs, symbolic expression as tool for developing organizations, and so on. Workshops focused on organization change, leadership, identity, ambience, formation, and continuity—always with particular attention to ritual, play, narrative, and aesthetic expression."[77] Implicit in the report was the feeling that the analysis of organizational life went beyond the documentation of history and ethnography to applications to improve life in the future.

The analysis of "organizations" is not restricted to corporations, although many of its models are drawn from them. One consideration is the influence of organizations on the generation of folklore. For instance, probably the most visible, if not the most collectible, form of modern folklore consists of satirical photocopied memos and cartoons found in many work places. Again and again, they make references to the dominance of organizational life, from illustrated chains of command to satirized lists of organizational rules. Modern legends similarly offer insight into the shifting perception of society. Among the emergent stories was a crop of legends about corporations and consumption: batter-fried rats; time on the kidney machine in exchange for the accumulation of cigarette wrappers; connections between large retailing organizations and satanic cults. In Gary Alan Fine's study of rumors that Pop Rocks candy had caused the death of a young child and then had been made illegal, he discovered that structural features of the preadolescent community (age, sex, Little League baseball team, school attended) dictated who was likely to have heard the story.[78] In looking at the relations of different levels of the social structure, the small frames of ethnography expanded. For Fine, questions of performance, communication, and symbolism could be subsumed under social structure. But in examining the social differentiation of society, the relativistic notion that plural groups are basic to performance buckled. Society appears to be more bureaucratic. Society has a social order, and folklore works at its different levels to question, support, and interpret it.

Folklore studies were, again, not alone in this current. Fine suggested that, indeed, folklore studies were late in joining a movement connecting "structural social sciences." As in other currents, a model of reality that had been proposed for the modern society came to be applied to cultural investigation. Indeed, both the individual artisan and the larger social order are parts of the same current, because they both look at a negotiated social order in different domains of organization. Of course, the organizational current is not the only investigation that is suited to problems of folklore, but it moves to the fore because it proposes to reveal what is of most concern in a future-oriented society—the present state of the modern world and its guiding structures for the future. Although the organizational model shows strong signs of emergence as a major current of folklore studies, it may not take hold, because American folklorists have, since World War II, been typically caught between the muses and the masses. They have been tied to an egalitarian and lateral outlook on society.[79] Yet, as folklore studies increasingly moves outside the academy, as it becomes more subject to organizational differentiation, and as it lodges in governmental agencies, foundations, corporations, museums, and libraries, then the keyword *organization* may balloon into a prominent theory of folklore studies.

Theories differ because the problems that folklorists faced and the society that they worked in changed. Transformations in theories reflect a changing favor for dominant models and metaphors taken from society. Yet there is continuity between the past and the present. As in the last 150 years, folklorists are again joining humanists and social scientists in probing tradition and subcultural identity in a society that appears to be ever more modern and uniform, ever more novel and individualized.[80] This is the great connecting theme among the currents of folklore studies. The theme has acted on, as well as reacted to, social change. It ties folklore studies to the broader movement of American intellectual history. Folklore studies, like other cultural studies, has centered on portions of the culture that are apparently undergoing and causing rapid change, or are remaining in spite of change.

I have observed that the temper of the times has had an influence on cultural studies, an influence that is commonly outside of the awareness of scholars. From the nineteenth century, folklore studies has moved from a societal preoccupation with the past to one with the present and now with the future. Scholarship has moved from the broad picture of history to the small frames of ethnography. Moving toward the future, folklorists predict the shape of tradition; more than documenting, they apply their study to act on culture.[81] Putting these developments in historical context has been a way to make connections between study and society, between a subject and its object. It has shown ways in which folkloristic views have been tied to societal standpoints.

Folklore studies has made considerable achievements during its intellectual history. It has introduced the keyword *folk* into public discourse. Its collections and theories have gone beyond the academy into the marketplace and the political arena. It has consolidated a host of disparate interests into a field of study and, later, into a profession. In America, folklore studies has become entwined with envisioning the nation's heritage. It therefore has become a force on public opinion and imagination. Folklore studies has provided a legacy of American lore, which has furnished an intensity of experience that was lacking in the standard historical and literary record. In describing folklore as basic to modern existence, folklore studies has offered a cultural depth to an apparently one-dimensional present. It has opened earthy realms of artistry for analysis. In collecting and presenting living traditions, folklore studies has encouraged the public to hear the true strains and to see the real things. It has made culture more concrete and more complex, by pointing to the many expressions of America's cultures, and, in so doing, has reminded the nation of social worlds beneath its surface. Folklore studies has sought traditions before they were gone or missed and has explained how they came to be or why they arise anew. The center of folklore studies remains in tradition, in explaining human experience that takes the form of recurrent, expressive responses to social life and environment. In its choice of subjects and in its approaches, folklore studies continues to comment on changes and continuities in society. Therein lies the "historical truths otherwise lost," pronounced in the last century. And herein now lies a legacy of cultural investigation as cultural act.

Notes

PREFACE

1. Raymond Williams, *Keywords: A Vocabulary of Culture and Society* (New York, 1976), x.
2. Lee J. Vance, "The Study of Folk-Lore," *Forum* 22 (1896/97): 249; Richard M. Dorson, "Preface," in *Handbook of American Folklore,* ed. Richard M. Dorson (Bloomington, Ind., 1983), x.
3. Richard M. Dorson, "Afterword," *Journal of the Folklore Institute* 10 (1973): 126.

CHAPTER 1. THE USABLE HIDDEN PAST OF FOLKLORE

1. Lee J. Vance, "Folk-Lore Studies," *Open Court* 1 (1887): 612.
2. Reprinted in John F. Watson, *Annals of Philadelphia and Pennsylvania* (Philadelphia, 1857), iv–v.
3. Philip S. Klein and Ari Hoogenboom, *A History of Pennsylvania* (University Park, Pa., 1980), 201–18; Thomas C. Cochran, *Frontiers of Change: Early Industrialism in America* (Oxford, 1981), 50–100.
4. "Step Gables and Clinkers," *Heritage* 1 (Nov.–Dec. 1984): 4.
5. John F. Watson, *Annals of Philadelphia and Pennsylvania* (Philadelphia, 1891), ix–x; Deborah Dependahl Waters, "Philadelphia's Boswell: John Fanning Watson," *Pennsylvania Magazine of History and Biography* 98 (1974): 3–52; Frank Sommer, "John F. Watson: First Historian of American Decorative Arts," *Antiques* 83 (1963): 300–303.
6. Watson, *Annals of Philadelphia* (1857), vi–vii.
7. Watson, *Annals of Philadelphia* (1891), x.
8. Watson, *Annals of Philadelphia* (1857), 12.
9. Ibid., 1.
10. Ibid., 2.
11. Friedrich Nietzsche, *The Gay Science* (1882; reprint, New York, 1974), 181. The Marcks quote is from "Die imperialistische Idee in der Gegenwart" (1903), which can be found in Stephen Kern, *The Culture of Time and Space, 1880–1918* (Cambridge, Mass., 1983), 240.
12. Lee J. Vance, "The Study of Folk-Lore," *Forum* 22 (1896/97): 249.
13. Theodore Dreiser, *Sister Carrie* (1900; reprint, New York, 1970), 3.

14. John Fiske, "Curtin's Myths and Folk-Lore of Ireland," *Atlantic Monthly* 66 (1890): 568.

15. Henry Childs Merwin, "On Being Civilized Too Much," *Atlantic Monthly* 79 (1897): 833–46.

16. Otis Mason, "The Natural History of Folklore," *Journal of American Folklore* 4 (1891): 103.

17. William Thoms, "Folklore," in *The Study of Folklore,* ed. Alan Dundes (Englewood Cliffs, N.J., 1965), 5.

18. The Christian Remembrancer, "The Study of Folk Lore," *Littell's Living Age* 94 (1866): 707.

19. Don Yoder, "The Folklife Studies Movement," *Pennsylvania Folklife* 13 (July 1963): 43–56; Åke Hultkrantz, *General Ethnological Concepts* (Copenhagen, 1960), 126–44, 242–49; Helmut Moller, "Aus den Anfangen der Volkskunde als Wissenschaft," *Zeitschrift für Volkskunde* 60 (1964): 218–41.

20. Charlotte Sophia Burne, *The Handbook of Folklore* (London, 1914), 1; George Laurence Gomme, *Ethnology in Folklore* (London, 1892), 2.

21. Daniel Brinton, "The Aims of Anthropology," *Proceedings of the American Association for the Advancement of Science* 44 (1895): 1–17.

22. F. B. Gummere, "Primitive Poetry and the Ballad," *Modern Philology* 1 (1903): 195; William K. McNeil, "A History of American Folklore Scholarship before 1908" (Ph.D. diss., Indiana University, 1980), 800.

23. T. F. Crane, "Recent Folk-Lore Publications," *Nation,* 12 June 1890, 475–76.

24. William Wells Newell, "On the Field and Work of a Journal of American Folk-Lore," *Journal of American Folklore* 1 (1888): 3–7, "Notes and Queries," ibid., 1 (1888): 79–81, and "Folk-Lore at the Columbian Exposition," ibid., 5 (1892): 239–40.

25. Fletcher S. Bassett, "The Folk-Lore Congress," in *The International Folk-Lore Congress of the World's Columbian Exposition,* ed. Helen Wheeler Bassett and Frederick Starr (Chicago, 1898), 21–22; Michael J. Bell, "The Folk-Lorist—Eighty Years After," in *The Folk-Lorist* (Philadelphia, 1973); William K. McNeil, "The Chicago Folklore Society and the International Folklore Congress of 1893," *Midwestern Journal of Language and Folklore* 11 (1985): 5–19; Fletcher S. Bassett, *The Folk-Lore Manual* (Chicago, 1892), 6–7.

26. Burton J. Bledstein, *The Culture of Professionalism* (New York, 1976), 80–128; Thomas L. Haskell, *The Emergence of Professional Social Science* (Urbana, Ill., 1977); Arthur S. Link, "The American Historical Association, 1884–1984: Retrospect and Prospect," *American Historical Review* 90 (1985): 1–17.

27. "Cuss-Words Used by the Thoughtless: Dr. Brinton Reads an Interesting Paper on This Subject to the Folk-Lore Society," *Philadelphia Inquirer,* 29 Dec. 1895, 3.

28. Otis T. Mason, *Woman's Share in Primitive Culture* (New York, 1894), 1.

29. Vance, "Folk-Lore Studies," 664.

30. Otis T. Mason, "The Natural History of Folk-Lore," 97.

31. Ibid., 98.

32. Mark Twain, *Mark Twain's Letters,* ed. Albert Bigelow Paine, vol. 2 (New York, 1929), 525–28.

33. "Third Annual Meeting of the American Folk-Lore Society," *Journal of American Folklore* 5 (1892): 1.

34. Hammond Lamont, "Fondness for Old Follies," *Atlantic Monthly* 81 (1905): 215–16.

35. William Schooling, "Fairy Tales and Science," *Westminster Review* 135 (1891): 165.

36. Bryan Hooker, "Fairy Tales," *Forum* 40 (1908): 375–76; Fiske, "Curtin's Myths and Folk-Lore," 568–72; "Dreams and the Subconscious," *Scribner's* 46 (Sept. 1909): 380.

37. Charles Darwin, *The Descent of Man*, 2d ed. (New York, 1874), 162–65, 707.

38. William I. Knapp, "Address of Welcome on Behalf of the Chicago Folk-Lore Society," in *The International Folk-Lore Congress of the World's Columbian Exposition*, ed. Bassett and Starr, 24; Edward Tylor, *The Origins of Culture* (1871; reprint, Gloucester, Mass., 1970), 24.

39. George W. Stocking, Jr., *Race, Culture, and Evolution* (1968; reprint, Chicago, 1982), 97.

40. Tylor, *Origins of Culture*, xvi.

41. T. K. Penniman, *A Hundred Years of Anthropology*, 3d ed. (London, 1965), 19.

42. Quoted in John M. Blum et al., *The National Experience*, 2d ed. (New York, 1968), 452.

43. Sigmund Freud, "The Uncanny," in *Collected Papers*, 5 vols. (London, 1956), 5:368–407.

44. Victorian travel is discussed by James Laver in *Manners and Morals in the Age of Optimism, 1848–1914* (New York, 1966), 164–77; T. J. Jackson Lears, *No Place of Grace* (New York, 1966), 164–77; John A. Jakle, *The Tourist* (Lincoln, Nebr., 1985), 1–83. Travel accounts are from J. B. Priestley, *Midnight on the Desert* (New York, 1937), 65–65; Lewis Gannett, *Sweet Land* (Garden City, N.Y., 1937), 66. The advertisement for travel among the Amish appeared in the 1980s and is a theme in the popular literature about the Pennsylvania plain sects from Phebe Earle Gibbons, *"Pennsylvania Dutch," and Other Essays* (Philadelphia, 1882), through Ann Hark, *Hex Marks the Spot in the Pennsylvania Dutch Country* (Philadelphia, 1938), and Edwin Valentine Mitchell, *It's an Old Pennsylvania Custom* (New York, 1947).

45. McNeil, "History of American Folklore Scholarship," 817–47.

46. Stewart Culin, "A Summer Trip among the Western Indians," *Bulletin of the Free Museum of Science and Art* 3 (1901): 1–175; Frank Hamilton Cushing, "My Adventures in Zuñi," *Century Illustrated Monthly Magazine* 25 (1882): 191–207, 500–511, and 26 (1883): 28–47.

47. Richard Cull, "On the Recent Progress of Ethnology," *Journal of the Ethnological Society of London* 3 (1854): 165.

48. Richard M. Dorson, *The British Folklorists* (Chicago, 1968), 299; Joseph Jacobs and Alfred Nutt, eds., *The International Folk-Lore Congress, 1891* (London, 1892).

49. Burne, *Handbook of Folklore*, v.

50. Giuseppe Cocchiara, *The History of Folklore in Europe*, trans. John N. McDaniel (Philadelphia, 1971); Francis A. de Caro, "Concepts of the Past in Folkloristics," *Western Folklore* 35 (1976): 3–22; Eugene E. Reed, "Herder, Primitivism and the Age of Poetry," *Modern Language Review* 60 (1965): 553–67; Georgianna R. Simpson, *Herder's Conception of "Das Volk"* (Chicago, 1921); Ellen J. Stekert, "Tylor's Theory of Survivals and National Romanticism: Their Influence on American Folk Song Collectors," *Southern Folklore*

Quarterly 32 (1968): 209–36; Burton Feldman and Robert Richardson, eds., *The Rise of Modern Mythology, 1680–1860* (Bloomington, Ind., 1972), 297–449; William A. Wilson, "Herder, Folklore, and Romantic Nationalism," *Journal of Popular Culture* 4 (1973): 819–35.

51. Richard Sennett, *The Fall of Public Man* (New York, 1974), 184–90.

52. George M. Beard, "Causes of American Nervousness," in *Democratic Vistas, 1860–1880,* ed. Alan Trachtenberg (New York, 1970), 238.

53. Edward P. Alexander, *Museums in Motion* (Nashville, Tenn., 1979), 31.

54. Stewart Culin, "The Perfect Collector" (typescript, Stewart Culin Papers, Brooklyn Museum, New York).

55. Otis T. Mason, *Woman's Share in Primitive Culture,* 2–3.

56. Anna Garlin Spencer, "The Primitive Working-Woman," *Forum* 46 (1911): 546–58.

57. J. J. Bachofen, *Myths, Religion, and Mother Right,* trans. Ralph Manheim (Princeton, N.J., 1967); Elizabeth Cady Stanton "The Matriarchate, or Mother-Age," in *Transactions of the National Council of Women of the United States* (Philadelphia, 1891), 218–27; Susan B. Anthony, "Comments," ibid., 227–30.

58. See James A. Farrer, *Primitive Manners and Customs* (London, 1879); Leopold Wagner, *Manners, Customs, and Observances* (London, 1894); William S. Walsh, *Curiosities of Popular Customs and of Rites, Ceremonies, Observances and Miscellaneous Antiquities* (Philadelphia, 1898).

59. Alice Kessler-Harris, *Out to Work: A History of Wage Earning Women in the United States* (New York, 1982); Daniel T. Rodgers, *The Work Ethic in Industrial America, 1850–1920* (Chicago, 1974), 182–209; Ella Wheeler Wilcox, "The Restlessness of the Modern Woman," *Cosmopolitan* 31 (1901): 314–17; "Women of Leisure," *Century* 60 (1900): 632–33.

60. George Wharton James, "Primitive Inventions," *Craftsman* 5 (1903): 125–37; Thorstein Veblen, "The Barbarian Status of Women," *American Journal of Sociology* 4 (1899): 503–14; William I. Thomas, "Woman and the Occupations," *American Magazine* 68 (1909): 463–70, and "Sex in Primitive Industry," *American Journal of Sociology* 4 (1899): 474–88; Lester Ward, "Our Better Halves," *Forum* 6 (1888): 266–75; Olive Schreiner, *Woman and Labor* (New York, 1911).

61. "The Women of the Exposition and the Woman's Work," in *History of the World's Fair* (Chicago, 1893), 163–192; Mrs. Potter Palmer, "Introduction to Woman's Department," in *The World's Columbian Exposition, Chicago, 1893* (Chicago, 1893), 437–56.

62. Sue Samuelson, "Women in the American Folklore Society, 1888–1892," *Folklore Historian* 2 (1985): 3–11.

63. Isabel Cushman Chamberlain, "Contributions toward a Bibliography of Folk-Lore Relating to Women," *Journal of American Folklore* 12 (1899): 32–37.

64. Samuelson, "Women in the American Folklore Society," 3–11.

65. Caroline French Benton, "A Year of Club Work: Myths and Folk-Lore," *Woman's Home Companion* 40 (Mar. 1913): 37–38.

66. Elsie Clews Parsons, "Femininity and Conventionality," *American Academy of Political and Social Science* 56 (1914): 47–53. For Parsons's life see Keith S. Chambers, "The Indefatigable Elsie Clews Parsons—Folklorist," *Western Folklore* 32 (1973): 180–98.

67. Warren I. Susman, *Culture as History* (New York, 1984), 131–41.

CHAPTER 3. THE PROFESSIONALIZATION
OF TIME AND SPACE

1. Stephen Kern, *The Culture of Time and Space, 1880–1918* (Cambridge, Mass., 1983), 211–13; Johannes Fabian, *Time and the Other: How Anthropology Makes Its Object* (New York, 1983); Henry Nash Smith, *Virgin Land: The American West as Symbol and Myth* (Cambridge, Mass., 1950); Jacob Riis, *How the Other Half Lives: Studies among the Tenements of New York* (New York, 1890).

2. George Laurence Gomme, *Folklore as an Historical Science* (London, 1908); Daniel Brinton, "The Aims of Anthropology," *Proceedings of the American Association for the Advancement of Science* 44 (1895): 1–17.

3. Richard Cull, "Remarks on the Nature, Objects, and Evidences of Ethnological Science," *Journal of the Ethnological Society of London* 3 (1854): 103.

4. Axel Olrik, "Epic Laws of Folk Narrative," in *The Study of Folklore,* ed. Alan Dundes (Englewood Cliffs, N.J., 1965), 129–41; Wilhelm F. H. Nicolaisen, "Time in Folk-Narrative," in *Folklore Studies in the Twentieth Century,* ed. Venetia Newall (Totowa, N.J., 1980), 314–19, and "Space in Folk Narrative," in *Folklore on Two Continents,* ed. Nikolai Burlakoff and Carl Lindahl (Bloomington, Ind., 1980), 14–18.

5. Lee J. Vance, "Folk-Lore Study in America," *Popular Science Monthly* 43 (1893): 587.

6. Susan Dwyer-Shick, "The American Folklore Society and Folklore Research in America, 1888–1940" (Ph.D. diss., University of Pennsylvania, 1979), 268–300.

7. Letter from William John McGee to Stewart Culin, 18 Feb. 1897 (National Anthropological Archives, Smithsonian Institution); letter from William John McGee to George A. Dorsey, 21 Jan. 1902 (National Anthropological Archives, Smithsonian Institution).

8. Marvin Harris, *The Rise of Anthropological Theory* (New York, 1968), 2.

9. Stephen Toulmin and June Goodfield, *The Discovery of Time* (New York, 1965), 232.

10. Edward Tylor, *Anthropology* (New York, 1881), 1–34, and "On a Method of Investigating the Development of Institutions; Applied to Laws of Marriage and Descent," *Journal of the Royal Anthropological Institute* 18 (1889): 245–69; George W. Stocking, Jr., *Race, Culture, and Evolution* (1968; reprint, Chicago, 1982), 69–132; Harris, *Rise of Anthropological Theory,* 150–62; Richard M. Dorson, ed., *Peasant Customs and Savage Myths* (Chicago, 1968), 181–216; Kern, *Culture of Time and Space,* 10–64.

11. Daniel Brinton, *The Basis of Social Relations,* ed. Livingston Farrand (New York, 1902), 51; Franz Boas, "The History of Anthropology," *Science* 20 (1904): 513–24.

12. Alexander F. Chamberlain, "Work Accomplished in the Study of American Indian Folk-Lore," *Journal of American Folklore* 15 (1902): 127–29; John Wesley Powell, "The Interpretation of Folk-Lore," *Journal of American Folklore* 8 (1895): 1–6, and "The Lessons of Folklore," *American Anthropologist* 2 (1900): 1–36.

13. Lewis Henry Morgan, *Ancient Society, Or Researches in the Lines of Human Progress from Savagery through Barbarism to Civilization,* annotated by Eleanor Burke Leacock (1877; reprint, Gloucester, Mass., 1974); Robert Lowie, *The History of Ethnological Theory* (New York, 1937), 54–67; McNeil,

"History of American Folklore Scholarship before 1908," 270–89; Curtis M. Hinsley, Jr., *Savages and Scientists: The Smithsonian Institution and the Development of American Anthropology, 1846–1910* (Washington, D.C., 1981), 125–43; Maurice Bloch, *Marxism and Anthropology* (Oxford, Eng., 1983), 1–62; William H. Shaw, "Marx and Morgan," *History and Theory* 23 (1984): 215–28.

14. Mason, "The Natural History of Folk-Lore," *Journal of American Folklore* 4 (1891): 97.

15. William Wells Newell, "Review of *The Sabbath in Puritan New England*," *Journal of American Folklore* 4 (1891): 356–57.

16. Mason, "Natural History of Folk-Lore," 101.

17. William Wells Newell, "Resignation," *Journal of American Folklore* 14 (1901): 56.

18. Lee J. Vance, "The Study of Folk-Lore," *Forum* (1896/97): 251; Allen H. Eaton, *Immigrant Gifts to American Life* (New York, 1932), 87–91.

19. Arnold van Gennep, *Folklore*, trans. Austin Fife (Middletown, Pa., 1985).

20. Frederick Jackson Turner, "The Significance of the Frontier in American History" *Annual Report of the American Historical Association for the Year 1893* (Washington, D.C., 1894), 197–227.

21. T. F. Crane, "The Diffusion of Popular Tales," *Journal of American Folklore* 1 (1888): 10; Franz Boas, "Dissemination of Tales among the Natives of North America," *Journal of American Folklore* 4 (1891): 13–20.

22. Wilhelm Schmidt, *The Culture Historical Method of Ethnology*, trans. S. A. Sieber (New York, 1939); Wilhelm Schmidt and Wilhelm Koppers, *Volker und Kulturen* (Regensburg, Ger., 1924); Fritz Graebner, "Die melanesiche Bogenkultur und ihre verwandten," *Anthropos* 4 (1909): 1031.

23. Friedrich Ratzel, *Anthropogeographie* (1882; reprint, Stuttgart, Ger., 1899), 236–38.

24. Franz Boas, *Baffin-Land: Geographische Ergebnisse einer in den Jahren 1883 und 1884 ausgeführten Forschungsreise* (Gotha, 1885), *The Central Eskimo* (Washington, D.C., 1888), and "The Limitations of the Comparative Method of Anthropology," *Science* 4 (1896): 901–8; Melville Herskovits, *Franz Boas: The Science of Man in the Making* (New York, 1953); Franz Boas, *A Franz Boas Reader*, ed. George W. Stocking, Jr. (Chicago, 1974), 1–156.

25. Franz Boas, "The Study of Geography," in *Race, Language and Culture* (New York, 1940), 639–47.

26. James Joyce, *Ulysses* (1922; reprint, New York, 1961), 668–69.

27. Boas, *A Franz Boas Reader*, 1.

28. Gladys Reichard, "Franz Boas and Folklore," in *Franz Boas, 1858–1942* (Memoirs of the American Anthropological Association, no. 61, 1943), 52; Melville Jacobs, "Folklore," in *The Anthropology of Franz Boas*, ed. Walter Goldschmidt (Memoirs of the American Anthropological Association, no. 89, 1959), 119.

29. Melville Herskovits, *The Myth of the Negro Past* (New York, 1941), and "Problem, Method, and Theory in Afro-American Studies," in *The New World Negro*, ed. Frances Herskovits (Bloomington, Ind., 1966), 54.

30. Melville Herskovits, "The Contribution of Afro-American Studies to Africanist Research," in *The New World Negro*, ed. Herskovits, 12–23; W. E. Burghardt Du Bois, ed., *The Negro American Family* (Atlanta, Ga., 1908).

31. Timothy H. H. Thoresen, "Folkloristics in A. L. Kroeber's Early Theory of Culture," *Journal of the Folklore Institute* 10 (1973): 41–55.

32. Stith Thompson, *The Folktale* (1946; reprint, Berkeley, Calif., 1977), 298–99.

33. Stith Thompson, "The Star Husband Tale," in *The Study of Folklore,* ed. Alan Dundes (Englewood Cliffs, N.J., 1965), 415–74.

34. Murray Wax, "The Limitations of Boas' Anthropology," *American Anthropologist* 58 (1956): 63–74.

35. Harris, *Rise of Anthropological Theory,* 260–63, 302–18; Leslie White, "The Social Organization of Ethnological Theory," *Rice University Studies* 52 (1966): 1–66; McNeil, "History of American Folklore Scholarship," 871–85.

36. Alan Dundes, "From Etic to Emic Units in the Structural Study of Folktales," *Journal of American Folklore* 75 (1962): 95–105, and "Introduction to The Star Husband Tale," in *The Study of Folklore,* 415; Peggy Martin, *Stith Thompson: His Life and His Role in Folklore Scholarship* (Bloomington, Ind., Folklore Publication Group Monograph Series no. 2, 1978), 30–36; Christine Goldberg, "The Historic-Geographic Method: Past and Future," *Journal of Folklore Research* 21 (1984): 1–18.

37. Bronislaw Malinowski, *Argonauts of the Western Pacific* (1922; reprint, Garden City, N.Y., 1954), xvi.

38. Ibid., 510.

39. Émile Durkheim, *The Elementary Forms of the Religious Life,* trans. J. W. Swain (1912; reprint, New York, 1947); William Robertson Smith, *The Religion of the Semites: The Fundamental Institutions* (1889; reprint, New York, 1957); Malinowski, *Argonauts of the Western Pacific,* 345–46.

40. Sir James G. Frazer, "Preface," in Malinowski, *Argonauts of the Western Pacific,* vii–xiv.

41. Fred Voget, *A History of Ethnology* (New York, 1975), 513–14; Lowie, *History of Ethnological Theory,* 196–229; Sir Edward Evans-Pritchard, *A History of Anthropological Thought* (New York, 1981), 153–69.

42. Bronislaw Malinowski, *Magic, Science and Religion* (1948; reprint, Garden City, N.Y., 1954), 79.

43. Malinowski, *Argonauts of the Western Pacific,* 515–16.

44. Bronislaw Malinowski, "Anthropology," *Encyclopaedia Britannica,* 13th ed., suppl. 1 (Chicago, 1926).

45. Bronislaw Malinowski, "Culture as a Determinant of Behavior," in *Factors Determining Human Behavior* (1937; reprint, New York, 1974), 133.

46. Alfred D. Chandler, "The Beginnings of 'Big Business' in American Industry," *Business History Review* 33 (1959): 1–31; Alan Trachtenberg, *The Incorporation of America: Culture and Society in the Gilded Age* (New York, 1982), 4.

47. Sinclair Lewis, *Arrowsmith* (1925; reprint, New York, 1961), 265.

48. Henry Jacoby, *The Bureaucratization of the World,* trans. Eveline Kanes (Berkeley, Calif., 1973), 1.

49. Kern, *The Culture of Time and Space,* 136–37; Donald M. Lowe, *History of Bourgeois Perception* (Chicago, 1982), 87–88; Sigmund Freud, *Introductory Lectures on Psychoanalysis* (1920; reprint, New York, 1966); William James, *Principles of Psychology* (New York, 1890); Roman Jakobson, *Selected Writings,* vol. 2 (The Hague, 1971), 711; Max Weber, "Politics as a Vocation," in *Man in Contemporary Society* (New York, 1955), 359–90.

50. Henry Ford, *My Life and Work* (Garden City, N.Y., 1923), 6; Warren Susman, "Culture Heroes: Ford, Barton, Ruth," in *Culture as History* (New York, 1984), 130.

51. Durkheim, *Elementary Forms of the Religious Life;* Voget, *History of Ethnology,* 483–91; Harris, *Rise of Anthropological Theory,* 477–82.

52. A. R. Radcliffe-Brown, "The Interpretation of Andamese Customs and Beliefs: Myths and Legends," in *Studies on Mythology,* ed. Robert Georges (Homewood, Ill., 1968), 49, "On the Concept of Function in Social Science," *American Anthropologist* 37 (1935): 395, and "The Interpretation of Andamese Customs," 53, 71.

53. Meyer Fortes, "Oedipus and Job in West African Religion," in *Anthropology of Folk Religion,* ed. Charles Leslie (New York, 1960), 39; Edmund Leach, "Myth as Justification for Faction and Social Change," in *Studies on Mythology,* ed. Robert Georges, 198.

54. Bronislaw Malinowski, *A Scientific Theory of Culture and Other Essays* (Chapel Hill, N.C., 1944), 169–70.

55. Evans-Pritchard, *History of Anthropological Thought,* 200; Lowie, *History of Ethnological Theory,* 230–49; Dorothy Gregg and Elgin Williams, "The Dismal Science of Functionalism," *American Anthropologist* 50 (1948): 594–611; Kingsley Davis, "The Myth of Functional Analysis as a Special Method in Sociology and Anthropology," *American Sociological Review* 24 (1959): 757–72; Harris, *Rise of Anthropological Theory,* 527.

56. Voget, *History of Ethnology,* 462.

57. William R. Bascom, "Folklore and Anthropology," in *The Study of Folklore,* ed. Alan Dundes, 25–33, and "Perhaps Too Much to Chew?" *Western Folklore* 40 (1981): 285–98. For more on the life of Bascom see Daniel Crowley and Alan Dundes, "William Russel Bascom (1912–81)," *Journal of American Folklore* 95 (1982): 465–67.

58. William R. Bascom, "Four Functions of Folklore," in *The Study of Folklore,* ed. Alan Dundes, 279–98. Bascom's fifth function of social integration and cohesion is particularly emphasized in Sergeij A. Tokarev, "Toward a Methodology for the Ethnographic Study of Material Culture," trans. Peter Voorheis, in *American Material Culture and Folklife,* ed. Simon J. Bronner (Ann Arbor, Mich., 1985), 77–96.

59. Bascom, "Four Functions of Folklore," 298.

60. Ibid., 290–91.

61. Frank Hoffman, *Analytical Survey of Anglo-American Traditional Erotica* (Bowling Green, Ohio, 1973), 93; Evon Z. Vogt, "Water Witching: An Interpretation of a Ritual Pattern in a Rural American Community," in *Reader in Comparative Religion: An Anthropological Approach,* ed. William A. Lessa and Evon Z. Vogt (Evanston, Ill., 1958), 340. For an extended discussion of this functional analysis see Evon Z. Vogt and Ray Hyman, *Water Witching, U.S.A.* (Chicago, 1959).

62. Roger Abrahams and Alan Dundes, "On Elephantasy and Elephanticide," *Psychoanalytic Review* 56 (1969): 225–41; Patrick B. Mullen, "The Function of Magic Folk Belief among Texas Coastal Fishermen," *Journal of American Folklore* 82 (1969): 214–25.

63. Henry Glassie, *All Silver and No Brass: An Irish Christmas Mumming* (Bloomington, Ind., 1975), 128.

64. Elliott Oring, "Three Functions of Folklore: Traditional Functionalism as Explanation in Folkloristics," *Journal of American Folklore* 81

(1976): 67–80, and "Everything Is a Shade of Elephant: An Alternative to a Psychoanalysis of Humor," *New York Folklore* 1 (1975): 149–60.

65. Christa Kamenetsky, *Children's Literature in Hitler's Germany* (Athens, Ohio, 1984) and "Folktale and Ideology in the Third Reich," *Journal of American Folklore* 90 (1977): 168–78. For comparative examples see William E. Simeone, "Fascists and Folklorists in Italy," *Journal of American Folklore* 91 (1978): 543–58; Felix Oinas, ed., *Folklore, Nationalism, and Politics* (Columbus, Ohio, 1978).

66. See Roger D. Abrahams and Susan Kalcik, "Folklore and Cultural Pluralism," in *Folklore in the Modern World,* ed. Richard M. Dorson (The Hague, 1978), 223–36; Roger D. Abrahams, "The Negro Stereotype: Negro Folklore and the Riots," in *The Urban Experience and Folk Tradition,* ed. Américo Paredes and Ellen Stekert (Austin, Tex., 1971), 65–85; William Hugh Jansen, "The Esoteric-Exoteric Factor in Folklore," in *The Study of Folklore,* ed. Alan Dundes, 43–51.

67. Robert K. Merton, "Manifest and Latent Functions," in *Social Theory and Social Structure* (Glencoe, Ill., 1949), 19–84; Jan Harold Brunvand, *The Study of American Folklore: An Introduction,* 2d ed. (New York, 1978); Carl Lindahl, J. Sanford Rikoon, and Elaine J. Lawless, *A Basic Guide to Fieldwork for Beginning Folklore Students* (Bloomington, Ind., Folklore Publications Group Monograph Series, no. 7, 1979).

68. Evans-Pritchard, *History of Anthropological Thought,* 199.

69. Alan Dundes, "The Functions of Folklore," in *The Study of Folklore,* ed. Alan Dundes, 278.

70. Meyer Fortes, "Social Anthropology at Cambridge since 1900," in *Readings in the History of Anthropology,* ed. Regna Darnell (New York, 1974), 438–39; Davis, "Myth of Functional Analysis," 71.

71. Marshall McLuhan, *Understanding Media: The Extensions of Man* (New York, 1964), 19.

72. Bronislaw Malinowski, *A Scientific Theory of Culture* (Chapel Hill, N.C., 1944), 71.

73. Stith Thompson, "Folklorist's Progress" (typescript, Indiana University Library, 1956); Dwyer-Shick, "American Folklore Society and Folklore Research in America, 1888–1940," 48–49.

74. Stith Thompson, "Advances in Folklore Studies," in *Anthropology Today,* ed. Alfred L. Kroeber (Chicago, 1953), 587.

75. Warren E. Roberts, *The Tale of the Kind and the Unkind Girls* (Berlin, 1958).

76. Fred Eggan, "One Hundred Years of Ethnology and Social Anthropology," in *One Hundred Years of Anthropology,* ed. J. O. Brew (Cambridge, Mass., 1968), 141; Alfred L. Kroeber, "A History of the Personality of Anthropology," in *Readings in the History of Anthropology,* ed. Regna Darnell, 324, 329; Melville Jacobs, *Patterns in Cultural Anthropology* (Homewood, Ill., 1964), 321–22; William Bascom, "Folklore and Anthropology," in *The Study of Folklore,* ed. Alan Dundes, 33.

77. Interview with Louis C. Jones, Cooperstown, N.Y., July 1982.

78. William Hugh Jansen, "Abraham 'Oregon' Smith: Pioneer, Folk Hero, and Tale Teller" (Ph.D. diss., Indiana University, 1949); John Mason Brewer, "Negro Preacher Tales from the Texas 'Brazos Bottoms'" (Master's thesis, Indiana University, 1949); Marie Campbell, "Olden Tales from across the Ocean Waters: A Collection of Seventy-eight European Folktales from the

Oral Tradition of Six Eastern Kentucky Narrators" (Ph.D. diss., Indiana University, 1956).

79. Herbert Halpert, "Folklore: Breadth versus Depth," *Journal of American Folklore* 71 (1958): 99; Neil V. Rosenberg, "Herbert Halpert: A Biographical Sketch," in *Folklore Studies in Honour of Herbert Halpert,* ed. Kenneth S. Goldstein and Neil V. Rosenberg (St. John's, Newfoundland, 1980), 1.

80. Francis Lee Utley, "Conflict and Promise in Folklore," *Journal of American Folklore* 65 (1952): 111; Richard M. Dorson, "Should There Be a Ph.D. in Folklore?" *American Council of Learned Societies Newsletter* 14 (Apr. 1963): 1.

81. Dorson, "Should There Be a Ph.D. in Folklore?" 8. See Dorson's comments on "Cultural Anthropologists" in *American Folklore and the Historian* (Chicago, 1971), 18–21.

82. H. L. Nieburg, *Culture Storm: Politics and the Ritual Order* (New York, 1973); Richard Sennett, *The Fall of Public Man* (New York, 1974); Edward Hall, *The Silent Language* (Garden City, N.Y., 1959); Edmund Leach, *Culture and Communication* (Cambridge, Eng., 1976); Warren I. Susman, "Culture and Communications," in *Culture as History,* 252–70; Dan Ben-Amos, "Toward a Definition of Folklore in Context," in *Toward New Perspectives in Folklore,* ed. Richard Bauman and Américo Paredes (Austin, Tex., 1972), 3–15; Dan Ben-Amos and Kenneth S. Goldstein, eds., *Folklore: Performance and Communication* (The Hague, 1975).

CHAPTER 4. FOLKLORE IN AN ERA OF COMMUNICATION

1. Samuel Eliot Morison, *The Oxford History of the American People,* vol. 3: *1869–1963* (New York, 1972), 253.

2. Leslie White, "History, Evolutionism, and Functionalism: Three Types of Interpretation of Culture," *Southwestern Journal of Anthropology* 1 (1945): 221–48; Daniel G. Brinton, "The Aims of Anthropology," *Proceedings of the American Association for the Advancement of Science* 44 (1895): 10.

3. Warren I. Susman, *Culture as History* (New York, 1984), 234.

4. Henry Marvin Belden, "The Study of Folk-Song in America," *Modern Philology* 2 (1905): 575; Gleason L. Archer, *History of Radio to 1926* (New York, 1938), 64–65; Stephen Kern, *The Culture of Time and Space, 1880–1920* (Cambridge, Mass., 1983), 65–67.

5. T. F. Crane, "Studies in Folklore," *Nation,* 21 Dec. 1916, suppl., 6.

6. J. H. Robertson, *The Story of the Telephone* (London, 1947), 116; Sir Ernest Satow, *A Guide to Diplomatic Practice* (London, 1917), 1:157; Kern, *Culture of Time and Space,* 259–86.

7. Franz Boas, "The History of Anthropology," in *Readings in the History of Anthropology,* ed. Regna Darnell (New York, 1974), 268; D. K. Wilgus, *Anglo-American Folksong Scholarship since 1898* (New Brunswick, N.J., 1959), 241.

8. Regna Darnell, "The Development of American Anthropology 1879–1920: From Bureau of American Ethnology to Franz Boas" (Ph.D. diss., University of Pennsylvania, 1969), 235.

9. Dan Ben-Amos, "A History of Folklore Studies: Why Do We Need It?" *Journal of the Folklore Institute* 10 (1973): 122.

10. Louis C. Jones, *Three Eyes on the Past: Exploring New York Folk Life* (Syracuse, N.Y., 1982), xix.

11. *The Arts of Life in America: A Series of Murals by Thomas Benton* (New York: Whitney Museum of American Art, 1932); Walter Blair and Franklin J. Meine, *Mike Fink: King of the Mississippi Keelboatmen* (1933; reprint, Westport, Conn., 1971); John A. Lomax and Alan Lomax, *American Ballads and Folk Songs* (New York, 1934); Walter Blair, *Native American Humor, 1800–1900* (New York, 1937); Richard M. Dorson, *Davy Crockett, American Comic Legend* (New York, 1939).

12. Richard M. Dorson's studies at Harvard appeared as *Davy Crockett, American Comic Legend* and *Jonathan Draws the Long Bow: New England Popular Tales and Legends* (Cambridge, Mass., 1946).

13. Jones, *Three Eyes on the Past,* xvii.

14. Donald M. Lowe, *History of Bourgeois Perception* (Chicago, 1982), 109; Kern, *Culture of Time and Space,* 287–312; Gertrude Stein, *Picasso* (Boston, 1959), 11.

15. Susman, *Culture as History,* 211–29.

16. B. A. Botkin, ed., *New York City Folklore* (New York, 1956), xv; Bruce Jackson, "Benjamin A. Botkin (1901–1975)," *Journal of American Folklore* 89 (1976): 1–6; Richard M. Dorson, *American Folklore and the Historian* (Chicago, 1971), 5–13.

17. William Bascom, "Folklore," in *Dictionary of Folklore, Mythology, and Legend,* ed. Maria Leach, 2 vols. (New York, 1949), 1:398; Ernest Sutherland Bates, "American Folk-Lore," *Saturday Review of Literature,* 10 July 1926, 913; Allen Eaton, *An Exhibition of the Rural Arts* (Washington, D.C., 1937), and "American Folk Arts," *Studio* 27 (June 1944): 201–3; Allen Eaton and Lucinda Crile, *Rural Handicrafts in the United States* (Washington, D.C., 1946).

18. Stith Thompson, "Folklore at Midcentury," *Midwest Folklore* 1 (1951): 5–12.

19. Richard M. Dorson, *American Folklore and the Historian,* 46, and *Bloodstoppers and Bearwalkers: Folk Tales of Immigrants, Lumberjacks and Indians* (Cambridge, Mass., 1952); Leonard Roberts, *South from Hell-fer-Sartin: Kentucky Mountain Folk Tales* (Lexington, Ky., 1955); Roger Abrahams, *Deep down in the Jungle: Negro Narrative Folklore from the Streets of Philadelphia* (Hatboro, Pa., 1964); George Korson, *Black Rock: Mining Folklore of the Pennsylvania Dutch* (Baltimore, Md., 1960); Austin Fife and Alta Fife, *Saints of Sage and Saddle: Folklore among the Mormons* (Bloomington, Ind., 1956).

20. Thompson, "Folklore at Midcentury," 6.

21. Ibid., 12.

22. Edward T. Hall, *The Silent Language* (1959; reprint, New York, 1968), 93, 169; Kenneth Burke, *A Grammar of Motives* (Berkeley, Calif., 1945), and *Attitudes toward History,* 3d ed. (Berkeley, Calif., 1984).

23. David Riesman, *The Lonely Crowd: A Study of the Changing American Character* (New Haven, Conn., 1950).

24. B. F. Skinner, *Science and Human Behavior* (New York, 1953), 15; Robert F. Berkhofer, Jr., *A Behavioral Approach to Historical Analysis* (New York, 1969), 6.

25. Henry D. Shapiro, *Appalachia on Our Mind: The Southern Mountains and Mountaineers in the American Consciousness, 1870–1920* (Chapel Hill, N.C., 1978), ix.

26. Harold D. Lasswell, "The Structure and Function of Communication in Society," in *Mass Communications,* ed. Wilbur Schramm (Urbana, Ill., 1949), 102–15.

27. Richard Wightman Fox, "Epitaph for Middletown: Robert S. Lynd and the Analysis of Consumer Culture," in *The Culture of Consumption,* ed. Richard Wightman Fox and T. J. Jackson Lears (New York, 1983), 101–42.

28. Robert Redfield, "The Folk Society," in *Sociology Full Circle: Contemporary Readings on Society,* ed. William Feigelman (New York, 1972), 61–72, and *The Little Community and Peasant Society and Culture* (Chicago, 1967).

29. Don Yoder, "The Folklife Studies Movement," *Pennsylvania Folklife* 13 (July 1963): 43–56, and "Folklife Studies in American Scholarship," in *American Folklife,* ed. Don Yoder (Austin, Tex., 1976), 3–18.

30. John Michael Vlach, "The Concept of Community and Folklife Study," in *American Material Culture and Folklife,* ed. Simon J. Bronner (Ann Arbor, Mich., 1985), 63.

31. Henry Glassie, *Passing the Time in Ballymenone: Culture and History of an Ulster Community* (Philadelphia, 1982), 13; Howard Wight Marshall, *Folk Architecture in Little Dixie: A Regional Culture in Missouri* (Columbia, Mo., 1981). For other views of community as defined by perceptions of residents see Maurice R. Stein, *The Eclipse of Community: An Interpretation of American Studies* (Princeton, N.J., 1960); Yi-Fu Tuan, *Space and Place: The Perspective of Experience* (Minneapolis, Minn., 1977), and *Segmented Worlds and Self: Group Life and Individual Consciousness* (Minneapolis, Minn., 1982).

32. Franz Boas, "The Ethnological Significance of Esoteric Doctrines," *Science,* n.s., 16 (1902): 872–74, and "Mythology and Folklore," in *General Anthropology,* ed. Franz Boas (Boston, 1938), 609–26; William Hugh Jansen, "The Esoteric-Exoteric Factor in Folklore," in *The Study of Folklore,* ed. Alan Dundes (Englewood Cliffs, N.J., 1965), 43–51.

33. Alan Dundes, "What Is Folklore?" in *The Study of Folklore,* ed. Alan Dundes, 2; Roger Abrahams, "Interpreting Folklore Ethnographically and Sociologically," in *Handbook of American Folklore,* ed. Richard M. Dorson (Bloomington, Ind., 1983), 345–50.

34. Michael Owen Jones, "L.A. Add-ons and Re-dos: Renovation in Folk Art and Architectural Design," in *Perspectives on American Folk Art,* ed. Ian M. G. Quimby and Scott T. Swank (New York, 1980), 362.

35. Dan Ben-Amos, "Toward a Definition of Folklore in Context," in *Toward New Perspectives in Folklore,* ed. Richard Bauman and Américo Paredes (Austin, Tex., 1972), 3–15; Barre Toelken, *The Dynamics of Folklore* (Boston, 1979), 50.

36. Alan Dundes, "Structuralism and Folklore," *Studia Fennica* 20 (1976): 75.

37. Robert Scholes, *Structuralism in Literature* (New Haven, Conn., 1974), 4; Kern, *The Culture of Time and Space,* 187–88.

38. Pierre Maranda and Elli-Kaija Köngäs Maranda, "Introduction," in *Structural Analysis of Oral Tradition,* ed. Pierre Maranda and Elli-Kaija Köngäs Maranda (Philadelphia, 1971), ix; Dundes, "Structuralism and Folklore," 89; Ulf Drobin, "Commentaries on Structuralism and Folklore," *Studia Fennica* 20 (1976): 108.

39. Svatava Pirkova-Jakobson, "Introduction," in Vladimir Propp, *Morphology of the Folktale,* trans. Laurence Scott, 2d ed., rev. Louis A. Wagner (Austin, Tex., 1968), xx.

40. A. I. Nikiforov, "Towards a Morphological Study of the Folktale," in *The Study of Russian Folklore,* ed. and trans. Felix J. Oinas and Stephen Soudakoff (The Hague, 1975), 155–62.

41. Propp, *Morphology*, 115.

42. Dundes, "Structuralism and Folklore," 83.

43. Henry Glassie, *Folk Housing in Middle Virginia: A Structural Analysis of Historic Artifacts* (Knoxville, Tenn., 1975), 41.

44. Kenneth Pike, *Language in Relation to a Unified Theory of the Structure of Human Behavior* (The Hague, 1967), 10.

45. Henry Glassie, "Structure and Function, Folklore and the Artifact," *Semiotica* 7 (1973): 340.

46. Alan Dundes and Carl Pagter, *Work Hard and You Shall Be Rewarded: Urban Folklore from the Paperwork Empire* (Bloomington, Ind., 1978), 189–91; Lowe, *History of Bourgeois Perception*, 131–39; Marshall Fishwick and Ray B. Browne, eds., *Icons of Popular Culture* (Bowling Green, Ohio, 1970); George H. Lewis, ed., *Side-Saddle on the Golden Calf: Social Structure and Popular Culture in America* (Pacific Palisades, Calif., 1972); H. L. Nieburg, *Culture Storm: Politics and the Ritual Order* (New York, 1973).

47. William Safire, *On Language* (New York, 1980); Edwin Newman, *Strictly Speaking* (Indianapolis, Ind., 1974); Robert Mueller, *Buzzwords* (New York, 1974); Herman A. Estrin and Donald V. Mehus, eds., *The American Language in the 1970's* (San Francisco, Calif., 1974); William W. Evans, "Language and the Lay Linguist," *American Speech* 52 (1977): 134–45; Sidney I. Landau, "Popular Meanings of Scientific and Technical Terms," *American Speech* 55 (1980): 204–9; David M. Maurer and Elesa Clay High, "New Words—Where Do They Come from and Where Do They Go?" *American Speech* 55 (1980): 184–94.

48. Richard Sennett, *The Fall of Public Man* (New York, 1974), 282–93; Nieburg, *Culture Storm*, 105–20; Victor Turner, ed., *Celebration: Studies in Festivity and Ritual* (Washington, D.C., 1982); Roger D. Abrahams, "Toward an Enactment-Centered Theory of Folklore," in *Frontiers of Folklore*, ed. William Bascom (Boulder, Colo., 1977), 79–120.

49. Victor Turner, *The Forest of Symbols: Aspects of Ndembu Ritual* (Ithaca, N.Y., 1967), 46.

50. Clifford Geertz, "Thick Description: Toward an Interpretive Theory of Culture," in *The Interpretation of Cultures* (New York, 1973), 3–30, and "Deep Play: Notes on the Balinese Cockfight," in *Myth, Symbol, and Culture*, ed. Clifford Geertz (New York, 1971), 1–38.

51. Thomas A. Burns and J. Stephen Smith, "The Symbolism of Becoming in the Sunday Service of an Urban Black Holiness Church," *Anthropological Quarterly* 51 (1978): 185–204; Gerald L. Pocius, "Hooked Rugs in Newfoundland: The Representation of Social Structure in Design," *Journal of American Folklore* 92 (1979): 273–84.

52. Alan Dundes, "Projection in Folklore: A Plea for Psychoanalytic Semiotics," in his *Interpreting Folklore* (Bloomington, Ind., 1980), 33–61.

53. I. C. Jarvie, "On the Limits of Symbolic Interpretation in Anthropology," *Current Anthropology* 17 (1976): 687–701; Dundes, "Projection in Folklore," 33.

54. Roger D. Abrahams, "Folklore in Culture: Notes toward an Analytic Method," in *Readings in American Folklore*, ed. Jan Harold Brunvand (New York, 1979), 392.

55. Dell Hymes, "The Ethnography of Speaking," in *Anthropology and Human Behavior*, ed. T. Gladwin and W. C. Sturtevant (Washington, D.C., 1962), 13–53, "Introduction: Toward Ethnographies of Communication,"

American Anthropologist 66 (1964): 1–34, and "Breakthrough into Performance," in *Folklore: Performance and Communication,* ed. Dan Ben-Amos and Kenneth S. Goldstein (The Hague, 1975), 11–74.

56. Richard Bauman and Joel Sherzer, "Preface," in *Explorations in the Ethnography of Speaking,* ed. Richard Bauman and Joel Sherzer (London, 1974), 3.

57. Dell Hymes, "The Contribution of Folklore to Sociolinguistic Research," in *Toward New Perspectives in Folklore,* ed. Américo Paredes and Richard Bauman, 50.

58. Richard Bauman, "Introduction," in *Toward New Perspectives in Folklore,* ed. Américo Paredes and Richard Bauman, xi–xv.

59. Ben-Amos, "Toward a Definition of Folklore in Context," 3–15; Roger D. Abrahams, "Personal Power and Social Restraint in the Definition of Folklore," 16–30; Richard Bauman, "Differential Identity and the Social Base of Folklore," 31–40; "On the Application of the Concepts of Active and Inactive Traditions to the Study of Repertory," 62–67, in *Toward New Perspectives,* ed. Américo Paredes and Richard Bauman.

60. Dan Ben-Amos and Kenneth S. Goldstein, "Introduction," 1–7, and Bruce A. Rosenberg, "Oral Sermons and Oral Narrative," 75–101, in *Folklore: Performance and Communication,* ed. Dan Ben-Amos and Kenneth S. Goldstein.

61. Ben-Amos and Goldstein, "Introduction," in *Folklore: Performance and Communication,* 1–7; Roger D. Abrahams, "Introductory Remarks to a Rhetorical Theory of Folklore," *Journal of American Folklore* 81 (1968): 143–58.

62. Richard Bauman, *Verbal Art as Performance* (Rowley, Mass., 1977), 11; Abrahams, "Toward an Enactment-Centered Theory of Folklore," 117.

63. Eugen Kagarow, "Folkloristik und Volkskunde," *Mitteilungen der schlesischen Gesellschaft fur Volkskunde* 30 (1929): 70–77; Richard M. Dorson, "Concepts of Folklore and Folklife Studies," in *Folklore and Folklife: An Introduction,* ed. Richard M. Dorson (Chicago, 1972), 45; Bruce Jackson, "Folkloristics," *Journal of American Folklore* 98 (1985): 95–101; Dan Ben-Amos, "On the Final (s) in 'Folkloristics,'" *Journal of American Folklore* 98 (1985): 334–36.

64. See the assessments in the 1970s and 1980s of the state of the discipline in Richard M. Dorson, "Folklore, Academe, and the Marketplace," in *Folklore and Fakelore: Essays toward a Discipline of Folk Studies* (Cambridge, Mass., 1976), *Folklore in the Modern World* (The Hague, 1978), and "The State of Folkloristics from an American Perspective," *Journal of Folklore Research* 19 (1982): 71–106; *The State of Folkloristics* (special issue of *New York Folklore* 9, nos. 3 and 4, 1983).

65. Lowe, *History of Bourgeois Perception,* 39; Sennett, *Fall of Public Man,* 313–36.

66. See Sennett, *The Fall of Public Man,* 1–27; Nieburg, *Culture Storm;* Jackson Lears, "Preface to the Paperback Edition," *No Place of Grace* (New York, 1981), xi–xiv; Marvin Harris, *America Now* (New York, 1979). Discussion of the problems of statistically measuring the changing American character is found in Michael Barton, "The Lonely Crowd in Minnesota: A Psychometric Approach to the Study of the Modern American Character," in *Prospects 7,* ed. Jack Salzman (New York, 1982), 365–90.

67. Wilbur Zelinsky, "Selfward Bound? Personal Preference Patterns and the Changing Map of American Society," *Economic Geography* 50 (1974): 175; Sennett, *The Fall of Public Man,* 313–15.

68. W. Edson Richmond, "Introduction," xviii; Henry Glassie, "Folkloristic Study of the American Artifact: Objects and Objectives," 381, in *Handbook of American Folklore,* ed. Richard M. Dorson.

69. Wilhelm F. H. Nicolaisen, "Names and Narratives," *Journal of American Folklore* 97 (1984): 268.

70. Alan Dundes, "Forum on Psychoanalytic Folklore" (American Folklore Society Meeting, San Diego, 1984); Elizabeth C. Fine, *The Folklore Text: From Performance to Print* (Bloomington, Ind., 1984), 203.

71. Dan Ben-Amos, "The Seven Strands of *Tradition:* Varieties in Its Meaning in American Folklore Studies," *Journal of Folklore Research* 21 (1984): 97–131; Gary Alan Fine, "The Third Force in Folkloristics: The Situational and Structural Properties of Tradition" (paper delivered at the American Folklore Society meeting, Cincinnati, Ohio, 1985). For examples of studies of cultural expressiveness that use performance as a take-off point see Michael Owen Jones, Bruce Giuliano, and Roberta Krell, eds., *Foodways and Eating Habits: Directions for Research* (Los Angeles, 1981); David J. Hufford, *The Terror That Comes in the Night: An Experience-Centered Study of Supernatural Assault Traditions* (Philadelphia, 1982); Moira Smith and Regina Bendix, eds., *Conversational Folklore* (special issue of *Folklore Forum* 17, no. 2, 1984); Abrahams, "Interpreting Folklore Ethnographically and Sociologically," 345–50.

72. Sandra K. D. Stahl, "The Personal Narrative as Folklore," *Journal of the Folklore Institute* 14 (1977): 9–30, and "A Literary Folkloristic Methodology for the Study of Meaning in Personal Narrative," *Journal of Folklore Research* 22 (1985): 45–69; Verni Greenfield, "Silk Purses from Sows' Ears: An Aesthetic Approach to Recycling," in *Personal Places: Perspectives on Informal Art Environments,* ed. Daniel Franklin Ward (Bowling Green, Ohio, 1984), 133–47, and *Making Do or Making Art: A Study of American Recycling* (Ann Arbor, Mich., 1985).

73. Nicolaisen, "Names and Narratives," 269–70.

74. Robert B. Denhardt, *In the Shadow of Organization* (Lawrence: Regents Press of Kansas, 1981); Walter F. Baber, *Organizing the Future: Matrix Models for the Postindustrial Polity* (University, Ala., 1983); Peter J. Frost et al., eds., *Organizational Culture* (Beverly Hills, Calif., 1985); Terrence E. Deal and Allan A. Kennedy, *Corporate Cultures: The Rites and Rituals of Corporate Life* (Reading, Mass., 1982); Howard S. Becker, *Art Worlds* (Berkeley, Calif., 1982); John Michael Vlach and Simon J. Bronner, eds., *Folk Art and Art Worlds* (Ann Arbor, Mich., 1986); Richard Wightman Fox and T. J. Jackson Lears, eds., *The Culture of Consumption* (New York, 1983); Gary Alan Fine, "Negotiated Orders and Oranizational Cultures," *Annual Review of Sociology* 10 (1984); 239–62.

75. "Folklore and Organizational Life," in *Folklore/Folklife* (Washington, D.C., 1984), 14; Robert H. Byington, "Letter to the Editor," *American Folklore Society Newsletter* 14 (Feb. 1985): 2; Robert S. McCarl, "Reply to Michael Owen Jones," *American Folklore Society Newsletter* 14 (June 1985): 2, 5; Alf H. Walle, "Comment on Byington," *American Folklore Society Newsletter* 14 (June 1985): 2–3; Michael Owen Jones, "On Folklorists Studying Organizations," *American Folklore Society Newsletter* 14 (Apr. 1985): 5–6, 8.

76. Richard M. Dorson, "Folklore in the Modern World," in *Folklore in the Modern World,* ed. Richard M. Dorson (The Hague, 1978), 23.

77. Michael Owen Jones, "Organizational Folklore and Corporate Culture," *American Folklore Society Newsletter* 12 (Oct. 1983): 3–4, 6.

78. For photocopied folklore see Dundes and Pagter, *Work Hard and You Shall Be Rewarded;* Simon J. Bronner, "Folklore in the Bureaucracy," in *Tools for Management,* ed. Frederick Richmond and Kathy Nazar (Harrisburg, Pa., 1984), 45–57. For organizational legends see Gary Alan Fine, "The Goliath Effect: Corporate Dominance and Mercantile Legends," *Journal of American Folklore* 98 (1965): 63–84, "The Kentucky Fried Rat: Legends and Modern Society," *Journal of the Folklore Institute* 17 (1980): 222–43, and "Folklore Diffusion through Interactive Social Networks: Conduits in a Preadolescent Community," *New York Folklore* 5 (1979): 87–126.

79. See Alan Dundes, "The American Concept of Folklore," *Journal of the Folklore Institute* 3 (1966): 226–49; Roger D. Abrahams and Susan Kalčik, "Folklore and Cultural Pluralism," in *Folklore in the Modern World,* ed. Richard M. Dorson (The Hague, 1978), 223–36; Henry Glassie, "The Moral Lore of Folklore," *Folklore Forum* 16 (1983): 123–52; Richmond, "Introduction," xiv.

80. Richard Bauman, "Folklore and the Forces of Modernity," *Folklore Forum* 16 (1983): 153–58; Wilhelm F. H. Nicolaisen, "Variant, Dialect, and Region: An Exploration in the Geography of Tradition," *New York Folklore* 6 (1980): 137–50; Linda Keller Brown and Kay Mussell, eds., *Ethnic and Regional Foodways in the United States: The Performance of Group Identity* (Knoxville, Tenn., 1984); Barbara Kirshenblatt-Gimblett, "The Future of Folklore Studies in America: The Urban Frontier," *Folklore Forum* 16 (1983): 175–234; Simon J. Bronner, *Grasping Things: Folk Material Culture and Mass Society in America* (Lexington, Ky., 1986).

81. See Lynwood Montell, "Academic and Applied Folklore: Partners for the Future," *Folklore Forum* 16 (1983): 159–74; Dick Sweterlitsch, ed., *Papers on Applied Folklore* (Folklore Forum Bibliographic and Special Series, no. 8, 1971); Charles Camp, "Developing a State Folklife Program," in *Handbook of American Folklore,* ed. Richard M. Dorson, 518–24; Michael Owen Jones, "A Feeling for Form, As Illustrated by People at Work," in *Folklore on Two Continents,* ed. Nikolai Burlakoff and Carl Lindahl (Bloomington, Ind., 1980), 260–69.

Bibliography

This bibliography includes works that have influenced me, lists my cited references, and suggests further readings on the subjects contained in this book. Like the chapters in this book, the bibliography tells what has been done in the past, but has an eye toward the future. I have devised categories that were useful to me, and my hope is that they can serve fellow investigators. Under "Background Works," I put works of general history, literature, arts, philosophy, and criticism that offer evidence of the historical and cultural context of folklore studies. In the next sections, I divide the bibliography of the history of American folklore studies into four categories: "Histories," "Surveys," "Biographies," and "Accounts of Meetings and Events." There will be overlap, especially between histories and surveys. It is useful to separate them, because their time perspectives differ. Surveys are more immediate than histories. Histories primarily dig into the past; surveys chart the intellectual landscape. "Biographies" is a broad category; it includes intellectual criticisms of important figures, autobiographies, obituaries, and tributes. The next four categories center on methods and theories. Besides separate categories for "Statements of Method" and "Statements of Theory," I have added lists of

"Collections" and "Studies." The collections stress the identification of folkloric texts, and the studies emphasize their interpretations. The list of collections and studies could easily be extended; I chose representative works that bring to the fore the methods and theories that I discuss in the book. The next three categories can be called reflections on folklore studies. They are divided into "Commentaries" on disciplinary issues, "Forecasts" for the future of folklore studies, and "Definitions" of folk and folklore. The final four categories provide books and articles that have to do with professionalism in folklore studies. The first category contains "Statements on Public and Applied Folklore," and the second covers "Statements on Higher Education." I close out the bibliography with folkloristic "Reference Works" (such as bibliographies and indices) and "Statements on Historiography."

BACKGROUND WORKS

Abbott, Lyman. *Henry Ward Beecher.* 1903. Reprint. New York: Chelsea House, 1980.

Allen, Frederick Lewis. *The Big Change: America Transforms Itself, 1900– 1950.* New York: Harper & Row, 1952.

Anderson, John Q. "Emerson and the Language of the Folk." In *Folk Travelers: Ballads, Tales, and Talk,* edited by Mody C. Boatright, Wilson M. Hudson, and Allen Maxwell, pp. 152–59. Dallas, Tex.: Southern Methodist University Press, 1953.

Archer, Gleason L. *History of Radio to 1926.* 1938. Reprint. New York: Arno Press, 1971.

Arts of Life in America: A Series of Murals by Thomas Benton, The. New York: Whitney Museum of American Art, 1932.

Baber, Walter F. *Organizing the Future: Matrix Models for the Post-Industrial Polity.* University: University of Alabama Press, 1983.

Barton, Bruce. *The Man Nobody Knows: A Discovery of Jesus.* Indianapolis, Ind.: Bobbs-Merrill, 1924.

Barton, Michael. "The Lonely Crowd in Minnesota: A Psychometric Approach to the Study of the Modern American Character." In *Prospects 7,* edited by Jack Salzman, pp. 365–90. New York: Burt Franklin, 1982.

Beard, Charles A., and Mary R. Beard. *The Rise of American Civilization.* 4 vols. New York: Macmillan, 1927–42.

Beard, George M. "Causes of American Nervousness." In *Democratic Vistas, 1860–1880,* edited by Alan Trachtenberg, pp. 238–47. New York: George Braziller, 1970.

Becker, Howard S. *Art Worlds.* Berkeley: University of California Press, 1982.

Berkhofer, Robert F., Jr. *A Behavioral Approach to Historical Analysis.* New York: Free Press, 1969.

Blair, Walter. *Native American Humor, 1800–1900.* New York: American Book Co., 1937.

Bledstein, Burton J. *The Culture of Professionalism: The Middle Class and the Development of Higher Education in America.* New York: W. W. Norton, 1976.

Bloch, Maurice. *Marxism and Anthropology.* Oxford: Clarendon Press, 1983.

Blum, John M.; Bruce Calton; Edmund S. Morgan; Arthur M. Schlesinger, Jr.; Kenneth M. Stampp; C. Vann Woodward. *The National Experience: A*

History of the United States. 2d ed. New York: Harcourt, Brace & World, 1968.

Boorstin, Daniel. *The Americans: The National Experience.* New York: Vintage Books, 1965.

————. *The Americans: The Democratic Experience.* New York: Vintage Books, 1973.

————. *The Discoverers: A History of Man's Search to Know His World and Himself.* New York: Random House, 1983.

Brown, Richard D. *Modernization: The Transformation of American Life, 1600–1865.* New York: Hill & Wang, 1976.

Browne, Ray B., and Ralph H. Wolfe, eds. *Directions and Dimensions in American Culture Studies in the 1980s.* Bowling Green, Ohio: Bowling Green State University Popular Press, 1979.

Burke, Kenneth. *A Grammar of Motives.* Berkeley: University of California Press, 1945.

————. *Studies in Symbolic Action.* New York: Vintage, 1957.

————. *Attitudes toward History.* 3d ed. Berkeley: University of California, 1984.

Cash, Wilbur J. *The Mind of the South.* New York: Knopf, 1941.

Cashman, Sean Dennis. *America in the Gilded Age: From the Death of Lincoln to the Rise of Theodore Roosevelt.* New York: New York University Press, 1984.

Ceram, C. W. *Gods, Graves, and Scholars: The Story of Archaeology.* 2d ed. New York: Bantam, 1972.

Chandler, Alf D. "The Beginnings of 'Big Business' in American Industry." *Business History Review* 3 (1959): 1–31.

Chenoweth, Lawrence. *The American Dream of Success: The Search for the Self in the Twentieth Century.* North Scituate, Mass.: Duxbury Press, 1974.

Cochran, Thomas C. *Frontiers of Change: Early Industrialism in America.* Oxford: Oxford University Press, 1981.

Commager, Henry Steele. *The American Mind: An Interpretation of American Thought and Character since the 1880s.* New Haven, Conn.: Yale University Press, 1950.

————. *The Study of History.* Columbus, Ohio: Charles E. Merrill, 1966.

Conkin, Paul K. *Puritans and Pragmatists: Eight Eminent American Thinkers.* 1968. Reprint. Bloomington: Indiana University Press, 1976.

Cox, Harvey. *The Secular City: Secularization and Urbanization in Theological Perspective.* Rev. ed. New York: Macmillan, 1966.

Darwin, Charles. *The Descent of Man.* 2d ed. New York: A. L. Burt, 1874.

Deal, Terrence E., and Allan A. Kennedy. *Corporate Cultures: The Rites and Rituals of Corporate Life.* Reading, Mass.: Addison-Wesley, 1982.

Denhardt, Robert B. *In the Shadow of Organization.* Lawrence: Regents Press of Kansas, 1981.

Dewey, John. *Art as Experience.* New York: Minton, Balch, & Co., 1934.

"Dreams and the Subconscious." *Scribner's* 46 (Sept. 1909): 380.

Dreiser, Theodore. *Sister Carrie.* 1900. Reprint. New York: W. W. Norton, 1970.

Dupré, Louis. *Marx's Social Critique of Culture.* New Haven, Conn.: Yale University Press, 1983.

Eichler, Lillian. *The Customs of Mankind.* Garden City, N.Y.: Doubleday, 1924.

Ellison, Ralph. *Invisible Man.* New York: Random House, 1952.

Estrin, Herman A., and Donald V. Mehus, eds. *The American Language in the 1970's*. San Francisco, Calif.: Boyd & Fraser, 1974.

Evans, William W. "Language and the Lay Linguist." *American Speech* 52 (1977): 134–45.

Evreinov, Nicolai Nikolaevich. *The Theatre in Life*. Edited and translated by Alexander I. Nazaroff. New York: Brentano's, 1927.

Fischer, David Hackett. *Growing Old in America*. Oxford: Oxford University Press, 1978.

Fishwick, Marshall, and Ray B. Browne, eds. *Icons of Popular Culture*. Bowling Green, Ohio: Bowling Green State University Popular Press, 1970.

Ford, Henry. *My Life and Work*. Garden City, N.Y.: Doubleday, Page & Co., 1923.

Fox, Richard Wightman. "Epitaph for Middletown: Robert S. Lynd and the Analysis of Consumer Culture." In *The Culture of Consumption*, edited by Richard Wightman Fox and T. J. Jackson Lears, pp. 101–42. New York: Pantheon, 1983.

———, and T. J. Jackson Lears, eds. *The Culture of Consumption: Critical Essays in American History, 1880–1980*. New York: Pantheon, 1983.

Freud, Sigmund. *Totem and Taboo: Some Points of Agreement between the Mental Lives of Savages and Neurotics*. 1913. Reprint. New York: W. W. Norton, 1951.

———. *Introductory Lectures on Psychoanalysis*. 1920. Reprint. New York: W. W. Norton, 1966.

———. *Civilization and Its Discontents*. 1930. Reprint. New York: W. W. Norton, 1961.

———. "The Uncanny." In *Collected Papers*. 5 vols., 5:368–407. London: Hogarth Press, 1956.

Gabriel, Ralph Henry, ed. *The Pageant of America: A Pictorial History of the United States*. 15 vols. New Haven, Conn.: Yale University Press, 1925–29.

Gottschalk, Louis. *Understanding History*. New York: Alfred A. Knopf, 1965.

Green, Harvey. *The Light of the Home: An Intimate View of the Lives of Women in Victorian America*. New York: Pantheon, 1983.

———. "Scientific Thought and the Nature of Children in America, 1820–1920." In *A Century of Childhood, 1820–1920*, pp. 121–37. Rochester, N.Y.: Margaret Woodbury Strong Museum, 1984.

Gutman, Herbert. *Work, Culture and Society in Industrializing America: Essays in American Working-Class and Social History*. New York: Vintage Books, 1976.

Hall, Edward. *The Silent Language*. Garden City, N.Y.: Doubleday, 1959.

———. *The Hidden Dimension*. Garden City, N.Y.: Doubleday, 1966.

Handy, Charles. *Understanding Organizations*. New York: Penguin Books, 1976.

Harris, Marvin. *America Now: The Anthropology of a Changing Culture*. New York: Simon & Schuster, 1981.

Hawthorne, Nathaniel. *Twice-Told Tales, and Other Short Stories*. 1837. Reprint. New York: Washington Square Press, 1965.

Hicks, Granville; Joseph North; Michael Gold; Paul Peters; Isidor Schneider; Alan Calmer, eds. *Proletarian Literature in the United States*. New York: International Publishers, 1935.

Higham, John, and Paul K. Conkin, eds. *New Directions in American Intellectual History*. Baltimore, Md.: Johns Hopkins University Press, 1979.

Hoffman, Daniel. *Form and Fable in American Fiction.* New York: W. W. Norton, 1961.

Hofstadter, Richard. "The Myth of the Happy Yeoman." In *American Vistas: 1877 to the Present,* edited by Leonard Dinnerstein and Kenneth T. Jackson, pp. 20–32. New York: Oxford University Press, 1971.

Hooker, Bryan. "Fairy Tales." *Forum* 40 (Oct. 1908): 375–76.

Howells, William Dean. *A Hazard of New Fortunes.* 1890. Reprint. New York: New American Library, 1965.

Iacocca, Lee A. *Iacocca: An Autobiography.* New York: Bantam, 1984.

Irving, Washington. *The Sketch Book.* 1818–20. Reprint. New York: Signet, 1961.

Jacoby, Henry. *The Bureaucratization of the World.* Translated by Eveline L. Kanes. Berkeley: University of California Press, 1973.

Jakle, John A. *The Tourist: Travel in Twentieth-Century North America.* Lincoln: University of Nebraska Press, 1985.

Jakobson, Roman. *Selected Writings.* The Hague: Mouton, 1971.

James, William. *Principles of Psychology.* New York: Henry Holt & Co., 1890.

Joyce, James. *Ulysses.* Paris: Shakespeare, 1922.

Kasson, John. *Civilizing the Machine: Technology and Republican Values in America, 1776–1900.* New York: Grossman, 1976.

Kauver, Gerald, and Gerald Sorensen, eds. *The Victorian Mind.* New York: Capricorn, 1969.

Kern, Stephen. *The Culture of Time and Space, 1880–1918.* Cambridge: Harvard University Press, 1983.

Kessler-Harris, Alice. *Out to Work: A History of Wage Earning Women in the United States.* New York: Oxford University Press, 1982.

Kevles, Daniel J. *The Physicists: The History of a Scientific Community in Modern America.* New York: Vintage Books, 1979.

Klein, Philip S., and Ari Hoogenboom. *A History of Pennsylvania.* 2d ed. University Park: Pennsylvania State University Press, 1980.

Koenig, Otto. "Behaviour Study and Civilization." In *The Nature of Human Behaviour,* edited by Gunter Altner, pp. 153–210. London: George Allen & Unwin, 1976.

Kuhn, Thomas S. *The Structure of Scientific Revolutions.* 2d ed. Chicago: University of Chicago Press, 1970.

Lamont, Hammond. "Fondness for Old Follies." *Nation,* 14 Sept. 1905, 215–16.

Landau, Sidney I. "Popular Meanings of Scientific and Technical Terms." *American Speech* 55 (1980): 204–9.

Larrabee, Eric. *The Self-Conscious Society.* Garden City, N.Y.: Doubleday, 1960.

Lasswell, Harold D. "The Structure and Function of Communication in Society." In *Mass Communications,* edited by Wilbur Schramm, pp. 102–15. Urbana: University of Illinois Press, 1949.

Laver, James. *Manners and Morals in the Age of Optimism, 1848–1914.* New York: Harper & Row, 1966.

Lears, T. J. Jackson. *No Place of Grace: Antimodernism and the Transformation of American Culture, 1880–1920.* New York: Pantheon, 1981.

Lewis, George H., ed. *Side-Saddle on the Golden Calf: Social Structure and Popular Culture in America.* Pacific Palisades, Calif.: Goodyear Publishing, 1972.

Lewis, Russell. "Everything under One Roof: World's Fairs and Department Stores in Paris and Chicago." *Chicago History* 12 (Fall 1983): 28–47.

Lewis, Sinclair. *Arrowsmith*. 1925. Reprint. New York: New American Library, 1961.

Lowe, Donald M. *History of Bourgeois Perception*. Chicago: University of Chicago Press, 1982.

McLuhan, Marshall. *Understanding Media: The Extensions of Man*. New York: McGraw-Hill, 1964.

Marks, Robert W., ed. *Great Ideas in Psychology: The Most Significant Writings of the Founders of Modern Psychology*. New York: Bantam, 1966.

Maurer, David W., and Elesa Clay High. "New Words—Where Do They Come From and Where Do They Go?" *American Speech* 55 (1980): 184–94.

Mead, George Herbert. *Mind, Self, and Society: From the Standpoint of a Social Behaviorist*. Edited by Charles W. Morris. 1934. Reprint. Chicago: University of Chicago Press, 1962.

Merwin, Henry Childs. "On Being Civilized Too Much." *Atlantic Monthly* 79 (June 1897): 838–46.

Miller, Perry. *The New England Mind: The Seventeenth Century*. New York: Macmillan, 1939.

———. *The New England Mind: From Colony to Province*. Cambridge: Harvard University Press, 1953.

Morison, Samuel Eliot. *The Oxford History of the American People*. Vol. 3: *1869–1963*. New York: Mentor, 1972.

Mueller, Robert Kirk. *Buzzwords: A Guide to the Language of Leadership*. New York: Van Nostrand Reinhold, 1974.

Murphey, Murray G. "The Place of Beliefs in Modern Culture." In *New Directions in American Intellectual History*, edited by John Higham and Paul K. Conkin, pp. 151–65. Baltimore, Md.: Johns Hopkins University Press, 1979.

Murphy, James K. "The Backwoods Characters of Will N. Harben." *Southern Folklore Quarterly* 39 (1975): 291–96.

Nash, Roderick, ed. *The Call of the Wild, 1900–1916*. New York: George Braziller, 1970.

Newman, Edwin. *Strictly Speaking: Will America Be the Death of English?* Indianapolis, Ind.: Bobbs-Merrill, 1974.

Nieburg, H. L. *Culture Storm: Politics and the Ritual Order*. New York: St. Martin's Press, 1973.

Nye, Russel Blaine. *The Cultural Life of the New Nation, 1776–1830*. New York: Harper & Row, 1960.

Packard, Vance Oakley. *The Status Seekers: An Exploration of Class Behavior in America and the Hidden Barriers That Affect You, Your Community, and Your Future*. New York: McKay, 1959.

Parrington, Vernon Louis. *Main Currents in American Thought: An Interpretation of American Literature from the Beginnings to 1920*. 3 vols. New York: Harcourt, Brace & Co., 1927–30.

Parsons, Elsie Clews. *American Indian Life*. 1922. Reprint. New York: Greenwich House, 1983.

Paulding, James Kirke. *The Dutchman's Fireside, A Tale*. New York: J & J Harper, 1831.

Perry, Lewis. *Intellectual Life in America: A History*. New York: Franklin Watts, 1984.

Peters, Thomas J., and Robert H. Waterman, Jr. *In Search of Excellence: Lessons from America's Best-Run Companies.* New York: Harper & Row, 1982.

Potter, David M. *People of Plenty: Economic Abundance and the American Character.* Chicago: University of Chicago Press, 1954.

Riesman, David. *The Lonely Crowd: A Study of the Changing American Character.* New Haven, Conn.: Yale University Press, 1950.

Riis, Jacob. *How the Other Half Lives: Studies among the Tenements of New York.* 1890. Reprint. Cambridge, Mass.: Belknap Press of Harvard University Press, 1970.

Rodgers, Daniel T. *The Work Ethic in Industrial America, 1850–1920.* Chicago: University of Chicago Press, 1974.

Rourke, Constance. *American Humor: A Study of the National Character.* Garden City, N.Y.: Doubleday, 1931.

———. *Roots of American Culture, The.* Edited by Van Wyck Brooks. New York: Harcourt, Brace & World, 1942.

Safire, William. *On Language.* New York: Times Books, 1981.

Satow, Sir Ernest. *A Guide to Diplomatic Practice.* London: Longmans, Green, & Co., 1917.

Schooling, William. "Fairy Tales and Science." *Westminster Review* 135 (1891): 165–76.

Schreiner, Olive. *Woman and Labor.* New York: Frederick A. Stokes, 1911.

Sedgwick, Ellery. "The American Genteel Tradition in the Early Twentieth Century." *American Studies* 25 (1984): 49–67.

Sennett, Richard. *The Fall of Public Man: On the Social Psychology of Capitalism.* New York: Vintage Books, 1974.

Shapiro, Henry D. *Appalachia on Our Mind: The Southern Mountains and Mountaineers in the American Consciousness, 1870–1920.* Chapel Hill: University of North Carolina Press, 1978.

Skinner, B. F. *Science and Human Behavior.* New York: Macmillan, 1953.

Smith, Henry Nash. *Virgin Land: The American West as Symbol and Myth.* Cambridge: Harvard University Press, 1950.

———, ed. *Popular Culture and Industrialism, 1865–1890.* Garden City, N.Y.: Doubleday, 1967.

Spencer, Anna Garlin. "The Primitive Working-Woman." *Forum* 46 (1911): 546–58.

Stanton, Elizabeth Cady. "The Matriarchate, or Mother-Age." In *Transactions of the National Council of Women of the United States,* pp. 218–30. Philadelphia: J. B. Lippincott, 1891.

Stein, Gertrude. *Picasso.* Boston: Beacon Press, 1959.

Stein, Maurice. *The Eclipse of Community: An Interpretation of American Studies.* Princeton, N.J.: Princeton University Press, 1960.

Susman, Warren I. *Culture as History: The Transformation of American Society in the Twentieth Century.* New York: Pantheon, 1984.

Thomas, William I. "Sex in Primitive Industry." *American Journal of Sociology* 4 (1899): 474–88.

———. "Woman and the Occupations." *American Magazine* 68 (1909): 463–70.

Tingsten, Herbert. *Victoria and the Victorians.* London: George Allen & Unwin, 1972.

Toulmin, Stephen, and June Goodfield. *The Discovery of Time.* New York: Harper & Row, 1965.

Trachtenberg, Alan. *Democratic Vistas, 1860–1880.* New York: George Braziller, 1970.

———. *The Incorporation of America: Culture and Society in the Gilded Age.* New York: Hill & Wang, 1982.

Tuan, Yi-Fu. *Space and Place: The Perspective of Experience.* Minneapolis: University of Minnesota Press, 1977.

———. *Segmented Worlds and Self: Group Life and Individual Consciousness.* Minneapolis: University of Minnesota Press, 1982.

Turner, Frederick Jackson. "The Significance of the Frontier in American History." *Annual Report of the American Historical Association for the Year 1893,* pp. 197–227. Washington, D.C.: Government Printing Office, 1894.

Twain, Mark. *The Adventures of Huckleberry Finn.* 1884. Reprint. New York: Signet, 1959.

———. *A Connecticut Yankee in King Arthur's Court.* 1889. Reprint. New York: Penguin, 1971.

———. *Mark Twain's Letters.* Edited by Albert Bigelow Paine. New York: Harper & Bros., 1929.

Veblen, Thorstein. "The Barbarian Status of Women." *American Journal of Sociology* 4 (1899): 503–14.

———. *The Theory of the Leisure Class.* 1899. Reprint. New York: Penguin Books, 1979.

———. *The Instinct of Workmanship and the State of the Industrial Arts.* 1914. Reprint. New York: Augustus M. Kelley, 1964.

Veysey, Laurence. "The Autonomy of American History Reconsidered." *American Quarterly* 31 (1979): 455–77.

Ward, Lester. "Our Better Halves." *Forum* 6 (1888): 266–75.

Warshaver, Gerald. "Bushwacked by Reality: The Significance of Stephen Crane's Interest in Rural Folklore." *Journal of the Folklore Institute* 19 (1982): 1–16.

Weber, Max. "Politics as a Vocation." In *Man in Contemporary Society.* New York: Columbia University Press, 1955.

Whyte, William Hollingsworth. *The Organization Man.* New York: Simon & Schuster, 1956.

Wilcox, Ella Wheeler. "The Restlessness of the Modern Woman." *Cosmopolitan* 31 (1901): 314–17.

Williams, Raymond. *The Country and the City.* New York: Oxford University Press, 1973.

———. *Keywords: A Vocabulary of Culture and Society.* New York: Oxford University Press, 1976.

———. *Marxism and Literature.* Oxford: Oxford University Press, 1977.

Wilson, Sloan. *The Man in the Gray Flannel Suit.* New York: Simon & Schuster, 1955.

Wish, Harvey. *The American Historian: A Social Intellectual History of the Writing of the American Past.* New York: Oxford University Press, 1960.

"Women of Leisure." *Century* 60 (1900): 632–33.

Zelinsky, Wilbur. "Selfward Bound? Personal Preference Patterns and the Changing Map of American Society." *Economic Geography* 50 (Apr. 1974): 143–79.

Zenderland, Leila, ed. *Recycling the Past: Popular Uses of American History.* Philadelphia: University of Pennsylvania Press, 1978.

HISTORIES

Alexander, Edward P. *Museums in Motion: An Introduction to the History and Functions of Museums.* Nashville, Tenn.: American Association for State and Local History, 1979.

Boas, Franz. "The History of Anthropology." *Science* 20 (1904): 513–24. Reprinted in *Readings in the History of Anthropology,* edited by Regna Darnell, pp. 260–73. New York: Harper & Row, 1974.

Boon, James A. *Other Tribes, Other Scribes: Symbolic Anthropology in the Comparative Study of Cultures, Histories, Religions, and Texts.* Cambridge: Cambridge University Press, 1982.

Bowler, Peter J. *The Eclipse of Darwinism: Anti-Darwinian Evolution Theories in the Decades around 1900.* Baltimore, Md.: Johns Hopkins University Press, 1983.

Bronner, Simon J. "The Hidden Past of Material Culture Studies in American Folkloristics." *New York Folklore* 8 (1982): 1–10.

———. "The Early Movements of Anthropology and Their Folkloristic Relationships." *Folklore* 95 (1984): 57–73.

———. "Introduction." In *American Folk Art: A Guide to Sources,* edited by Simon J. Bronner, pp. xi–xxvii. New York: Garland Publishing, 1984.

———. "Folklore Collectors in the South." In *Encyclopedia of Southern Culture,* ed. William Ferris and Charles Wilson. Chapel Hill: University of North Carolina Press, 1987.

Buckley, Bruce R. "New Beginnings and Old Ends: Museums, Folklife, and the Cooperstown Experiment." *Folklore Historian* 1 (1984): 24–31.

Burstein, Sona Rosa. "Eighty Years of Folklore: Evaluations and Reevaluations." *Folklore* 69 (1958): 73–92.

"Chicago Folk-Lore Society, The." *Folk-Lorist* 1 (1892/93): 8.

Clark, Joseph D. "Fifty Years of Meetings and Programs of the North Carolina Folklore Society." *North Carolina Folklore* 12 (1964): 27–32.

Cocchiara, Giuseppe. *The History of Folklore in Europe.* Translated by John N. McDaniel. Philadelphia: Institute for the Study of Human Issues, 1971.

Darnell, Regna. "The Development of American Anthropology, 1879–1920: From Bureau of American Ethnology to Franz Boas." Ph.D. diss., University of Pennsylvania, 1969.

———. "The Emergence of Academic Anthropology at the University of Pennsylvania." *Journal of the History of the Behavioral Sciences* 6 (1970): 80–92.

———. "The Professionalization of American Anthropology." *Social Science Information* 10 (1971): 83–103.

———. "American Anthropology and the Development of Folklore Scholarship, 1890–1920." *Journal of the Folklore Institute* 10 (1973): 23–40.

———, ed. *Readings in the History of Anthropology.* New York: Harper & Row, 1974.

de Caro, F. A. "Oral History and Folklore in Seventeenth Century England." *Kentucky Folklore Record* 28 (1982): 33–39.

Dewhurst, C. Kurt. "The Role of Exhibitions, Fairs, and Expositions in the Study of Folk Art Study." *Kentucky Folklore Record* 29 (1983): 83–88.

Dorson, Richard M. *The British Folklorists: A History.* Chicago: University of Chicago Press, 1968.

————, ed. *Folklore Research around the World: A North American Point of View.* Port Washington, N.Y.: Kennikat Press, 1973.

————. *The Birth of American Studies.* Bloomington, Ind.: Indiana University Publications, 1976.

Dundes, Alan. "Nationalistic Inferiority Complexes and the Fabrication of Fakelore: A Reconsideration of Ossian, the *Kinder-und Hausmarchen,* the *Kalevala,* and Paul Bunyan." *Journal of Folklore Research* 22 (1985): 5–18.

Dwyer-Shick, Susan. "The Development of Folklore and Folklife Research in the Federal Writers' Project, 1935–1943." *Keystone Folklore* 20 (1975): 5–31.

————. "The American Folklore Society and Folklore Research in America, 1888–1940." Ph.D. diss., University of Pennsylvania, 1979.

Eggan, Fred. "One Hundred Years of Ethnology and Social Anthropology." In *One Hundred Years of Anthropology,* edited by J. O. Brew, pp. 119–52. Cambridge: Harvard University Press, 1968.

Evans-Pritchard, Sir Edward. *A History of Anthropological Thought.* New York: Basic Books, 1981.

Feldman, Burton, and Robert D. Richardson, eds. *The Rise of Modern Mythology, 1680–1860.* Bloomington: Indiana University Press, 1972.

Fortes, Meyer. "Social Anthropology at Cambridge since 1900." In *Readings in the History of Anthropology,* edited by Regna Darnell, pp. 426–39. New York: Harper & Row, 1974.

Franklin, Phyllis. "English Studies in America: Reflections on the Development of a Discipline." *American Quarterly* 30 (1978): 21–38.

Freeman, John Finley. "University Anthropology: Early Departments in the United States." *Kroeber Anthropological Society Papers* 32 (1965): 530–38.

Freund, Hugo A. "Published State Folklore." *Western Folklore* 42 (1983): 215–27.

Gillespie, Angus K. "Pennsylvania Folk Festivals in the 1930s." *Pennsylvania Folklife* 26 (Fall 1976), 2–11.

Gomme, Allan. "The Folk-Lore Society: Whence and Whither." *Folklore* 63 (1952): 1–18.

Grobman, Neil R. "Eighteenth-Century Scottish Philosophers on Oral Tradition." *Journal of the Folklore Institute* 10 (1973): 187–95.

————. "The Role of Popular Nineteenth-Century Periodical Literature in Shaping Afro-American Religious Folklore Scholarship." *New York Folklore* 2 (1976): 43–60.

Hallowell, A. Irving. "Anthropology in Philadelphia." In *The Philadelphia Anthropological Society: Papers Presented on Its Golden Anniversary,* edited by Jacob W. Gruber, pp. 1–31. Philadelphia: Temple University Press, 1967.

Hand, Wayland D. "Foreword." In *Idaho Folklife: Homesteads to Headstones,* edited by Louie W. Attebery, pp. vii–ix. Salt Lake City: University of Utah Press, 1985.

Harrah-Conforth, Bruce. "Indiana Folklore Roots." *American Folklore Society Newsletter* 14 (Apr. 1985): 1.

Harris, Marvin. *The Rise of Anthropological Theory.* New York: Harper & Row, 1968.

Haskell, Thomas L. *The Emergence of Professional Social Science.* Urbana: University of Illinois Press, 1977.

Hatch, Elvin. *Theories of Man and Culture.* New York: Columbia University Press, 1973.

Hautala, Jonko. *Finnish Folklore Research, 1828–1918.* Helsinki: Tilgmann, 1968.

Hinsley, Curtis M., Jr. *Savages and Scientists: The Smithsonian Institution and the Development of American Anthropology, 1846–1910.* Washington, D.C.: Smithsonian Institution Press, 1981.

Hodgen, Margaret T. *Early Anthropology in the Sixteenth and Seventeenth Centuries.* Philadelphia: University of Pennsylvania Press, 1964.

Hymes, Dell. "Notes toward a History of Linguistic Anthropology." *Anthropological Linguistics* 5 (1963): 59–103.

Jackson, Bruce, ed. *The Negro and His Folklore in Nineteenth Century Periodicals.* Austin: University of Texas Press, 1967.

Jones, Louis C. "HWT: NYSCT: BBB: NYFS." *New York Folklore Quarterly* 14 (1958): 177–88.

Judd, Neil. *The Bureau of American Ethnology: A Partial History.* Norman: University of Oklahoma Press, 1967.

Kamenetsky, Christa. "Folktale and Ideology in the Third Reich." *Journal of American Folklore* 90 (1977): 168–78.

———. *Children's Literature in Hitler's Germany.* Athens: Ohio University Press, 1984.

Köngäs-Maranda, Elli-Kaija. "The Roots of the Two Ethnologies, and Ethnilogy." *Folklore Forum* 15 (1982): 51–68.

Leach, MacEdward. "The Men Who Made Folklore a Scholarly Discipline." In *Our Living Traditions: An Introduction to American Folklore,* edited by Tristram P. Coffin, pp. 15–23. New York: Basic Books, 1968.

Leaf, Murray J. *Man, Mind, and Science: A History of Anthropology.* New York: Columbia University Press, 1979.

Link, Arthur S. "The American Historical Association, 1884–1984: Retrospect and Prospect." *American Historical Review* 90 (1985): 1–17.

Lowie, Robert H. *The History of Ethnological Theory.* New York: Holt, Rinehart & Winston, 1937.

———. "Reminiscences of Anthropological Currents in America Half a Century Ago." *American Anthropologist* 58 (1956): 995–1016.

MacDurdy, George Grant. "Twenty Years of Section H, Anthropology." *Science* 15 (1902): 532, 534.

McNeil, William K. "A History of American Folklore Scholarship before 1908." Ph.D. diss., Indiana University, 1980.

———. "The First American Collectors of African Folklore." *Kentucky Folklore Record* 28 (1982): 40–47.

———. "History in American Folklore: A Historical Perspective." *Western Folklore* 41 (1982): 30–35.

McNutt, James Charles. "Beyond Regionalism: Texas Folklorists and the Emergence of a Post-Regional Consciousness." Ph.D. diss., University of Texas, 1982.

Marshall, Howard Wight. "Folklife and the Rise of American Folk Museums." *Journal of American Folklore* 90 (1977): 391–413.

Pauly, Philip J. "The World and All That Is in It: The National Geographic Society, 1888–1918." *American Quarterly* 31 (1979): 517–32.

Penniman, T. K. *A Hundred Years of Anthropology.* 3d ed. London: G. Duckworth, 1965.

Pound, Louise. "The American Dialect Society: A Historical Sketch." *Publications of the American Dialect Society* 17 (1952): 3–28.

Ray, Verne F., and Nancy Oestrich Lurie. "The Contributions of Lewis and Clark to Ethnography." *Journal of the Washington Academy of Sciences* 44 (1954): 360–72.

Reed, Eugene E. "Herder, Primitivism and the Age of Poetry." *Modern Language Review* 60 (1965): 553–67.

Reich, Wendy. "The Uses of Folklore in Revitalization Movements." *Folklore* 82 (1971): 233–44.

Reuss, Richard A. "American Folklore and Left Wing Politics: 1927–1957." Ph.D. diss., Indiana University, 1971.

————, ed. *American Folklore Historiography.* Special issue of the *Journal of the Folklore Institute,* vol. 10, no. 3, June–August 1973.

Robacker, Earl F. "The Rise of Interest in Folk Art." *Pennsylvania Folklife* 10 (Spring 1959): 20–29.

Samuelson, Sue. "Women in the American Folklore Society, 1888–1892." *Folklore Historian* 2 (1985): 3–11.

Seward, Adrienne Lanier. "The Legacy of Early Afro-American Folklore Scholarship." In *Handbook of American Folklore,* edited by Richard M. Dorson, pp. 48–56. Bloomington: Indiana University Press, 1983.

Simeone, William E. "Fascists and Folklorists in Italy." *Journal of American Folklore* 91 (1978): 543–58.

Smith, Georgina. "Literary Sources and Folklore Studies in the Nineteenth Century: A Re-assessment of Armchair Scholarship." *Lore and Language* 2 (1978): 26–42.

Smith, John David. "The Unveiling of Slave Folk Culture, 1865–1920." *Journal of Folklore Research* 21 (1984): 47–62.

Stekert, Ellen J. "Tylor's Theory of Survivals and National Romanticism: Their Influence on Early American Folksong Collectors." *Southern Folklore Quarterly* 32 (1968): 209–36.

"Step Gables and Clinkers: Birth of the Historic Preservation Idea." *Heritage* 1 (Nov.–Dec. 1984): 1–4.

Stocking, George W., Jr. "'Cultural Darwinism' and 'Philosophical Idealism' in E. B. Tylor: A Special Plea for Historicism in the History of Anthropology." *Southwestern Journal of Anthropology* 21 (1965): 130–47.

————. *Race, Culture, and Evolution: Essays in the History of Anthropology.* Rev. ed. Chicago: University of Chicago Press, 1982.

————, ed. *Objects and Others: Essays on Museums and Material Culture.* Madison: University of Wisconsin Press, 1985.

Taylor, Archer. "Precursors of the Finnish Method of Folklore Study." *Modern Philology* 25 (1928): 481–91.

————, and Wayland Hand. "Twenty-five Years of Folklore Study in the West." *Western Folklore* 25 (1966): 229–43.

Voget, Fred. *A History of Ethnology.* New York: Holt, Rinehart & Winston, 1975.

Whisnant, David E. *All That Is Native and Fine: The Politics of Culture in an American Region.* Chapel Hill: University of North Carolina Press, 1983.

Wilgus, D. K. *Anglo-American Folksong Scholarship since 1898.* New Brunswick, N.J.: Rutgers University Press, 1959.

Williams, John Alexander. "Radicalism and Professionalism in Folklore Studies: A Comparative Perspective." *Journal of the Folklore Institute* 11 (1974): 211–34.

Wilson, William A. "Herder, Folklore, and Romantic Nationalism." *Journal of Popular Culture* 4 (1973): 819–35.

Wise, Gene. " 'Paradigm Dramas' in American Studies: A Cultural and Institutional History of the Movement." *American Quarterly* 31 (1979): 293–337.

Yoder, Don. "The Folklife Studies Movement." *Pennsylvania Folklife* 13 (July 1963), 43–56.

———. "Folklife in Pennsylvania: An Historical Survey." *Keystone Folklore* 1 (1982): 8–20.

Zumwalt, Rosemary. "American Folkloristics: The Literary and Anthropological Roots." Ph.D. diss., University of California at Berkeley, 1982.

SURVEYS

Anderson, Jay. *Time Machines: The World of Living History.* Nashville, Tenn.: American Association for State and Local History, 1984.

Barbeau, C. Marius. "The Field of European Folk-Lore in America." *Journal of American Folklore* 32 (1919): 185–97.

———. "The Folklore Movement in Canada." *Journal of American Folklore* 56 (1943): 166–68.

Bascom, William R. "Afro-American Studies." *Proceedings of the International Congress of Americanists* 6 (1979): 591–95.

Bates, Ernest Sutherland. "American Folk-Lore." *Saturday Review of Literature,* 10 July 1926, 913.

Baughman, Ernest W. "Folklore to the Fore." *English Journal* 32 (1943): 206–9.

Bauman, Richard, and Roger Abrahams with Susan Kalčik. "American Folklore and American Studies." *American Quarterly* 28 (1976): 360–78.

Belden, H. M. "The Study of Folk-Song in America." *Modern Philology* 2 (1905): 573–79.

Ben-Amos, Dan. "The Seven Strands of *Tradition:* Varieties in Its Meaning in American Folklore Studies." *Journal of Folklore Research* 21 (1984): 97–131.

Boas, Franz. "The Smithsonian Institution and Its Affiliated Bureaus." *Science* 16 (1902): 801–3.

Botkin, Benjamin. "WPA and Folklore Research." *Southern Folklore Quarterly* 3 (1939): 7–15.

Brinton, Daniel. "The Aims of Anthropology." *Proceedings of the American Association for the Advancement of Science* 44 (1895): 1–17.

Bronner, Simon J. "Recent Folk Art Publications: A Review Essay." *Mid-South Folklore* 6 (1978): 27–30.

———. "Concepts in the Study of Material Aspects of American Folk Culture." *Folklore Forum* 12 (1979): 133–72.

———. "Modern Anthropological Trends and Their Folkloristic Relationships." *Folklife* 19 (1981): 66–83.

———. " 'Visible Proofs': Material Culture Study in American Folkloristics." *American Quarterly* 35 (1983): 316–38. Revised and reprinted in *Material*

   Culture: A Research Guide, edited by Thomas J. Schlereth, pp. 127–54.
   Lawrence: University Press of Kansas, 1985.
———. "The State of Folkloristics: Introduction." *New York Folklore* 9 (1983):
   1–3.
———. "The Idea of the Folk Artifact." In *American Material Culture and
   Folklife,* edited by Simon J. Bronner, pp. 3–39. Ann Arbor, Mich.: UMI
   Research Press, 1985.
Brunvand, Jan Harold. "New Directions for the Study of American Folklore."
   Folklore 82 (1971): 25–35.
———. *The Study of American Folklore: An Introduction.* 2d ed: New York: W.
   W. Norton. 1978.
Carriere, Joseph M. "The Present State of French Folklore Studies in North
   America." *Southern Folklore Quarterly* 10 (1946): 219–26.
Chamberlain, Alexander. "Work Accomplished in the Study of American
   Indian Folk-Lore." *Journal of American Folklore* 15 (1902): 127–29.
Chapple, Edward. "The Unbounded Reaches of Anthropology as a Research
   Science, and Some Working Hypotheses." *American Anthropologist* 82
   (1980): 741–58.
Crane, T. F. "Recent Folk-Lore Publications." *Nation,* 12 June 1890, 475–76.
———. "The Study of Popular Tales." *Chautauquan* 16 (1892/93): 180–85.
———. "Studies in Folklore." *Nation,* suppl., 21 Dec. 1916, 6.
Cull, Richard. "Nature, Objects, and Evidence of Ethnological Science."
   Journal of Ethnological Society of London 3 (1854): 103–11.
———. "On the Recent Progress of Ethnology." *Journal of the Ethnological
   Society of London* 3 (1854): 165–77; 4 (1856): 104–19, 297–316.
Davidson, Donald. "Current Attitudes towards Folklore." *Tennessee Folklore
   Society Bulletin* 6 (1940): 44–51.
de Caro, Francis A. "Concepts of the Past in Folkloristics." *Western Folklore* 35
   (1976): 3–22.
Dégh, Linda. "Approaches to Folklore Research among Immigrant Groups."
   Journal of American Folklore 79 (1966): 551–56.
———. "Comment on 'Anthropological Research Action and Education in
   Modern Nations: With Special Reference to the U.S.A.'" *Current Anthro-
   pology* 9 (1968): 256–57.
———. "The Study of Ethnicity in Modern European Ethnology." *Journal of
   the Folklore Institute* 12 (1975): 113–30.
Dorsey, George A. "The Department of Anthropology of the Field Columbian
   Museum—A Review of Six Years." *American Anthropologist* 2 (1900):
   247–65.
Dorson, Richard M. "Folklore Studies in the United States Today." *Folklore* 62
   (1951): 353–66.
———. "Five Directions in American Folklore." *Midwest Folklore* 1 (1951):
   149–65.
———. "Current Folklore Theories." *Current Anthropology* 4 (1963): 93–112.
———. "The American Folklore Scene, 1963." *Folklore* 74 (1963): 433–49.
———. *American Folklore and the Historian.* Chicago: University of Chicago
   Press, 1971.
———. "Concepts of Folklore and Folklife Studies." In *Folklore and Folklife:
   An Introduction,* edited by Richard M. Dorson, pp. 1–50. Chicago: Univer-
   sity of Chicago Press, 1972.

————. "Mythology and Folklore." In *Annual Review of Anthropology,* edited by Bernard J. Siegel, pp. 107–26. Palo Alto, Calif.: Annual Reviews, 1973.

————. "The Folklore Boom, 1977." *Journal of the Folklore Institute* 15 (1978): 81–90.

————. "Folklore in the Modern World." In *Folklore in the Modern World,* edited by Richard M. Dorson, pp. 11–51. The Hague: Mouton, 1978.

————. "The State of Folkloristics from an American Perspective." *Journal of the Folklore Institute* 19 (1982): 71–106.

————, ed. *Handbook of American Folklore.* Bloomington: Indiana University Press, 1983.

Dunaway, David K., and Willa K. Baum, eds. *Oral History: An Interdisciplinary Anthology.* Nashville, Tenn.: American Association for State and Local History, 1984.

Dundes, Alan. "Trends in Content Analysis: A Review Article." *Midwest Folklore* 12 (1962): 31–38.

————. "The American Concept of Folklore." *Journal of the Folklore Institute* 3 (1966): 226–49.

————. "North American Indian Folklore Studies." *Journal de la Société des americanistes* 56 (1967): 53–79.

Fabian, Johannes. *Time and the Other: How Anthropology Makes Its Object.* New York: Columbia University Press, 1983.

Foster, John Wilson. "The Plight of Current Folklore Theory." *Southern Folklore Quarterly* 32 (1968): 237–48.

Gaidoz, H. "Folklore in the United States (1885)." Translated by Charles Oliver and edited by William K. McNeil. *Folklore Historian,* special supplement, 1 (1984): 1–12.

Gayton, Ann H., ed. "Folklore Research in North America: Reports of the Committee on Research in Folklore, 1945 and 1946." *Journal of American Folklore* 60 (1947): 350–416.

————. "Perspectives in Folklore." *Journal of American Folklore* 64 (1951): 147–50.

Georges, Robert A. "From Folktale Research to the Study of Narrating." *Studia Fennica* 20 (1976): 159–68.

Glassie, Henry. "Folkloristic Study of the American Artifact: Objects and Objectives." In *Handbook of American Folklore,* edited by Richard M. Dorson, pp. 376–83. Bloomington: Indiana University Press, 1983.

Goldenweiser, Alexander A. "Recent Trends in American Anthropology." *American Anthropologist* 43 (1941): 151–63.

Gomme, George Laurence. "Folk-Lore and the Folk-Lore Society." *Antiquary* 1 (1880): 13–15.

Goode, G. Browne. "The Condition and Progress of the United States National Museum during the Year Ending June 30, 1894." In *Report of the United States National Museum,* pp. 3–44. Washington, D.C.: Government Printing Office, 1896.

Halpert, Herbert. "Some Undeveloped Areas in American Folklore." *Journal of American Folklore* 70 (1957): 249–305.

Hand, Wayland D. "North American Folklore Societies." *Journal of American Folklore* 56 (1943): 161–91.

————. "American Folklore after Seventy Years: Survey and Prospects." *Journal of American Folklore* 73 (1960): 1–11.

———. "Folklore and Mythology at UCLA." *Western Folklore* 23 (1964): 35–38.

———. "Status of European and American Legend Study." *Current Anthropology* 6 (1965): 439–46.

———. "Folklore Societies and the Research Effort." *Keystone Folklore Quarterly* 14 (1969): 97–104.

———. "Comparative Folk Medicine: The New Agendum." *Folklore Forum* 16 (1983): 249–61.

Henderson, M. Carole. "Folklore Scholarship and the Sociopolitical Milieu in Canada." *Journal of the Folklore Institute* 10 (1973): 97–108.

Herskovits, Melville. "Folklore after a Hundred Years: A Problem in Redefinition." *Journal of American Folklore* 59 (1946): 89–100.

Honko, Lauri, and Pekka Laaksonen, eds. *Trends in Nordic Tradition Research.* Helsinki: Suomalaisen Kirjallisuuden Seura, 1983.

Jabbour, Alan. "American Folklore Studies: The Tradition and the Future." *Folklore Forum* 16 (1983): 235–48.

Jackson, Bruce. "Things That from a Long Way off Look Like Flies." *Journal of American Folklore* 98 (1985): 131–47.

Jacobs, Melville. *Pattern in Cultural Anthropology.* Homewood, Ill.: Dorsey, 1964.

Jones, Michael Owen. "The Study of Traditional Furniture: Review and Preview." *Keystone Folklore Quarterly* 12 (1967): 233–45.

———. "The Study of Folk Art Study: Reflections on Images." In *Folklore Today: A Festschrift for Richard M. Dorson,* edited by Linda Dégh, Henry Glassie, Felix J. Oinas, pp. 291–303. Bloomington: Research Center for Language and Semiotic Studies, Indiana University, 1976.

Köngäs-Maranda, Elli-Kaija. "The Concept of Folklore." *Midwest Folklore* 13 (1963): 69–88.

Kroeber, Alfred Louis. "Berkeley Folk-Lore Club." *American Anthropologist* 8 (1906): 437–38.

Leland, Charles G. "American Studies of Native Folk-Lore." *Critic* 9 (1888): 194.

Limón, José. "Western Marxism and Folklore: A Critical Introduction." *Journal of American Folklore* 96 (1983): 34–52.

Lowie, Robert H. "Contemporary Trends in American Cultural Anthropology." *Sociologus* 5 (1955): 113–21.

Malinowski, Bronislaw. "Anthropology." *Encyclopaedia Britannica.* 13th ed., suppl., vol. 1. Chicago: Encyclopaedia Britannica, 1926.

Newell, William Wells. "Folk-Lore Studies and Folk-Lore Societies." *Journal of American Folklore* 8 (1895): 231–41.

Oinas, Felix J., ed. *Folklore, Nationalism, and Politics.* Columbus, Ohio: Slavica Publishers, 1978.

Paredes, Americo. "Concepts about Folklore in Latin America and the United States." *Journal of the Folklore Institute* 6 (1969): 20–38.

Pound, Louise. "The Scholarly Study of Folklore." *Western Folklore* 11 (1952): 100–108.

Remembrancer, Christian. "Folk Lore." *Littell's Living Age* 94 (1866): 707–35.

Richmond, W. Edson. "Introduction." In *Handbook of American Folklore,* edited by Richard M. Dorson, pp. xi–xix. Bloomington: Indiana University Press, 1983.

Riedl, Norbert. "Folklore and the Study of Material Aspects of Folk Culture." *Journal of American Folklore* 79 (1966): 557–63.

Rikoon, J. Sanford. "Ethnic Food Traditions: A Review and Preview of Folklore Scholarship." *Kentucky Folklore Record* 28 (1982): 12–25.

Rooth, Anna Birgitta. "Scholarly Tradition in Folktale Research." *Fabula* 1 (1958): 193–200.

Schlereth, Thomas J. "Material Culture Studies in America, 1876–1976." In *Material Culture Studies in America,* edited by Thomas J. Schlereth, pp. 1–75. Nashville, Tenn.: American Association for State and Local History, 1982.

Stern, Stephen. "Ethnic Folklore and the Folklore of Ethnicity." *Western Folklore* 36 (1977): 7–32.

Tax, Sol, and Leslie G. Freeman, eds. *Horizons of Anthropology.* Chicago: Aldine Publishing, 1977.

Taylor, Archer. "Some Trends and Problems in Studies of the Folktale." *Studies in Philology* 37 (1940): 1–25.

———. "Trends in the Study of Folksong, 1937–1950." *Southern Folklore Quarterly* 17 (1953): 97–113.

———. "The Classics of Folklore." *ARV* 20 (1964): 113–24.

Thompson, Stith. "American Folklore after Fifty Years." *Journal of American Folklore* 51 (1938): 1–9.

———. "Folklore at Midcentury." *Midwest Folklore* 1 (1951): 5–12.

———. "Advances in Folklore Studies." In *Anthropology Today: An Encyclopedic Inventory,* edited by Alfred L. Kroeber, pp. 587–96. Chicago: University of Chicago Press, 1955.

Vance, Lee J. "Folk-Lore Studies." *Open Court* 1 (1887): 612–13, 662–65.

———. "Prof. Crane's Studies in Folk-Lore." *Critic* 9 (1888): 13–14.

———. "The Study of American Folk-Lore." *Critic* 9 (1888): 233.

———. "Folk-Lore Study in America." *Popular Science Monthly* 43 (1893): 586–98.

———. "The Study of Folk-Lore." *Forum* 22 (1896/1897): 249–56.

Wilson, William A. "The Study of Mormon Folklore." *Utah Historical Quarterly* 44 (1976): 317–28.

Wolf, Eric R. *Anthropology.* New York: W. W. Norton, 1974.

Yoder, Don. "Folklife Studies in American Scholarship." In *American Folklife,* edited by Don Yoder, pp. 3–18. Austin: University of Texas Press, 1976.

Zemljanova, L. M. "The Struggle between the Reactionary and Progressive Forces in Contemporary American Folkloristics." *Journal of the Folklore Institute* 1 (1964): 130–44.

———. *Sovremennaia amerikanskaia folkloristika* (Contemporary American folkloristics). Moscow: USSR Academy of Sciences, 1975.

BIOGRAPHIES

Alexander, Edward P. *Museum Masters: Their Museums and Their Influence.* Nashville, Tenn.: American Association for State and Local History, 1983.

Alvey, Gerald R. "Phillips Barry and Anglo-American Folksong Scholarship." *Journal of the Folklore Institute* 10 (1973): 67–95.

———. "Wm. Hugh Jansen (1914–1979)." *Journal of American Folklore* 93 (1980): 57–59.

Bascom, William R. "Malinowski's Contribution to the Study of Folklore." *Folklore* 94 (1983): 163–72.

Beck, Horace. "MacEdward Leach (1896–1967)." *Keystone Folklore Quarterly* 12 (1967): 193–98.

Bell, Michael Edward. "Harry Middleton Hyatt's Quest for the Essence of Human Spirit." *Journal of the Folklore Institute* 16 (1979): 1–27.

Bell, Michael J. "William Wells Newell and the Foundation of American Folklore Scholarship." *Journal of the Folklore Institute* 10 (1973): 7–21.

———. "The Relation of Mentality to Race: William Wells Newell and the Celtic Hypothesis." *Journal of American Folklore* 92 (1979): 25–43.

Berman, Milton. *John Fiske: The Evolution of a Popularizer.* Cambridge: Harvard University Press, 1961.

Birdsall, Esther K. "Some Notes on the Role of George Lyman Kittredge in American Folklore Studies." *Journal of the Folklore Institute* 10 (1973): 57–66.

Boas, Franz. "Tribute to W. W. Newell." *Journal of American Folklore* 20 (1907): 63–66.

Bonney, Charles C. "Lieutenant Fletcher S. Bassett." In *The International Folk-Lore Congress of the World's Columbian Exposition,* edited by Helen Wheeler Bassett and Frederick Starr, pp. 15–16. 1898. Reprint. New York: Arno Press, 1980.

Botkin, Benjamin. "Louise Pound (1872–1958)." *Western Folklore* 18 (1959): 201–2.

Boyer, Ruth M. "Anna Hadwick Gayton (1899–1977)." *Journal of American Folklore* 91 (1978): 834–41.

Briscoe, Virginia Wolf. "Ruth Benedict: Anthropological Folklorist." *Journal of American Folklore* 92 (1979): 445–76.

Bronner, Simon J. "Charlotte Sophia Burne, British Folklorist: A Re-examination." *Folklore Women's Communication,* no. 24 (Spring 1981): 14–19.

———. "Stewart Culin, Museum Magician." *Pennsylvania Heritage* 11 (Summer 1985): 4–11.

Brookes, Stella Brewer. *Joel Chandler Harris—Folklorist.* 1950. Reprint. Athens: University of Georgia Press, 1972.

Brown, Rollo W. "Kitty of Harvard." *Atlantic Monthly* 182 (1948): 65–69.

Brunvand, Jan Harold. "Richard M. Dorson (1916–1981)." *Journal of American Folklore* 95 (1982): 347–53.

Burson, Anne C. "Alexander Haggerty Krappe and His Science of Comparative Folklore." *Journal of the Folklore Institute* 19 (1982): 167–96.

Chamberlain, Alexander F. "In Memoriam: Horatio Hale." *Journal of American Folklore* 10 (1897): 60.

———. "Daniel Garrison Brinton." *Journal of American Folklore* 12 (1899): 115.

Chambers, Keith S. "The Indefatigable Elsie Clews Parsons—Folklorist." *Western Folklore* 32 (1973): 180–98.

Cochran, Robert. *Vance Randolph: An Ozark Life.* Urbana: University of Illinois Press, 1985.

Crawford, M. D. C. "Tribute to Robert Stewart Culin." *Brooklyn Museum Quarterly* 16 (1929): 88–89.

Crowley, Daniel, and Alan Dundes. "William Russel Bascom (1912–1981)." *Journal of American Folklore* 95 (1982): 465–67.

Culin, Stewart. "Remarks on Frank Hamilton Cushing." *American Anthropologist* 2 (1900): 375–77.

Darnell, Regna Diebold. "Daniel Garrison Brinton: An Intellectual Biography." Master's thesis, University of Pennsylvania, 1967.

de Caro, Francis. "G. L. Gomme: The Victorian Folklorist as Ethnohistorian." *Journal of the Folklore Institute* 19 (1982): 107–18.

Dexter, Ralph W. "Putnam's Problems Popularizing Anthropology." *American Scientist* 54 (1966): 315–22.

———. "The Role of F. W. Putnam in Developing Anthropology at the American Museum of Natural History." *Curator* 19 (1976): 303–10.

———. "F. W. Putnam as Secretary of the American Association for the Advancement of Science (1873–1898)." *Essex Institute Historical Collections* 118 (1982): 106–18.

Dorsey, George. "Stewart Culin." *American Magazine* 45 (1913): 37.

Dorson, Richard M. "Melville J. Herskovits (1895–1963)." *Journal of American Folklore* 76 (1963): 249–50.

———. "MacEdward Leach (1896–1967)." *Journal of American Folklore* 81 (1968): 103–4.

———. "Elsie Clews Parsons: Feminist and Folklorist." *AFFword* 1 (1971): 1–4.

———. "John W. Ashton (1900–1971)." *Folklore Forum* 4 (1971): i–ii.

———. "In Memoriam: Edwin C. Kirkland (1902–1972)." *Southern Folklore Quarterly* 37 (1973): 123–25.

———. "Stith Thompson (1885–1976)." *Journal of American Folklore* 90 (1977): 3–7.

———. "The Legend of the Missing Pajamas and Other Sad Sagas." *Journal of the Folklore Institute* 14 (1977): 115–24.

———. "Harry Hyatt and His Sister." *Journal of the Folklore Institute* 16 (1979): 127–29.

———. "Katharine Briggs, James Delargy, Vance Randolph." *Journal of the Folklore Institute* 18 (1981): 91–93.

Dundes, Alan. "Robert Lee J. Vance: American Folklore Surveyor of the 1890s." *Western Folklore* 23 (1964): 27–34.

Emrich, Duncan. " 'Folklore': William John Thoms." *California Folklore Quarterly* 5 (1946): 355–74.

Firth, Raymond, ed. *Man and Culture: An Evaluation of the Works of Malinowski.* London: Routledge & Kegan Paul, 1960.

Flanagan, John T. "A Pioneer in Indian Folklore: James A. Jones." *New England Quarterly* 12 (1939): 443–53.

Garrison, Theodore Roosevelt. "John Greenleaf Whittier: Pioneer Regionalist and Folklorist." Ph.D. diss., University of Wisconsin, 1960.

Gay, E. Jane. *With the Nez Perces: Alice Fletcher in the Field, 1889–1892.* Lincoln: University of Nebraska Press, 1981.

Georges, Robert A. "Elli Kaija Köngäs Maranda (1932–1982)." *Journal of American Folklore* 96 (1983): 460–61.

Gilbert, G. K. "John Wesley Powell." *Science* 16 (1902): 561–67.

Gillespie, Angus K. *Folklorist of the Coal Fields: George Korson's Life and Work.* University Park: Pennsylvania State University Press, 1980.

Goldfrank, Esther S. "Gladys Amanda Reichard (1893–1955)." *Journal of American Folklore* 69 (1957): 53–54.

Gordon, Dudley C. "Charles F. Lummis: Pioneer American Folklorist." *Western Folklore* 28 (1969): 175–81.

Green, Archie. "John Neuhaus: Wobbly Folklorist." *Journal of American Folklore* 73 (1960): 391–99.

Green, Jesse. "Introduction." In *Zuñi: Selected Writings of Frank Hamilton Cushing,* edited by Jesse Green, pp. 3–34. Lincoln: University of Nebraska Press, 1979.

Grobman, Neil R. "David Hume: Mythologist." *New York Folklore* 3 (1977): 115–30.

Halpert, Herbert. "Vance Randolph (1892–1980)." *Journal of American Folklore* 94 (1981): 345–50.

Hand, Wayland D. "Newbell Niles Puckett (1898–1967)." *Journal of American Folklore* 80 (1967): 341–42.

——. "MacEdward Leach (1896–1967)." *Western Folklore* 27 (1968): 43–44.

——. "Archer Taylor (1890–1973)." *Journal of American Folklore* 87 (1974): 3–9.

——. "Louis C. Jones and the Study of Folk Belief, Witchcraft and Popular Medicine in America." *New York Folklore* 1 (1975): 7–14.

——, and Frances M. Tally. "Superstition, Custom and Ritual Magic: Harry M. Hyatt's Approach to the Study of Folklore." *Journal of the Folklore Institute* 16 (1979): 28–43.

Harris, Robert E. "Archdeacon of Comma Hounds: My Friend Stith Thompson." *Vagabond* 3 (1926): 68–73.

Hart, Walter Morris. "Professor Child and the Ballad." *Publications of the Modern Language Association* 21 (1906): 807.

Haskew, Eula. "Charles Godfrey Leland: Collector of Folk-Lore." Master's thesis, Columbia University, 1928.

Heisley, Michael. "Lummis and Mexican-American Folklore." In *Chas. F. Lummis—The Centennial Exhibition Commemorating His Tramp across the Continent,* edited by Daniela P. Moneta, pp. 60–67. Los Angeles: Southwest Museum, 1985.

Helm, June, ed. *Pioneers of American Anthropology: The Uses of Biography.* Seattle: University of Washington Press, 1966.

Herold, Amos L. *James Kirke Paulding: Versatile American.* 1926. Reprint. New York: AMS Press, 1966.

Herskovits, Melville. *Franz Boas: The Science of Man in the Making.* New York: Scribners, 1953.

Herzog, George. "Phillips Barry." *Journal of American Folklore* 51 (1938): 439–41.

Hough, Walter. "Alice Cunningham Fletcher." *American Anthropologist* 25 (1923): 255.

Hyder, Clyde Kenneth. *George Lyman Kittredge: Teacher and Scholar.* Lawrence: University of Kansas Press, 1962.

Hymes, Dell. "Alfred Louis Kroeber." *Language* 37 (1961): 1–28.

Jackson, Bruce. "Benjamin A. Botkin (1901–1975)." *Journal of American Folklore* 89 (1976): 1–6.

Jacobs, Melville. "Folklore." In *The Anthropology of Franz Boas,* edited by Walter Goldschmidt, pp. 119–38. Memoirs of the American Anthropological Association, no. 89, 1959.

Jagendorf, Moritz. "Charles Godfrey Leland, Neglected Folklorist." *New York Folklore Quarterly* 19 (1963): 211–19.

Jones, Louis C. "Helen Fraser." *New York Folklore* 6 (1980): 109–10.
Jones, Michael Owen. "Francis Hindes Groome: Scholar Gypsy and Gypsy Scholar." *Journal of American Folklore* 80 (1967): 71–80.
Karpeles, Maud. *Cecil Sharp: His Life and Work.* Chicago: University of Chicago Press, 1967.
Klymasz, Robert B. "V. D. Bonch-Bruevich and the Lenin Connection in New World Folkloristics." *Journal of American Folklore* 93 (1980): 317–24.
Kroeber, Alfred Louis. "Frederic Ward Putnam." *American Anthropologist* 17 (1915): 712–18.
———. "Elsie Clews Parsons." *American Anthropologist* 45 (1943): 252–55.
Kroeber, Theodora. *Alfred Kroeber: A Personal Configuration.* Berkeley: University of California Press, 1970.
la Flesche, Francis. "Alice C. Fletcher." *Science* 57 (1923): 115.
"Lieut. Fletcher S. Bassett, U.S.N." *Journal of American Folklore* 5 (1893): 319.
Lowie, Robert H. "Franz Boas (1858–1942)." *Journal of American Folklore* 57 (1944): 59–64.
Luomala, Katherine. "Martha Warren Beckwith: A Commemorative Essay." *Journal of American Folklore* 75 (1962): 341–53.
McCann, Gordon. "'Come See Us When You Can': Some Memories of Vance Randolph." *Mid-America Folklore* 9 (1981): 29–33.
McNeil, William K. "Mary Henderson Eastman, Pioneer Collector of American Folklore." *Southern Folklore Quarterly* 39 (1975): 271–89.
———. "Lafcadio Hearn, American Folklorist." *Journal of American Folklore* 91 (1978): 947–67.
———. "James Athearn Jones: Pioneer American Folklorist." In *Folklore on Two Continents,* edited by Nikolai Burlakoff and Carl Lindahl, pp. 321–27. Bloomington, Ind.: Trickster Press, 1980.
———. "Mary Alicia Owen, Collector of Afro-American and Indian Lore in Missouri." *Missouri Folklore Society Journal* 2 (1980): 1–14.
———. "Richard M. Dorson (1916–1981)." *Mid-America Folklore* 9 (1981): 71–72.
Martin, Peggy. *Stith Thompson: His Life and His Role in Folklore Scholarship.* Bloomington, Ind.: Folklore Publication Group Monograph Series, no. 2, 1978.
Matthews, Washington. "Frank Hamilton Cushing." *American Anthropologist* 2 (1900): 372.
Meadows, Paul. *John Wesley Powell: Frontiersman of Science.* Lincoln: University of Nebraska Press, 1952.
Merriam, Alan P. "Melville Jean Herskovits (1895–1963)." *American Anthropologist* 66 (1964): 83–91.
Miller, E. Joan Wilson. "Vance Randolph, Folklorist." *Mid-South Folklore* 3 (1947): 63–70.
Moneta, Daniela P., ed. *Chas. F. Lummis—The Centennial Exhibition Commemorating His Tramp across the Continent.* Los Angeles: Southwest Museum, 1985.
Moses, L. G. *The Indian Man: A Biography of James Mooney.* Urbana: University of Illinois Press, 1984.
Mullen, Patrick. "Francis Lee Utley (1907–1974)." *Keystone Folklore* 19 (1974): 129–42.
Oinas, Felix J. "V. Ja. Propp (1895–1970)." *Journal of American Folklore* 84 (1971): 338–40.

————. "Elli-Kaija Köngäs Maranda: In Memoriam." *Folklore Forum* 15 (1982): 115-23.

Peabody, Charles. "Frederic Ward Putnam." *Journal of American Folklore* 28 (1915): 302-6.

Pennell, Elizabeth Robins. *Charles Godfrey Leland: A Biography.* 2 vols. Boston: Houghton Mifflin, 1906.

Powell, John Wesley. "James Owen Dorsey." *Smithsonian Institution Annual Report for 1895,* pp. 53-54. Washington, D.C.: Government Printing Office, 1896.

Primiano, Leonard Norman. "A. Irving Hallowell: His Contributions to Folklore Studies." *New York Folklore* 9 (1983): 43-54.

"Professor Child." *Atlantic Monthly* 78 (1896): 737-42.

Read, Allen Walker. "Tribute to Rossell Hope Robbins." *New York Folklore* 9 (1983): 1-8.

Reichard, Gladys. "Franz Boas and Folklore." In *Franz Boas, 1858-1942,* pp. 52-57. Memoirs of the American Anthropological Association, no. 61, 1943.

Reichard, Harry Hess. "John Baer Stoudt, D.D.: An Appreciation." *Pennsylvania German Folklore Society Annual,* vol. 9, pp. 220-29. Allentown, Pa.: Schlechter's, 1946.

Resek, Carl. *Lewis Henry Morgan: American Scholar.* Chicago: University of Chicago Press, 1960.

Reuss, Richard A., ed. *Roads into Folklore: Festschrift in Honor of Richard M. Dorson.* Folklore Forum Bibliographic and Special Series, no. 14, 1975.

Richmond, W. Edson. "Richard Mercer Dorson." *Journal of the Folklore Institute* 18 (1981): 95-96.

Roberts, Warren E. "Stith Thompson: His Major Work and a Bibliography." *ARV* 21 (1965): 5-20.

————. "Stith Thompson, 1885-1976." *Midwestern Journal of Language and Folklore* 2 (1976): 5-10.

Robinson, Fred Norris. "William Wells Newell." *Journal of American Folklore* 20 (1907): 59-60.

Roemer, Danielle M. "Henry Carrington Bolton: American Chemist and Folklorist." *Kentucky Folklore Record* 28 (1982): 61-70.

Rosenberg, Neil V. "Herbert Halpert: A Biographical Sketch." In *Folklore Studies in Honour of Herbert Halpert,* edited by Kenneth S. Goldstein and Neil V. Rosenberg, pp. 1-14. St. John's: Memorial University of Newfoundland, 1980.

Rosenstein, Donna Gail. "'Historic Human Tools': Henry Chapman Mercer and His Collection, 1897-1930." Master's thesis, University of Delaware, 1977.

Rowe, John Howland. "Alfred Louis Kroeber, 1876-1960." *American Antiquity* 27 (1962): 395-415.

————. "Anna Hadwick Gayton, 1899-1977." *American Anthropologist* 80 (1978): 653-56.

Schafer, Joseph, ed. *Memoirs of Jeremiah Curtin.* Madison: State Historical Society of Wisconsin, 1940.

Scherman, Tony. "A Man Who Mined Musical Gold in the Southern Hills" (Cecil Sharp). *Smithsonian* 16 (Apr. 1985): 173-96.

Shaw, William H. "Marx and Morgan." *History and Theory* 23 (1984): 215-28.

Smith, Marion. "Gladys Amanda Reichard." *American Anthropologist* 58 (1956): 913–16.

Smith, Robert J. "The Creditable Max Muller." In *Studies in Symbolism and Cultural Communication,* edited by F. Allan Hanson, pp. 90–109. Lawrence: University of Kansas Publications in Anthropology, 1982.

Sommer, Frank. "John F. Watson: First Historian of American Decorative Arts." *Antiques* 83 (1963): 300–303.

Spier, Leslie. "Franz Boas and Some of His Views." *Acta Americana* 1 (1943): 108–27.

———. "Elsie Clews Parsons." *American Anthropologist* 45 (1943): 244–51.

Stekert, Ellen. "Benjamin Albert Botkin, 1901–1975." *Western Folklore* 34 (1975): 335–38.

Stern, Bernhard J. *Lewis Henry Morgan: Social Evolutionist.* Chicago: University of Chicago Press, 1931.

Steward, Julian H. "Alfred Louis Kroeber, 1876–1960." *American Anthropologist* 63 (1961): 1038–60.

Thompson, Laurence C. "Melville Jacobs (1902–1971)." *American Anthropologist* 80 (1978): 640–46.

Thompson, Stith. "John Avery Lomax, 1867–1948." *Journal of American Folklore* 61 (1948): 305–6.

———. "Recollections of an Itinerant Folklorist." In *Mesquite and Willow,* edited by Mody C. Boatright, Wilson M. Hudson, and Allen Maxwell, pp. 118–28. Dallas, Tex.: Southern Methodist University Press, 1957.

———. "J. Frank Dobie, 1888–1964." *Journal of American Folklore* 78 (1965): 62–63.

———. "Reminiscences of an Octogenarian Folklorist." *Asian Folklore Studies* 27 (1968): 107–45.

Thoresen, Timothy H. H. "Folkloristics in A. L. Kroeber's Early Theory of Culture." *Journal of the Folklore Institute* 10 (1973): 41–55.

Van Dommelen, David B. "Allen Eaton: In Quest of Beauty." *American Craft* 45 (June–July 1985): 35–39.

Varesano, Angela-Marie Joanna. "Charles Godfrey Leland: The Eclectic Folklorist." Ph.D. diss., University of Pennsylvania, 1979.

Vlach, John Michael. "Holger Cahill as Folklorist." *Journal of American Folklore* 98 (1985): 148–62.

Vorpagel, Becky. "Daniel Brinton's Concept of Folklore." *New York Folklore* 9 (1983): 31–42.

Walton, David A. "Joel Chandler Harris as Folklorist: A Reassessment." *Keystone Folklore Quarterly* 11 (1966): 21–26.

Ward, Donald J. "Archer Taylor (1890–1973)." *Fabula* 15 (1974): 124–27.

Waters, Deborah Dependahl. "Philadelphia's Boswell: John Fanning Watson." *Pennsylvania Magazine of History and Biography* 98 (1974): 3–52.

Wilgus, D. K. "Francis Lee Utley (1907–1974)." *Western Folklore* 33 (1974): 202–4.

Willis, William S., Jr. "Franz Boas and the Study of Black Folklore." In *The New Ethnicity: Perspectives from Ethnology,* edited by John W. Bennett, pp. 307–34. St. Paul, Minn.: West Publishing, 1975.

Zumwalt, Rosemary. "Henry Rowe Schoolcraft, 1793–1864: His Collection and Analysis of the Oral Narratives of American Indians." *Kroeber Anthropological Society Papers,* nos. 53 and 54 (1978): 44–57.

ACCOUNTS OF MEETINGS AND EVENTS

Bassett, Fletcher S. "Department of Literature, Preliminary Address of the Committees on a Folk-Lore Congress." *Journal of American Folklore* 5 (1892): 249–50.

——. "The Folk-Lore Congress." In *The International Folk-Lore Congress of the World's Columbian Exposition*, edited by Helen Wheeler Bassett and Frederick Starr, pp. 17–23. 1898. Reprint. New York: Arno Press, 1980.

Brinton, Daniel. *Report upon the Collections Exhibited at the Columbian Historical Exposition at Madrid, 1892–1893.* Washington, D.C.: Government Printing Office, 1895.

Congrès international des traditions populaires. Paris: Bibliotheque des Annales Economiques, 1891.

Congrès international des traditions populaires. Paris: J. Maisonneuve, 1902.

Culin, Stewart. "Exhibit of Games in the Columbian Exposition." *Journal of American Folklore* 6 (1893): 205–27.

——. "Retrospect of the Folk-Lore of the Columbian Exposition." *Journal of American Folklore* 7 (1894): 51–59.

——, ed. *Brinton Memorial Meeting.* Philadelphia: American Philosophical Society, 1900.

Dorson, Richard M. "The 1962 Folklore Institute of America." *Midwest Folklore* 13 (1963): 89–96.

——. "The Anglo-American Folklore Conference." *Journal of the Folklore Institute* 7 (1970): 91–92.

——. "The UCLA Conference on American Folk Legend." *New York Folklore Quarterly* 27 (1971): 97–112.

——. "Introduction." In *Folklore in the Modern World,* edited by Richard M. Dorson, pp. 3–9. The Hague: Mouton, 1978.

Eaton, Allen. *An Exhibition of the Rural Arts.* Washington, D.C.: United States Department of Agriculture, 1937.

"Fiftieth Anniversary of the American Folk-Lore Society." *Journal of American Folklore* 51 (1938): 100–101.

"First Annual Meeting of the American Folk-Lore Society." *Journal of American Folklore* 3 (1890): 1–16.

Informal Notes on Transactions and Lectures: Second Folklore Institute of America. Bloomington: Indiana University, 1946.

Jacobs, Joseph, and Alfred Nutt, eds. *International Folk-Lore Congress: Papers and Transactions.* London: Folk-Lore Society, 1892.

Jones, Michael Owen. "Corporate Natives Confer on Culture." *American Folklore Society Newsletter* 13 (Oct. 1984): 6, 8.

Knapp, William I. "Address of Welcome on Behalf of the Chicago Folk-Lore Society." In *The International Folk-Lore Congress of the World's Columbian Exposition,* edited by Helen Wheeler Bassett and Frederick Starr, pp. 24–25. 1898. Reprint. New York: Arno Press, 1980.

Kroeber, Alfred Louis. "Folk-Lore Meetings in California." *American Anthropologist* 8 (1906): 435–36.

McNeil, William K. "The Chicago Folklore Society and the International Folklore Congress of 1893." *Midwestern Journal of Language and Folklore* 11 (1985): 5–19.

Mason, J. Alden. "Brinton Anniversary." *Journal of American Folklore* 51 (1938): 106–7.

Newell, William Wells. "Folk-Lore at the Columbian Exposition." *Journal of American Folklore* 5 (1892): 239–40.

———. "Congresses at the Columbian Exposition." *Journal of American Folklore* 5 (1892): 247–48.

———. "Resignation." *Journal of American Folklore* 14 (1901): 56.

"Proceedings of the Boston Branch." *Journal of American Folklore* 3 (1890): 77, 165–67.

"Proceedings of the California Folk-Lore Meetings, Berkeley Folk-Lore Club and the California Branch." *Journal of American Folklore* 18 (1905): 248–49, 305–11.

"Proceedings of the Cambridge Branch." *Journal of American Folklore* 6 (1893): 315–18.

"Proceedings of the Missouri Branch." *Journal of American Folklore* 21 (1908): 83–84.

"Proceedings of the Montreal Branch." *Journal of American Folklore* 5 (1892): 155–58.

"Proceedings of the Philadelphia Chapter." *Journal of the American Folklore Society* 3 (1890): 77, 164.

"Scientists Make Great Progress, Folk-Lore Is Discussed." *Philadelphia Inquirer*, 28 Dec. 1895, 3.

"Second Annual Meeting of the American Folk-Lore Society." *Journal of American Folklore* 4 (1891): 1–12.

"Third Annual Meeting of the American Folk-Lore Society." *Journal of American Folklore* 5 (1892): 1–8.

Thompson, Stith. "Local Meeting of the Texas Folk-Lore Society." *Journal of American Folklore* 28 (1915): 307.

———. "Congrès International de Folklore." *Journal of American Folklore* 51 (1938): 95–96.

———. "Folklore Conferences at Indiana University." *Journal of American Folklore* 63 (1950): 459.

———, ed. *Four Symposia on Folklore.* Bloomington: Indiana University Press, 1953.

Weigle, Marta. "CCC Charts Course for 1988–89." *American Folklore Society Newsletter* 14 (1985): 1, 5–6.

"William Wells Newell Memorial Meeting." *Journal of American Folklore* 20 (1907): 59–66.

"World's Wonder Toys at Brooklyn Museum." *Playthings* (May 1920): 105–10.

STATEMENTS OF METHOD

Abrahams, Roger D. "Folklore in Culture: Notes toward an Analytic Method." In *Readings in American Folklore,* edited by Jan Harold Brunvand, 390–403. New York: W. W. Norton, 1979.

Azbelev, S. N. "A Proposal for the International Systematization of Saints' Legends and Sagen." Translated by Ronald J. Meyer. *Folklore Forum* 10 (1977): 21–25.

Barry, Phillips. "The Collection of Folk-Song." *Journal of American Folklore* 27 (1914): 77–78.

Bascom, William R. "Folklore and Anthropology." In *The Study of Folklore,* edited by Alan Dundes, pp. 25–33. Englewood Cliffs, N.J.: Prentice-Hall, 1965.

Bassett, Fletcher S. *The Folk-Lore Manual.* Chicago: Chicago Folk-Lore Society, 1892.

Bauman, Richard. "The Field Study of Folklore in Context." In *Handbook of American Folklore,* edited by Richard M. Dorson, pp. 362–68. Bloomington: Indiana University Press, 1983.

Bausinger, Hermann. "The Renascence of Soft Methods: Being Ahead by Waiting." *Folklore Forum* 10 (1977): 1–8.

Beckwith, Martha Warren. *Folklore in America: Its Scope and Method.* Poughkeepsie, N.Y.: Vassar College, Folklore Foundation, 1931.

Bierhorst, John. "American Indian Verbal Art and the Role of the Literary Critic." *Journal of American Folklore* 88 (1975): 401–8.

Boas, Franz. "Museums of Ethnology and Their Classification." *Science* 9 (1887): 587–89.

——. "The Limitations of the Comparative Method of Anthropology." *Science* 4 (1896): 901–8.

——. "Mythology and Folklore." In *General Anthropology,* edited by Franz Boas, pp. 609–26. Boston: D. C. Heath, 1938.

Boggs, Ralph Steele. "Folklore Classification." *Southern Folklore Quarterly* 13 (1949): 161–226.

Bronner, Simon J. "Reflections on Field Research in the Folklife Sciences." *New York Folklore* 6 (1980): 151–60.

——. "The Paradox of Pride and Loathing and Other Problems." In *Foodways and Eating Habits: Directions for Research,* edited by Michael Owen Jones, Bruce Guiliano, and Roberta Krell, pp. 115–24. Los Angeles: California Folklore Society, 1981.

——. "Historical Methodology in Folklore: Introduction." *Western Folklore* 41 (1982): 28–29.

——. "Malaise or Revelation? Observations on the 'American Folklore' Polemic." *Western Folklore* 41 (1982): 52–61.

——. "Folklore and the Behavioral Sciences." *Anthropos* 79 (1984): 251–55.

——. "Researching Material Folk Culture in the Modern American City." In *American Material Culture and Folklife,* edited by Simon J. Bronner, pp. 221–35. Ann Arbor, Mich.: UMI Research Press, 1985.

——, and Stephen Stern. "American Folklore vs. Folklore in America: A Fixed Fight?" *Journal of the Folklore Institute* 17 (1980): 76–84.

Brunvand, Jan Harold. *A Guide for Collectors of Folklore in Utah.* Salt Lake City: University of Utah Press, 1971.

Burne, Charlotte Sophia. *The Handbook of Folklore.* London: Sidgwick & Jackson, 1914.

Carpenter, Inta Gale, ed. *Folklorists in the City: The Urban Field Experience.* Special Issue of *Folklore Forum,* vol. 11, no. 3, 1978.

de Caro, Francis. "Studying American Folklore in Printed Sources." In *Handbook of American Folklore,* edited by Richard M. Dorson, pp. 411–21. Bloomington: Indiana University Press, 1983.

Dorson, Richard M. "Collecting Oral Folklore in the United States." In *Buying the Wind: Regional Folklore in the United States,* edited by Richard M. Dorson, pp. 1–20. Chicago: University of Chicago Press, 1964.

——. *American Folklore and the Historian.* Chicago: University of Chicago Press, 1971.

——. "Techniques of the Folklorist." In *Folklore: Selected Essays,* by Richard M. Dorson, pp. 11–32. Bloomington: Indiana University Press, 1972.

————. "The Use of Printed Sources." In *Folklore and Folklife: An Introduction,* edited by Richard M. Dorson, pp. 465–78. Chicago: University of Chicago Press, 1972.

————. "Folklore in America vs. American Folklore." *Journal of the Folklore Institute* 15 (1978): 97–112.

————. "Rejoinder to 'American Folklore vs. Folklore in America: A Fixed Fight?'" *Journal of the Folklore Institute* 17 (1980): 85–89.

Dundes, Alan. "On The Psychology of Collecting Folklore." *Tennessee Folklore Society Bulletin* 28 (1962): 65–74.

————. "The Study of Folklore in Literature and Culture: Identification and Interpretation." *Journal of American Folklore* 78 (1965): 136–42.

————. "Ways of Studying Folklore." In *Our Living Traditions: An Introduction to American Folklore,* edited by Tristram Potter Coffin, pp. 37–47. New York: Basic Books, 1968.

————. "Metafolklore and Oral Literary Criticism." In *Essays in Folkloristics,* by Alan Dundes, pp. 38–49. Meerut, India: Folklore Institute, 1978.

Evans, E. Estyn. "The Cultural Geographer and Folklife Research." In *Folklore and Folklife,* edited by Richard M. Dorson, pp. 517–32. Chicago: University of Chicago Press, 1972.

Fenton, Alexander. "An Approach to Folk Life Studies." *Keystone Folklore Quarterly* 12 (1967): 5–21.

Ferris, William R., Jr. "The Collection of Racial Lore: Approaches and Problems." *New York Folklore Quarterly* 27 (1971): 261–79.

Folklore and Literary Criticism: A Dialogue. Special Issue of the *Journal of the Folklore Institute,* vol. 18, nos. 2 and 3, 1981.

Georges, Robert A., and Michael Owen Jones. *People Studying People: The Human Element in Fieldwork.* Berkeley: University of California Press, 1980.

Goddard, Pliny Earle. "The Relation of Folk-Lore to Anthropology." *Journal of American Folklore* 38 (1915): 18–23.

Goldberg, Christine. "The Historic-Geographic Method: Past and Future." *Journal of Folklore Research* 21 (1984): 1–18.

Goldstein, Kenneth S. *A Guide for Fieldworkers in Folklore.* Hatboro, Pa.: Folklore Associates, 1964.

Gomme, George Laurence, ed. *The Handbook of Folklore.* London: D. Nutt, 1890.

Gregory, James. "The Myth of the Male Ethnographer and the Woman's World." *American Anthropologist* 86 (1894): 316–27.

Grobman, Neil R. "Adam Ferguson's Influence on Folklore Research: The Analysis of Methodology and the Oral Epic." *Southern Folklore Quarterly* 38 (1974): 11–22.

Halpert, Herbert. "Folklore: Breadth Versus Depth." *Journal of American Folklore* 71 (1958): 97–103.

Honko, Lauri. "The Role of Fieldwork in Tradition Research." *Ethnologia Scandinavica* 7 (1977): 75–90.

————. "Methods in Folk Narrative Research." *Ethnologia Europaea* 11 (1979/80): 6–27.

Hymes, Dell. "The Contribution of Folklore to Sociolinguistic Research." *Journal of American Folklore* 84 (1971): 42–50.

Jenkins, J. Geraint. "Field-Work Documentation in Folk-Life Studies." *Journal of the Royal Anthropological Institute* 90 (1960): 250–71.

————. "The Uses of Artifacts and Folk Art in the Folk Museum." In *Folklore and Folklife: An Introduction,* edited by Richard M. Dorson, pp. 497–516. Chicago: University of Chicago Press, 1972.

Jones, Michael Owen. "Alternatives to Local (Re-) Surveys of Incidental Depth Projects." *Western Folklore* 35 (1976): 217–26.

————. "In Progress: 'Fieldwork—Theory and Self.'" *Folklore and Mythology Studies* 1 (1977): 1–22.

Kaplan, Abraham. *The Conduct of Inquiry: Methodology for Behavioral Science.* Scranton, Pa.: Chandler, 1964.

Ketner, Kenneth Laine. "The Role of Hypotheses in Folkloristics." *Journal of American Folklore* 86 (1973): 114–30.

Kirshenblatt-Gimblett, Barbara. "Studying Immigrant and Ethnic Folklore." In *Handbook of American Folklore,* edited by Richard M. Dorson, pp. 39–47. Bloomington: Indiana University Press, 1983.

Krohn, Kaarle. *Folklore Methodology.* Translated by Roger L. Welsch. Austin: University of Texas Press, 1971.

Langlois, Janet, and Philip LaRonge. "Using a Folklore Archive." In *Handbook of American Folklore,* edited by Richard M. Dorson, pp. 391–96. Bloomington: Indiana University Press, 1983.

Leach, MacEdward. "Problems of Collecting Oral Literature." *Publications of the Modern Language Association* 77 (1962): 335–40.

————, and Henry Glassie. *A Guide for Collectors of Oral Traditions and Folk Cultural Material in Pennsylvania.* Harrisburg: Pennsylvania Historical and Museum Commission, 1968.

Lindahl, Carl; J. Sanford Rikoon; and Elaine J. Lawless. *A Basic Guide to Fieldwork for Beginning Folklore Students.* Bloomington, Ind.: Folklore Publication Group Monograph Series, no. 7, 1979.

List, George. "Fieldwork: Recording Traditional Music." In *Folklore and Folklife: An Introduction,* edited by Richard M. Dorson, pp. 445–54. Chicago: University of Chicago Press, 1972.

————. "Archiving." In *Folklore and Folklife: An Introduction,* edited by Richard M. Dorson, pp. 455–64. Chicago: University of Chicago Press, 1972.

MacDonald, Donald A. "Fieldwork: Collecting Oral Literature." In *Folklore and Folklife: An Introduction,* edited by Richard M. Dorson, pp. 407–30. Chicago: University of Chicago Press, 1972.

Malinowski, Bronislaw. *A Diary in the Strict Sense of the Term.* New York: Harcourt, Brace & World, 1967.

Maniak, Angela. "Bibliographies and Indexes in American Folklore Research." In *Handbook of American Folklore,* edited by Richard M. Dorson, pp. 447–51. Bloomington: Indiana University Press, 1983.

Moore, Willard B. "Folklore Research and Museums." In *Handbook of American Folklore,* edited by Richard M. Dorson, pp. 402–10. Bloomington: Indiana University Press, 1983.

Newell, William Wells. "On The Field and Work of a Journal of American Folk-Lore." *Journal of American Folklore* 1 (1888): 3–7.

————. "Necessity of Collecting the Traditions of Native Races." *Journal of American Folklore* 1 (1888): 162–63.

————. "Additional Collection Essential to Correct Theory in Folk-Lore and Mythology." *Journal of American Folklore* 3 (1890): 23–32.

————. "The Study of Folklore." *Transactions of the New York Academy of Sciences* 9 (1890): 134–36.

———. "Topics for Collection of Folk-Lore." *Journal of American Folklore* 4 (1891): 151–58.

Nicolaisen, Wilhelm F. H. "Folklore and Geography: Towards an Atlas of American Folk Culture." *New York Folklore Quarterly* 29 (1973): 3–20.

———. "Personal Names in Traditional Ballads: A Proposal for a Ballad Onomasticon." *Journal of American Folklore* 94 (1981): 229–32.

Paredes, Américo. "On Ethnographic Work among Minority Groups: A Folklorist's Perspective." *New Scholar* 6 (1977): 1–32.

Pentikainen, Juha. "Depth Research." *Acta Ethnographica Academiae Scientiarum Hungaricae* 21 (1972): 127–51.

Philadelphia Chapter of the American Folklore Society. "Folk-Lore: Hints for the Local Study of Folk-Lore in Philadelphia and Vicinity." *Journal of American Folklore* 3 (1890): 78–80.

Powell, John Wesley. "The Interpretation of Folk-Lore." *Journal of American Folklore* 8 (1895): 1–6.

Reuss, Richard, and Ellen Stekert. "The Uses of Folklore by the Historian." *Historical Society of Michigan Chronicle* 7 (1971): 9–16.

Riedl, Norbert. "Folklore vs. 'Volkskunde.'" *Tennessee Folklore Society Bulletin* 31 (1965): 47–53.

Roberts, Warren. "Fieldwork: Recording Material Culture." In *Folklore and Folklife: An Introduction,* edited by Richard M. Dorson, pp. 431–44. Chicago: University of Chicago Press, 1972.

Schmidt, Wilhelm. *The Culture Historical Method of Ethnology: The Scientific Approach to the Racial Question.* Translated by S. A. Sieber. New York: Fortuny's Publishers, 1939.

Semple, Ellen Churchill. *Influences of Geographic Environment, On the Basis of Ratzel's System of Anthro-Geography.* New York: H. Holt, 1911.

Stahl, Sandra K. D. "Studying Folklore and American Literature." In *Handbook of American Folklore,* edited by Richard M. Dorson, pp. 422–33. Bloomington: Indiana University Press, 1983.

Thompson, Stith. *The Folktale.* 1946. Reprint. Berkeley: University of California Press, 1977.

———. "Narrative Motif-Analysis as a Folklore Method." In *Beitrage zur vergleichenden Erzahlforschung,* edited by K. Ranke, pp. 2–9. Helsinki: Folklore Fellows Communication, no. 161, 1955.

———. "Fifty Years of Folktale Indexing." In *Humaniora: Essays in Literature, Folklore, Bibliography,* pp. 49–57. Locust Valley, N.Y.: J. J. Augustin, 1960.

Titon, Jeff Todd. "The Life Story." *Journal of American Folklore* 93 (1980): 276–92.

———. "Stance, Role, and Identity in Fieldwork among Folk Baptists and Pentecostals." *American Music* 3 (1985): 16–24.

Toelken, Barre. *The Dynamics of Folklore.* Boston: Houghton Mifflin, 1979.

Tokarev, Sergeij A. "Toward a Methodology for the Ethnographic Study of Material Culture." Translated by Peter Voorheis. In *American Material Culture and Folklife,* edited by Simon J. Bronner, pp. 77–96. Ann Arbor, Mich.: UMI Research Press, 1985.

Tylor, Edward. *Anthropology: An Introduction to the Study of Man and Civilization.* 1881. Reprint. New York: D. Appleton, 1904.

―――. "On a Method of Investigating the Development of Institutions; Applied to Laws of Marriage and Descent." *Journal of the Royal Anthropological Institute* 18 (1889): 245–69.

van Gennep, Arnold. *Folklore.* Translated by Austin Fife. Middletown, Pa.: Folklore Historian, 1985.

Vlach, John Michael. "The Concept of Community and Folklife Study." In *American Material Culture and Folklife,* edited by Simon J. Bronner, pp. 63–76. Ann Arbor: UMI Research Press, 1985.

Wildhaber, Robert. "Folk Atlas Mapping." In *Folklore and Folklife: An Introduction,* edited by Richard M. Dorson, pp. 479–96. Chicago: University of Chicago Press, 1972.

Wilgus, D. K. "Collecting Musical Folklore and Folksong." In *Handbook of American Folklore,* edited by Richard M. Dorson, pp. 369–75. Bloomington: Indiana University Press, 1983.

STATEMENTS OF THEORY

Abrahams, Roger D. "Introductory Remarks to a Rhetorical Theory of Folklore." *Journal of American Folklore* 81 (1968): 143–58.

―――. "Folklore and Literature as Performance." *Journal of the Folklore Institute* 9 (1972): 75–94.

―――. "Toward an Enactment-Centered Theory of Folklore." In *Frontiers of Folklore,* edited by William Bascom, pp. 79–120. Boulder, Colo.: Westview Press, 1977.

―――. "Interpreting Folklore Ethnographically and Sociologically." In *Handbook of American Folklore,* edited by Richard M. Dorson, pp. 345–50. Bloomington: Indiana University Press, 1983.

Armstrong, Robert Plant. "What's Red, White, and Blue and Syndetic?" *Journal of American Folklore* 95 (1982): 327–46.

Bascom, William R. "The Myth-Ritual Theory." *Journal of American Folklore* 70 (1957): 103–14.

―――. "Four Functions of Folklore." In *The Study of Folklore,* edited by Alan Dundes, pp. 279–98. Englewood Cliffs, N.J.: Prentice-Hall, 1965.

―――. "Folklore, Verbal Art, and Culture." *Journal of American Folklore* 83 (1973): 374–81.

―――, ed. *Frontiers of Folklore.* Boulder, Colo.: Westview Press, 1977.

Bauman, Richard. "Towards a Behavioral Theory of Folklore." *Journal of American Folklore* 82 (1969): 167–70.

―――. *Verbal Art as Performance.* Rowley, Mass.: Newbury House, 1977.

―――, and Américo Paredes, eds. *Toward New Pespectives in Folklore.* Austin: University of Texas Press, 1972.

Ben-Amos, Dan. "The Context of Folklore: Implications and Prospects." In *Frontiers of Folklore,* edited by William Bascom, pp. 36–53. Boulder, Colo.: Westview, 1977.

―――. "The Ceremony of Innocence." *Western Folklore* 83 (1979): 47–52.

Blair, John G. "Structuralism, American Studies, and the Humanities." *American Quarterly* 30 (1978): 261–81.

Bringeus, Nils-Arvid. "The Communicative Aspect in Ethnology and Folklore." *Ethnologia Scandinavica* 9 (1979): 5–17.

Bronner, Simon J. " 'Learning of the People': Folkloristics in the Study of Behavior and Thought." *New York Folklore* 9 (1983): 75–88.

————. "Toward a Philosophy of Folk Objects." In *Personal Places: Perspectives on Informal Art Environments,* edited by Daniel Ward, pp. 171–77. Bowling Green, Ohio: Bowling Green State University Popular Press, 1984.

Burns, Thomas A. "Folkloristics: A Conception of Theory." *Western Folklore* 36 (1977): 109–34.

Carvalho-Neto, Paulo de. *The Concept of Folklore.* Coral Gables, Fla.: University of Miami Press, 1971.

Cashion, Gerald, ed. *Conceptual Problems in Contemporary Folklore Study.* Folklore Forum Bibliographic and Special Series, no. 12, 1974.

Chomsky, Noam. *Reflections on Language.* New York: Pantheon, 1975.

Crane, T. F. "The Diffusion of Popular Tales." *Journal of American Folklore* 1 (1888): 8–15.

Davis, Kingsley. "The Myth of Functional Analysis as a Special Method in Sociology and Anthropology." *American Sociological Review* 24 (1959): 757–72.

Dégh, Linda. "The Biology of Storytelling." *Folklore Preprint Series,* vol. 7 (Mar. 1979).

Dolgin, Janet L.; David S. Kemnitzer; and David M. Schneider, eds. *Symbolic Anthropology: A Reader in the Study of Symbols and Meanings.* New York: Columbia University Press, 1977.

Dorson, Richard M. "Theories of Myth and the Folklorist." *Daedalus* 88 (1959): 280–90.

Drobin, Ulf. "Commentaries on Structuralism and Folklore." *Studia Fennica* 20 (1976): 107–9.

Dundes, Alan. "From Etic to Emic Units in the Structural Study of Folktales." *Journal of American Folklore* 75 (1962): 95–105.

————. "The Devolutionary Premise in Folklore Theory." *Journal of the Folklore Institute* 6 (1969): 5–19.

————. *Analytic Essays in Folklore.* The Hague: Mouton, 1975.

————. "Structuralism and Folklore." *Studia Fennica* 20 (1976): 75–93.

————. "Projection in Folklore: A Plea for Psychoanalytic Semiotics." *Modern Language Notes* 91 (1976): 1500–1533. Reprinted in *Interpreting Folklore,* by Alan Dundes, pp. 33–61. Bloomington: Indiana University Press, 1980.

————, ed. *Sacred Narrative: Readings in the Theory of Myth.* Berkeley: University of California Press, 1984.

Edwards, Carol L. "The Parry-Lord Theory Meets Operational Structuralism." *Journal of American Folklore* 96 (1983): 151–69.

Ellis, A. B. "Evolution in Folklore." *Popular Science Monthly* 48 (1895): 93–104.

Farrer, J. A. "Comparative Folk-lore." *Cornhill Magazine* 33 (1876): 41–60.

Fine, Elizabeth C. *The Folklore Text: From Performance to Print.* Bloomington: Indiana University Press, 1984.

Fine, Gary Alan. "Evaluating Psychoanalytic Folklore: Are Freudians Ever Right?" *New York Folklore* 10 (1984): 5–20.

————. "Negotiated Orders and Organizational Cultures." *Annual Review of Sociology* 10 (1984): 239–62.

————. "The Third Force in Folkloristics: The Situational and Structural Properties of Tradition." Paper read at the American Folklore Society meeting, Cincinnati, Ohio, 1985.

Fiske, John. "Evolution of Language." North American Review 97 (1863): 450–61.

Foster, John Wilson. "The Plight of Current Folklore Theory." Southern Folklore Quarterly 32 (1968): 237–48.

Gardner, Howard. The Quest for Mind: Piaget, Lévi-Strauss, and the Structuralist Movement. New York: Vintage, 1972.

Geertz, Clifford. "Thick Description: Toward an Interpretive Theory of Culture." In The Interpretation of Cultures, by Clifford Geertz, pp. 3–30. New York: Basic Books, 1973.

Georges, Robert A. "Toward an Understanding of Storytelling Events." Journal of American Folklore 82 (1969): 313–28.

———. "Toward a Resolution of the Text/Context Controversy." Western Folklore 39 (1980): 34–40.

Glassie, Henry. "Structure and Function, Folklore and the Artifact." Semiotica 7 (1973): 313–51.

Goffman, Erving. The Presentation of Self in Everyday Life. Garden City, N.Y.: Doubleday, 1959.

———. Behavior in Public Places: Notes on the Social Organization of Gatherings. New York: Free Press, 1963.

Gomme, George Laurence. Ethnology in Folklore. London: K. Paul, Trench, Trubner, & Co., 1892.

———. Folklore as an Historical Science. London: Methuen, 1908.

Gray, Asa. Darwiniana: Essays and Reviews Pertaining to Darwinism. New York: D. Appleton, 1888.

Green, Archie. "Interpreting Folklore Ideologically." In Handbook of American Folklore, edited by Richard M. Dorson, pp. 351–58. Bloomington: Indiana University Press, 1983.

Gregg, Dorothy, and Elgin Williams. "The Dismal Science of Functionalism." American Anthropologist 50 (1948): 594–611.

Hale, Horatio. Ethnography and Philology. Philadelphia: C. Sherman, 1846.

———. "'Above' and 'Below': A Mythological Disease of Language." Journal of American Folklore 3 (1890): 177–90.

Harris, Marvin. Cultural Materialism: The Struggle for a Science of Culture. New York: Vintage Books, 1979.

Hodgen, Margaret. "Geographical Diffusion as a Criterion of Age." American Anthropologist 44 (1942): 345–68.

Honko, Lauri. "Empty Texts, Full Meanings: On Transformal Meaning in Folklore." Journal of Folklore Research 22 (1985): 37–44.

Hymes, Dell. "The Ethnography of Speaking." In Anthropology and Human Behavior, edited by T. Gladwin and W. C. Sturtevant, pp. 13–53. Washington, D.C.: Anthropological Society of Washington, 1962.

———. "Introduction: Toward Ethnographies of Communication." American Anthropologist 66 (1964): 1–34.

Jain, Ravindra K., ed. Text and Context: The Social Anthropology of Tradition. Philadelphia: Institute for the Study of Human Issues, 1977.

Jakobson, Roman, and Petr Bogatyrev. "Folklore as a Special Form of Creation." Translated by John M. O'Hara. Folklore Forum 13 (1980): 1–22.

Janelli, Roger L. "Toward A Reconciliation of Micro- and Macro-Level Analyses of Folklore." Folklore Forum 9 (1976): 59–66.

Jansen, William Hugh. "The Esoteric-Exoteric Factor in Folklore." In The Study of Folklore, edited by Alan Dundes, pp. 43–51. Englewood Cliffs, N.J.: Prentice-Hall, 1965.

Jarvie, I. C. "On the Limits of Symbolic Interpretation in Anthropology." *Current Anthropology* 17 (1976): 687–701.

Jones, Michael Owen. "Another America: Toward a Behavioral History Based on Folkloristics." *Western Folklore* 41 (1982): 43–51.

Jones, Steven. "Slouching towards Ethnography: The Text/Context Controversy Reconsidered." *Western Folklore* 38 (1979): 42–47.

Ketner, Kenneth Laine. "Identity and Existence in the Study of Human Traditions." *Folklore* 87 (1976): 192–200.

Kroeber, Alfred Louis. *Anthropology: Culture Patterns and Processes.* 1923. Reprint. New York: Harcourt, Brace & World, 1968.

la Barre, Weston. "Folklore and Psychology." *Journal of American Folklore* 61 (1948): 382–90.

Leach, Edmund. *Culture and Communication: The Logic by Which Symbols Are Connected.* Cambridge: Cambridge University Press, 1976.

Levin, Judith. "The Text Is Not a Thing: The Not-So-Grand Dichotomy Reconsidered." *New York Folklore* 8 (1982): 49–58.

Lévi-Strauss, Claude. *Structural Anthropology.* Translated by Claire Jacobson and Brooke Grundfest Schoepf. Garden City, N.Y.: Doubleday, 1967.

Lomax, Alan. *Folk Song Style and Culture.* 1968. Reprint. New Brunswick, N.J.: Transaction Books, 1978.

Lubbock, John. *The Origin of Civilisation and the Primitive Condition of Man.* 1870. Reprint. Chicago: University of Chicago Press, 1978.

Malinowski, Bronislaw. "Culture as a Determinant of Behavior." In *Factors Determining Human Behavior,* pp. 133–68. Cambridge: Harvard University, 1936.

———. *A Scientific Theory of Culture.* Chapel Hill: University of North Carolina Press, 1944.

Manly, John Matthews. "Literary Forms and the New Theory of the Origin of the Species." *Modern Philology* 4 (1907): 577–95.

Maranda, Elli-Kaija. "The Concept of Folklore." *Midwest Folklore* 13 (1963): 69–87.

———, and Pierre Maranda. "Structural Models in Folklore." *Midwest Folklore* 12 (1962): 133–92.

Maranda, Pierre, and Elli-Kaija Köngäs Maranda, eds. *Structural Analysis of Oral Tradition.* Philadelphia: University of Pennsylvania Press, 1971.

Mason, Otis. "The Natural History of Folklore." *Journal of American Folklore* 4 (1891): 97–105.

Meletinsky, E. M. "Perspective et limites de l'étude structural du folklore." *Studia Fennica* 20 (1976): 94–101.

Merton, Robert K. *Social Theory and Social Structure: Toward the Codification of Theory and Research.* Glencoe, Ill.: Free Press, 1949.

Murase, Anne. "Personality and Lore." *Western Folklore* 34 (1975): 171–86.

Newell, William Wells. "Individual and Collective Characteristics in Folk-Lore." *Journal of American Folklore* 19 (1906): 1–15.

Nicolaisen, Wilhelm F. H. "Variant, Dialect, and Region: An Exploration in the Geography of Tradition." *New York Folklore* 6 (1980): 137–49.

Nikiforov, A. I. "Towards a Morphological Study of the Folktale." In *The Study of Russian Folklore,* edited and translated by Felix J. Oinas and Stephen Soudakoff, pp. 155–62. The Hague: Mouton, 1975.

Olrik, Axel. "Epic Laws of Folk Narrative." In *The Study of Folklore,* edited by Alan Dundes, pp. 129–41. Englewood Cliffs, N.J.: Prentice-Hall, 1965.

Oring, Elliott. "Three Functions of Folklore: Traditional Functionalism as Explanation in Folkloristics." *Journal of American Folklore* 81 (1976): 67–80.

———. "Traditional Functionalism: Once More with Feeling." *Journal of American Folklore* 90 (1977): 73–75.

———. "Dyadic Traditions." *Journal of Folklore Research* 21 (1984): 19–28.

Pace, David. "Beyond Morphology: Lévi-Strauss and the Analysis of Folktales." *Folklore Forum* 10 (1977): 1–7.

Pike, Kenneth. *Language in Relation to a Unified Theory of the Structure of Human Behavior.* The Hague: Mouton, 1967.

Powell, John Wesley. "The Lessons of Folklore." *American Anthropologist* 2 (1900): 1–36.

———. "Introduction." In *Zuñi Folk Tales*, by Frank Hamilton Cushing, pp. vii–xvii. New York: G. P. Putnam's Sons, 1901.

Propp, Vladimir. *Morphology of the Folktale.* 2d ed. Translated by Laurence Scott and revised by Louis A. Wagner. Austin: University of Texas Press, 1968.

Radcliffe-Brown, A. R. "On the Concept of Function in Social Science." *American Anthropologist* 37 (1935): 394–402.

Ratzel, Friedrich. *The History of Mankind (Völkerkunde).* 3 vols. Translated by A. J. Butley. London: Macmillan, 1896–98.

Redfield, Robert. "The Natural History of the Folk Society." *Social Forces* 31 (1953): 224–28.

"Rival Folklore Theories." *Academy and Literature* 52 (1897): 124–25.

Scholes, Robert. *Structuralism in Literature.* New Haven, Conn.: Yale University Press, 1974.

Segal, Dmitri. "Folklore, Text, and Social Context." *PTL: A Journal for Descriptive Poetics and Theory of Literature* 1 (1976): 367–82.

Skeels, Dell. "Two Psychological Patterns Underlying the Morphologies of Propp and Dundes." *Southern Folklore Quarterly* 31 (1967): 244–61.

Sumner, William Graham. *Folkways: A Study of the Sociological Importance of Usages, Manners, Customs, Mores and Morals.* Boston: Ginn, 1906.

Sydow, Carl W. von. *Selected Papers on Folklore.* Copenhagen: Rosenkilde & Bagger, 1948.

Tylor, Edward Burnett. *The Origins of Culture* and *Religion in Primitive Culture* (Primitive Culture). 1871. Reprint. Gloucester, Mass.: Peter Smith, 1970.

Utley, Francis Lee. "The Migration of Folktales: Four Channels to the Americas." *Current Anthropology* 15 (1974): 5–27.

———. "The Folktale: Life History vs. Structuralism." In *Varia Folklorica*, edited by Alan Dundes, pp. 1–22. The Hague: Mouton, 1978.

Walle, Alf H. "On the Role of Functionalism in Contemporary Folkloristics." *Journal of American Folklore* 90 (1977): 68–72.

Wax, Murray. "The Limitations of Boas' Anthropology." *American Anthropologist* 58 (1956): 63–74.

White, Leslie. "History, Evolutionism, and Functionalism: Three Types of Interpretation of Culture." *Southwestern Journal of Anthropology* 1 (1945): 221–48.

———. " 'Diffusion vs. Evolution': An Anti-Evolutionist Fallacy." *American Anthropologist* 47 (1945): 339–56.

———. "The Social Organization of Ethnological Theory." *Rice University Studies* 52 (1966): 1–66.

Wilgus, D. K. "'The Text is the Thing.'" *Journal of American Folklore* 86 (1973): 241–52.

Wilson, William A. "The Evolutionary Premise in Folklore Theory and the 'Finnish Method.'" *Western Folklore* 35 (1976): 241–49.

———. "Richard M. Dorson's Theory for American Folklore: A Finnish Analogue." *Western Folklore* 41 (1982): 36–42.

Young, Katharine. "The Notion of Context." *Western Folklore* 44 (1985): 122–32.

Zan, Yigal. "The Text/Context Controversy: An Explanatory Perspective." *Western Folklore* 41 (1982): 1–27.

Zipes, Jack. *Breaking the Magic Spell: Radical Theories of Folk and Fairy Tales.* Austin: University of Texas Press, 1979.

COLLECTIONS

Allies, Jabez. *The British, Roman, and Saxon Antiquities and Folk-Lore of Worcestershire.* 2d ed. London: John Russell Smith, 1856.

Babcock, W. H. "Charms for Young Women." *Journal of American Folklore* 1 (1888): 164–65.

Baker, Ronald. *Folklore in the Writings of Rowland E. Robinson.* Bowling Green, Ohio: Bowling Green State University Popular Press, 1973.

———. *Hoosier Folk Legends.* Bloomington: Indiana University Press, 1982.

Bassett, Fletcher S. *Legends and Superstitions of the Sea and of Sailors.* 1885. Reprint. Detroit: Singing Tree Press, 1971.

Bayard, Samuel P., ed. *Dance to the Fiddle, March to the Fife: Instrumental Folk Tunes in Pennsylvania.* University Park: Pennsylvania State University Press, 1982.

Bergen, Fanny. "On the Eastern Shore." *Journal of American Folklore* 2 (1889): 295–300.

———. *Animal and Plant Lore.* Memoirs of the American Folklore Society, no. 7, 1899.

Blair, Walter, and Franklin J. Meine. *Mike Fink: King of the Mississippi Keelboatmen.* 1933. Reprint. Westport, Conn.: Greenwood, 1971.

Boas, Franz. *The Social Organization and the Secret Societies of the Kwakiutl Indians.* Report of the United States National Museum for 1895. Washington, D.C.: Government Printing Office, 1897.

———. *Kwakiutl Tales.* New York: Columbia University Press, 1910.

———. *Tsmishian Mythology.* 1916. Reprint. New York: Johnson Reprint, 1970.

Boatright, Mody C. *Folklore of the Oil Industry.* Dallas, Tex.: Southern Methodist University Press, 1963.

Botkin, Benjamin A., ed. *A Treasury of American Folklore.* New York: Crown, 1944.

———. *A Treasury of New England Folklore.* New York: Crown, 1947.

———. *A Treasury of Southern Folklore.* New York: Crown, 1949.

———. *New York City Folklore.* New York: Random House, 1956.

Brendle, Rev. Thomas R., and William S. Troxell. *Pennsylvania German Folk Tales, Legends, Once-upon-a-Time Stories, Maxims, and Sayings.* Norristown: Pennsylvania German Society, 1944.

Brewer, John Mason. "Negro Preacher Tales from the Texas 'Brazos Bottoms.'" Master's thesis, Indiana University, 1949.

Brinton, Daniel Garrison. "Reminiscences of Pennsylvania Folk-Lore." *Journal of American Folklore* 5 (1892): 177–85.

Campbell, Marie. "Survivals of Old Folk Drama in the Kentucky Mountains." *Journal of American Folklore* 51 (1938): 10–24.

———. "Olden Tales from across the Ocean Waters: A Collection of Seventy-Eight European Folktales from the Oral Tradition of Six Eastern Kentucky Narrators." Ph.D. diss., Indiana University, 1956.

Coffin, Tristram Potter, and Hennig Cohen, eds. *Folklore in America*. Garden City, N.Y.: Doubleday, 1966.

———. *Folklore from the Working Folk of America*. Garden City, N.Y.: Doubleday, 1974.

Crane, Thomas Frederick. *Italian Popular Tales*. Boston: Houghton Mifflin, 1883.

Culin, Stewart. *Korean Games, with Notes on the Corresponding Games of China and Japan*. Philadelphia: University of Pennsylvania Press, 1895.

———. "A Summer Trip among the Western Indians." *Bulletin of the Free Museum of Science and Art* 3 (1901): 1–175.

———. *Games of the North American Indians*. 1907. Reprint. New York: Dover, 1975.

Currier, John McNab. "Contributions to the Folk-Lore of New England." *Journal of American Folklore* 2 (1889): 291–94.

Curtin, Jeremiah. "European Folk-Lore in the United States." *Journal of American Folklore* 2 (1889): 56–59.

———. *Myths and Folk-Lore of Ireland*. Boston: Little, Brown, & Co., 1890.

Cushing, Frank Hamilton. "My Adventures in Zuñi." *Century Illustrated Monthly Magazine* 25 (1882): 191–207, 500–511; 26 (1883): 28–47.

———. *Zuñi Folk Tales*. New York: G. P. Putnam's Sons, 1901.

Dorson, Richard M. *Davy Crockett, American Comic Legend*. New York: Rockland Editions, 1939.

———. *Jonathan Draws the Long Bow: New England Popular Tales and Legends*. Cambridge: Harvard University Press, 1946.

———. *Bloodstoppers and Bearwalkers: Folk Tales of Immigrants, Lumberjacks, and Indians*. Cambridge: Harvard University Press, 1952.

———, ed. *Buying the Wind: Regional Folklore in the United States*. Chicago: University of Chicago Press, 1964.

———. *American Negro Folktales*. New York: Fawcett, 1967.

———. *America in Legend: Folklore from the Colonial Period to the Present*. New York: Pantheon, 1973.

Eaton, Allen. "American Folk Arts." *Studio* 27 (June 1944): 201–3.

———, and Lucinda Crile. *Rural Handicrafts in the United States*. Washington, D.C.: United States Department of Agriculture, 1946.

Farrer, James A. *Primitive Manners and Customs*. London: Chatto & Windus, 1879.

Fletcher, Alice C. "Glimpses of Child-life among the Omaha Tribe of Indians." *Journal of American Folklore* 1 (1888): 115–23.

Gardner, Emelyn E. *Folklore from the Schoharie Hills*. Ann Arbor: University of Michigan Press, 1937.

Gibbons, Phebe Earle. *"Pennsylvania Dutch," and Other Essays*. Philadelphia: J. B. Lippincott, 1882.

Halpert, Herbert. "Folktales and Legends from the New Jersey Pines: A Collection and a Study." Ph.D. diss., Indiana University, 1947.

Hark, Ann. *Hex Marks the Spot in the Pennsylvania Dutch Country.* Philadelphia: J. B. Lippincott, 1938.

Hearn, Lafcadio. *Some Chinese Ghosts.* Boston: Roberts Bros., 1887.

––––––. "Out of the Street: Japanese Folk Songs." *Atlantic Monthly* 73 (1896): 347–51.

Henderson, William. *Notes on the Folklore of the Northern Counties of England and the Borders.* London: W. Satchell, 1866.

Hoffman, W. J. "Folk-Lore of the Pennsylvania Germans." *Journal of American Folklore* 1 (1888): 125–35.

Hurston, Zora Neale. *Mules and Men: Negro Folktales and Voodoo Practices in the South.* 1935. Reprint. New York: Harper & Row, 1970.

Hyatt, Harry Middleton. *Folk-Lore from Adams County, Illinois.* New York: Alma Egan Hyatt Foundation, 1935.

Jansen, William Hugh. "Abraham 'Oregon' Smith: Pioneer, Folk Hero, and Tale Teller." Ph.D. diss., Indiana University, 1949.

Knortz, Karl. *Zur Amerikanischen Volkskunde.* Tubingen: H. Laupp'sche Buchhandlung, 1905.

Korson, George. *Black Rock: Mining Folklore of the Pennsylvania Dutch.* Baltimore, Md.: Johns Hopkins University Press, 1960.

Kroeber, A. L. *Yurok Myths.* Berkeley: University of California Press, 1978.

Lomax, John A., and Alan Lomax. *American Ballads and Folk Songs.* New York: Macmillan, 1934.

Mercer, Henry C. "Folklore: Notes Taken at Random." *A Collection of Papers Read before the Bucks County Historical Society,* vol. 2, pp. 406–16. Riegelsville, Pa.: B. F. Fackentahl, 1909.

––––––. "The Tools of the Nation Maker." *A Collection of Papers Read before the Bucks County Historical Society,* vol. 3, pp. 469–81. Riegelsville, Pa.: B. F. Fackenthal, 1909.

Mitchell, Edwin Valentine. *It's an Old Pennsylvania Custom.* New York: Bonanza Books, 1948.

Moore, Arthur K. "Specimens of the Folktales from Some Antebellum Newspapers of Louisiana." *Louisiana Historical Quarterly* 32 (1949): 723–58.

Morgan, Lewis Henry. *League of the Ho-de-no-sau-nee, or Iroquois.* 1851. Reprint. New York: Corinth Books, 1962.

Phillips, Henry, Jr. "First Contribution to the Folklore of Philadelphia and Its Vicinity." *Proceedings of the American Philosophical Society* 25 (1888): 159–70.

Pound, Louise. *Nebraska Folklore.* Lincoln: University of Nebraska Press, 1959.

Randolph, Vance. *Ozark Magic and Folklore.* 1947. Reprint. New York: Dover, 1964.

––––––. *We Always Lie to Strangers: Tall Tales from the Ozarks.* New York: Columbia University Press, 1951.

––––––. *The Devil's Pretty Daughter, and Other Ozark Folk Tales.* New York: Columbia University Press, 1955.

––––––. *Sticks in the Knapsack, and Other Ozark Folk Tales.* New York: Columbia University Press, 1958.

————. *Hot Springs and Hell, and Other Folk Jests and Anecdotes from the Ozarks*. Hatboro, Pa.: Folklore Associates, 1965.

————. *Pissing in the Snow, and Other Ozark Folk Tales*. Urbana: University of Illinois Press, 1976.

Reuss, Richard A. " 'That Can't Be Alan Dundes. Alan Dundes is Taller than That!' The Folklore of Folklorists." *Journal of American Folklore* 87 (1974): 303–17.

Roberts, Leonard. *South from Hell-fer-Sartin: Kentucky Mountain Folk Tales*. Lexington: University of Kentucky Press, 1955.

————. *Up Cutshin and Down Greasy: Folkways of a Kentucky Mountain Family*. Lexington: University of Kentucky Press, 1959.

Rush, Benjamin. *An Account of the Manners of the German Inhabitants of Pennsylvania*. Annotated by Theodore E. Schmauk. 1789. Reprint. Lancaster, Pa.: Pennsylvania-German Society, 1910.

Schoolcraft, Henry Rowe. *Algic Researches: Comprising Inquiries Respecting the Mental Characteristics of the North American Indians*. 2 vols. New York: Harper & Bros., 1839.

————. *Notes on the Iroquois; Or Contributions to American History, Antiquities, and General Ethnology*. Albany, N.Y.: Erastus H. Pease, 1847.

————. *Personal Memoirs of a Residence of Thirty Years with the Indian Tribes of the American Frontiers*. Philadelphia: Lippincott, Grambo, & Co., 1851.

————. *The Myth of Hiawatha and Other Oral Legends, Mythologic and Allegoric, of the North American Indians*. Philadelphia: J. B. Lippincott, 1856.

Scott, Walter, ed. *Minstrelsy of the Scottish Border*. 1802. Reprint. New York: Thomas Y. Crowell, 1931.

————. *Letters on Demonology and Witchcraft*. London: Murray, 1830.

————. *Northern Antiquities, or, An Historical Account of the Manners, Customs, Religion, and Laws, Maritime Expeditions and Discoveries, Language and Literature of the Ancient Scandinavians*. London: H. G. Bohn, 1847.

Sternberg, Thomas. *The Dialect and Folk-Lore of Northamptonshire*. London: J. R. Smith, 1851.

Thompson, Harold W. *Body, Boots and Britches: Folktales, Ballads and Speech from Country New York*. 1939. Reprint. Syracuse, N.Y.: Syracuse University Press, 1979.

Thoms, William John. *Lays and Legends of Various Nations, Illustrative of Their Traditions, Popular Literature, Manners, Customs and Superstitions*. London: G. Lowie, 1834.

————, ed. *Anecdotes and Traditions, Illustrative of Early English History and Literature*. London: J. B. Nichols & Son, 1839.

————. *Choice Notes from "Notes and Queries": Folk-Lore*. London: G. Bell, 1859.

Wagner, Leopold. *Manners, Customs, and Observances: Their Origin and Signification*. London: W. Heinemann, 1894.

Walsh, William S. *Curiosities of Popular Customs and of Rites, Ceremonies, Observances, and Miscellaneous Antiquities*. Philadelphia: J. B. Lippincott, 1898.

Ward, Donald, ed. and trans. *The German Legends of the Brothers Grimm*. 2 vols. Philadelphia: Institute for the Study of Human Issues, 1981.

Watson, John F. *Annals of Philadelphia and Pennsylvania in the Olden Time*. 2 vols. 1830. Rev. ed. Philadelphia: Elijah Thomas, 1857.

————. *Annals of Philadelphia and Pennsylvania in the Olden Time.* 3 vols. Enlarged by Willis P. Hazard. 1830. Rev. ed. Philadelphia: Edwin S. Stuart, 1891.

————. *Historic Tales of the Olden Time, Containing Olden Time Researches and Reminiscences of New York City.* New York: G. & C. Carvyl, 1832.

————. *Historic Tales of Olden Time, Concerning the Early Settlement and Progress of Philadelphia and Pennsylvania.* Philadelphia: E. Littell & T. Holden, 1833.

Williams, Phyllis H. *South Italian Folkways in Europe and America.* 1938. Reprint. New York: Russell & Russell, 1969.

STUDIES

Abrahams, Roger D. *Deep Down in the Jungle: Negro Narrative Folklore from the Streets of Philadelphia.* Hatboro, Pa.: Folklore Associates, 1964. 2d ed. Chicago: Aldine Publishing, 1970.

————. "The Negro Stereotype: Negro Folklore and the Riots." In *The Urban Experience and Folk Tradition,* edited by Américo Paredes and Ellen Stekert, pp. 69–85. Austin: University of Texas Press, 1971.

————. "Negotiating Respect: Patterns of Presentation among Black Women." *Journal of American Folklore* 88 (1975): 58–63.

————. "The Most Embarrassing Thing That Ever Happened: Conversational Stories in a Theory of Enactment." *Folklore Forum* 10 (1977): 9–15.

————. "Storytelling Events: Wake Amusements and the Structure of Nonsense on St. Vincent." *Journal of American Folklore* 95 (1982): 389–414.

————, and Alan Dundes. "On Elephantasy and Elephanticide." *Psychoanalytic Review* 56 (1969): 225–41.

————; Kenneth Goldstein; Wayland D. Hand, eds. *By Land and by Sea: Studies in the Folklore of Work and Leisure, Honoring Horace P. Beck on his Sixty–fifth Birthday.* Hatboro, Pa.: Legacy Books, 1985.

Bachofen, J. J. *Myths, Religion, and Mother Right.* Translated by Ralph Manheim. Princeton, N.J.: Princeton University Press, 1967.

Baker, Ronald L. "The Influence of Mass Culture on Modern Legends." *Southern Folklore Quarterly* 40 (1976): 367–76.

Bascom, William Russell. *Ifa Divination: Communication between Gods and Men in West Africa.* Bloomington: Indiana University Press, 1969.

————. *Contributions to Folkloristics.* Meerut, India: Folklore Institute, 1981.

Bauman, Richard, and Roger D. Abrahams, eds. *"And Other Neighborly Names": Social Process and Cultural Image in Texas Folklore.* Austin: University of Texas Press, 1981.

Bauman, Richard, and Joel Sherzer, eds. *Explorations in the Ethnography of Speaking.* Cambridge: Cambridge University Press, 1974.

Ben-Amos, Dan. *Sweet Words: Storytelling Events in Benin.* Philadelphia: Institute for the Study of Human Issues, 1975.

————, ed. *Folklore Genres.* Austin: University of Texas Press, 1976.

————, and Kenneth S. Goldstein, eds. *Folklore: Performance and Communication.* The Hague: Mouton, 1975.

Boas, Franz. *Baffin-Land: Geographische Ergebnisse einer in den Jahren 1883 und 1884 ausgeführten Forschungsreise.* Gotha, Ger.: Justus Perthes, 1885.

———. *The Central Eskimo*. Report of the Bureau of American Ethnology 1884–85. Washington, D.C.: Smithsonian Institution, 1888.

———. "Dissemination of Tales among the Natives of North America." *Journal of American Folklore* 4 (1891): 13–20.

———. "The Ethnological Significance of Esoteric Doctrines." *Science*, n.s., 16 (1902): 872–74.

———. *Race, Language and Culture*. New York: Free Press, 1940.

———. *A Franz Boas Reader: The Shaping of American Anthropology, 1883–1911*. Edited by George W. Stocking, Jr. Chicago: University of Chicago Press, 1974.

Bogoras, Waldemar. "The Folk-Lore of Northeastern Asia as Compared with that of Northwestern America." *American Anthropologist* 4 (1902): 577–683.

Brinton, Daniel G. *Essays of an Americanist*. Philadelphia: Porter & Coates, 1890.

———. *The Myths of the New World: A Treatise on the Symbolism and Mythology of the Red Race of America*. Philadelphia: D. McKay, 1896.

———. *Religions of Primitive Peoples*. New York: G. P. Putnam's Sons, 1897.

———. *The Basis of Social Relations*. Edited by Livingston Farrand. New York: Putnam, 1902.

Bronner, Simon J. " 'Let Me Tell It My Way': Joke Telling by a Father and Son." In *Humor and the Individual*, edited by Elliott Oring, pp. 18–36. Los Angeles: California Folklore Society, 1984.

———. "Folklore in the Bureaucracy." In *Tools for Management*, edited by Frederick Richmond and Kathy Nazar, pp. 45–57. Harrisburg, Pa.: PEN Publications, 1984.

———. *Chain Carvers: Old Men Crafting Meaning*. Lexington: University Press of Kentucky, 1985.

———, ed. *American Material Culture and Folklife*. Ann Arbor, Mich.: UMI Research Press, 1985.

———. *Grasping Things: Folk Material Culture and Mass Society in America*. Lexington: University Press of Kentucky, 1986.

Brunvand, Jan Harold. "The Study of Contemporary Folklore: Jokes." *Fabula* 13 (1972): 1–19.

Burlakoff, Nikolai, and Carl Lindahl, eds. *Folklore on Two Continents: Essays in Honor of Linda Dégh*. Bloomington, Ind.: Trickster Press, 1980.

Burns, Thomas A. "Fifty Seconds of Play: Expressive Interaction in Context." *Western Folklore* 37 (1978): 1–29.

———, and J. Stephen Smith. "The Symbolism of Becoming in the Sunday Service of an Urban Black Holiness Church." *Anthropological Quarterly* 51 (1978): 185–204.

Chamberlain, Alexander F. *The Child and Childhood in Folk-Thought*. New York: Macmillan, 1896.

———. "Mythology and Folklore of Invention." *Journal of American Folklore* 17 (1904): 14–22.

Crane, Thomas Frederick. *Italian Social Customs of the Sixteenth Century, and Their Influence on the Literatures of Europe*. New Haven, Conn.: Yale University Press, 1920.

Culin, Stewart. *China in America: A Study in the Social Life of the Chinese in the Eastern Cities of the United States*. Philadelphia: privately printed, 1887.

————. "The Origin of Ornament." *Free Museum of Science and Art Bulletin* 2 (1900): 235–43.

————. "America, the Cradle of Asia." *Proceedings of the American Association for the Advancement of Science* 52 (1903): 493–500.

Cushing, Frank Hamilton. "Primitive Motherhood." In *The Work and Words of the National Congress of Mothers*, pp. 3–47. New York: D. Appleton, 1897.

Dégh, Linda; Henry Glassie; and Felix J. Oinas, eds. *Folklore Today: A Festschrift for Richard M. Dorson.* Bloomington: Research Center for Language and Semiotic Studies, Indiana University, 1976.

Dégh, Linda, and Andrew Vazsonyi. "The Hypothesis of Multi-Conduit Transmission in Folklore." In *Folklore: Performance and Communication*, edited by Dan Ben-Amos and Kenneth S. Goldstein, pp. 207–51. The Hague: Mouton, 1975.

Denby, Priscilla. "Folklore in the Mass Media." *Folklore Forum* 4 (1971): 113–21.

Dennys, N. B. *The Folk-Lore of China, and Its Affinities with that of the Aryan and Semitic Races.* London: Trübnerad, 1876.

Dorson, Richard M. *American Folklore.* Chicago: University of Chicago Press, 1959.

————. "The Shaping of Folklore Traditions in the United States." *Folklore* 78 (1967): 161–83.

————, ed. *Peasant Customs and Savage Myths: Selections from the British Folklorists.* Chicago: University of Chicago Press, 1968.

————. *Folklore: Selected Essays.* Bloomington: Indiana University Press, 1972.

————. *Folklore and Fakelore: Essays toward a Discipline of Folk Studies.* Cambridge: Harvard University Press, 1976.

————, ed. *Folklore in the Modern World.* The Hague: Mouton, 1978.

————. *Land of the Millrats.* Cambridge: Harvard University Press, 1981.

Du Bois, W. E. Burghardt, ed. *The Negro American Family.* Atlanta, Ga.: Atlanta University Press, 1908.

Dundes, Alan. "Brown County Superstitions." *Midwest Folklore* 11 (1961): 25–56.

————. *Morphology of North American Indian Folktales.* Folklore Fellows Communications 195. Helsinki, Finland: Suomalainen Tiedeakatemia, 1964.

————, ed. *The Study of Folklore.* Englewood Cliffs, N.J.: Prentice-Hall, 1965.

————. "Folk Ideas as Units of World View." *Journal of American Folklore* 84 (1971): 93–103.

————, ed. *Mother Wit from the Laughing Barrel: Readings in the Interpretation of Afro-American Folklore.* Englewood Cliffs, N.J.: Prentice-Hall, 1973.

————, ed. *Varia Folklorica.* The Hague: Mouton, 1978.

————. *Interpreting Folklore.* Bloomington: Indiana University Press, 1980.

————, and Carl Pagter. *Work Hard and You Shall Be Rewarded: Urban Folklore from the Paperwork Empire.* Bloomington: Indiana University Press, 1978.

Durkheim, Émile. *The Elementary Forms of the Religious Life.* Translated by J. W. Swain. 1912. Reprint. New York: Free Press, 1965.

Eaton, Allen H. *Immigrant Gifts to American Life.* New York: Russell Sage Foundation, 1932.

Farrer, Claire R., ed. *Women and Folklore.* Austin: University of Texas Press, 1975.

Fife, Austin, and Alta Fife. *Saints of Sage and Saddle: Folklore among the Mormons*. Bloomington: Indiana University Press, 1956.

Fine, Gary Alan. "Folklore Diffusion through Interactive Social Networks: Conduits in a Preadolescent Community." *New York Folklore* 5 (1979): 87–126.

――――. "The Kentucky Fried Rat: Legends and Modern Society." *Journal of the Folklore Institute* 17 (1980): 222–43.

――――. "The Goliath Effect: Corporate Dominance and Mercantile Legends." *Journal of American Folklore* 98 (1985): 63–84.

Fiske, John. *Myths and Myth-Makers: Old Tales and Superstitions Interpreted by Comparative Mythology*. 1873. Reprint. Boston: Houghton Mifflin, 1887.

Fortes, Meyer. *Oedipus and Job in West African Religion*. London: Cambridge University Press, 1959.

――――. "Oedipus and Job in West African Religion." In *Anthropology of Folk Religion*, edited by Charles M. Leslie, pp. 5–49. New York: Vintage, 1960.

Frantz, Ray W. "The Role of Folklore in Huckleberry Finn." *American Literature* 28 (1956): 314–27.

Frazer, James George. *The Golden Bough: A Study in Magic and Religion*. 12 vols. 1911–14. Reprint. New York: St. Martin's Press, 1966.

Geertz, Clifford. "Deep Play: Notes on the Balinese Cockfight." In *The Interpretation of Cultures*, by Clifford Geertz, pp. 412–54. New York: Basic Books, 1973.

Georges, Robert A., ed. *Studies in Mythology*. Homewood, Ill.: Dorsey Press, 1968.

Glassie, Henry. *Pattern in the Material Folk Culture of the Eastern United States*. Philadelphia: University of Pennsylvania Press, 1968.

――――. *All Silver and No Brass: An Irish Christmas Mumming*. Bloomington: Indiana University Press, 1975.

――――. *Folk Housing in Middle Virginia: A Structural Analysis of Historic Artifacts*. Knoxville: University of Tennessee Press, 1975.

――――. *Passing the Time in Ballymenone: Culture and History of an Ulster Community*. Philadelphia: University of Pennsylvania Press, 1982.

Goldstein, Kenneth S., and Neil V. Rosenberg, eds. *Folklore Studies in Honour of Herbert Halpert*. St. John's: Memorial University of Newfoundland, 1980.

Graebner, Fritz. "Die melanesische Bogenkultur und ihre venwandten." *Anthropos* 4 (1909): 726–80, 998–1032.

Greenfield, Verni. "Silk Purses from Sows' Ears: An Aesthetic Approach to Recycling." In *Personal Places: Perspectives on Informal Art Environments*, edited by Daniel Franklin Ward, pp. 133–47. Bowling Green, Ohio: Bowling Green State University Popular Press, 1984.

――――. *Making Do or Making Art: A Study of American Recycling*. Ann Arbor, Mich.: UMI Research Press, 1985.

Gummere, F. B. "Primitive Poetry and the Ballad." *Modern Philology* 1 (1903): 193–202, 217–234, 373–90.

Gumperz, John J., and Dell Hymes, eds. *Directions in Sociolinguistics: The Ethnography of Communication*. New York: Holt, Rinehart & Winston, 1972.

Haddon, Alfred C. *Evolution in Art, As Illustrated by the Life-Histories of Designs*. 1895. Reprint. New York: AMS Press, 1979.

Hand, Wayland, ed. *American Folk Lege a A Symposium.* Berkeley: University of California Press, 1971.

Handler, Richard, and Jocelyn Linnekin. "Tradition, Genuine or Spurious." *Journal of American Folklore* 97 (1984): 273–90.

Hanson, F. Allan, ed. *Studies in Symbolism and Cultural Communication.* Lawrence: University of Kansas Publications in Anthropology, no. 14, 1982.

Herskovits, Frances, ed. *The New World Negro.* Bloomington: Indiana University Press, 1966.

Herskovits, Melville J. *The Myth of the Negro Past.* 1941. Reprint. Boston: Beacon Press, 1958.

Hufford, David J. *The Terror That Comes in the Night: An Experience-Centered Study of Supernatural Assault Traditions.* Philadelphia: University of Pennsylvania Press, 1982.

Hymes, Dell. "Breakthrough into Performance." In *Folklore: Performance and Communication,* edited by Dan Ben-Amos and Kenneth S. Goldstein, pp. 11–74. The Hague: Mouton, 1975.

International Folk-Lore Association: Papers Read at Memphis, Atlanta and Chicago. Chicago: International Folk-Lore Association, 1896.

Ives, Edward. *Joe Scott: The Woodsman-Songmaker.* Urbana: University of Illinois Press, 1978.

Jackson, Bruce, ed. *Folklore and Society: Essays in Honor of Benjamin A. Botkin.* Hatboro, Pa.: Folklore Associates, 1966.

James, George Wharton. "Primitive Inventions." *Craftsman* 5 (1903): 125–37.

Jansen, William Hugh. "Classifying Performance in the Study of Verbal Folklore." In *Studies in Folklore,* edited by W. Edson Richmond, pp. 110–18. Bloomington: Indiana University Press, 1957.

Jenkins, Geraint, ed. *Studies in Folk Life: Essays in Honor of Iorwerth C. Peate.* London: Routledge & Kegan Paul, 1969.

Jones, Louis C. *Three Eyes on the Past: Exploring New York Folk Life.* Syracuse, N.Y.: Syracuse University Press, 1982.

Jones, Michael Owen. *The Hand Made Object and Its Maker.* Berkeley: University of California Press, 1975.

———. "L.A. Add-ons and Re-dos: Renovation in Folk Art and Architectural Design." In *Perspectives on American Folk Art,* edited by Ian M. G. Quimby and Scott T. Swank, pp. 325–63. New York: W. W. Norton, 1980.

———, Bruce Giuliano, and Roberta Krell, eds. *Foodways and Eating Habits: Directions for Research.* Los Angeles: California Folklore Society, 1981.

Jordan, Rosan A., and Susan J. Kalčik, eds. *Women's Folklore, Women's Culture.* Philadelphia: University of Pennsylvania Press, 1985.

Krappe, Alexander. *The Science of Folklore.* New York: W. W. Norton, 1964.

Langlois, Janet L. "The Belle Isle Bridge Incident: Legend Dialectic and Semiotic System in the 1943 Detroit Race Riots." *Journal of American Folklore* 96 (1983): 183–99.

Lawless, Elaine J. "Making a Joyful Noise: An Ethnography of Communication in the Pentecostal Religious Service." *Southern Folklore Quarterly* 44 (1980): 1–22.

Leach, Edmund. "Myth as Justification for Faction and Social Change." In *Studies on Mythology,* edited by Robert A. Georges, pp. 184–98. Homewood, Ill.: Dorsey Press, 1968.

Leslie, Charles M., ed. *Anthropology of Folk Religion.* New York: Vintage, 1960.

Lessa, William A., and Evon Z. Vogt, eds. *Reader in Comparative Religion: An Anthropological Approach.* Evanston, Ill.: Row, Peterson, & Co., 1958.

Lord, Albert B. *The Singer of Tales.* Cambridge: Harvard University Press, 1960.

McCarl, Robert S. " 'You've Come a Long Way—And Now This Is Your Retirement': An Analysis of Performance in Fire Fighting Culture." *Journal of American Folklore* 97 (1984): 393–422.

McGuire, J. D. *A Study of the Primitive Methods of Drilling.* Report of the United States National Museum for 1894. Washington, D.C.: Smithsonian Institution, 1896.

Malinowski, Bronislaw. *Argonauts of the Western Pacific.* 1922. Reprint. New York: E. P. Dutton, 1961.

———. *Magic, Science and Religion.* 1948. Reprint. Garden City, N.Y.: Doubleday, 1954.

Marrett, Robert. *Psychology and Folk-Lore.* New York: Macmillan, 1920.

Marshall, Howard Wight. *Folk Architecture in Little Dixie: A Regional Culture in Missouri.* Columbia: University of Missouri Press, 1981.

Mason, Otis T. *Woman's Share in Primitive Culture.* New York: D. Appleton, 1894.

———. *The Origins of Invention: A Study of Industry among Primitive Peoples.* 1895. Reprint. Freeport, N.Y.: Books for Libraries Press, 1972.

———. *Primitive Travel and Transportation.* Report of the United States National Museum for 1894. Washington, D.C.: Smithsonian Institution, 1896.

Morgan, Lewis Henry. *Ancient Society: Or Researches in the Lines of Human Progress from Savagery through Barbarism to Civilization.* 1877. Reprint. Gloucester, Mass.: Peter Smith, 1974.

Mullen, Patrick B. "The Function of Magic Folk Belief among Texas Coastal Fishermen." *Journal of American Folklore* 82 (1969): 214–25.

Newall, Venetia, ed. *Folklore Studies in the Twentieth Century.* Totowa, N.J.: Rowman & Littlefield, 1980.

Nicolaisen, Wilhelm F. H. "Time in Folk-Narrative." In *Folklore Studies in the Twentieth Century,* edited by Venetia Newall, pp. 314–19. Totowa, N.J.: Rowman & Littlefield, 1980.

———. "Space in Folk Narrative." In *Folklore on Two Continents,* edited by Nikolai Burlakoff and Carl Lindahl, pp. 14–18. Bloomington, Ind.: Trickster Press, 1980.

———. "Names and Narratives." *Journal of American Folklore* 97 (1984): 259–72.

Odum, Howard W. *Folk, Region, and Society: Selected Papers.* Edited by Katharine Jocher. Chapel Hill: University of North Carolina Press, 1964.

Oring, Elliott. "Whalemen and Their Songs: A Study of Folklore and Culture." *New York Folklore Quarterly* 27 (1971): 130–52.

———. "Everything Is a Shade of Elephant: An Alternative to a Psychoanalysis of Humor." *New York Folklore* 1 (1975): 149–60.

———. "Jokes and Their Relation to Sigmund Freud." In *Humor and the Individual,* edited by Elliott Oring, pp. 37–48. Los Angeles: California Folklore Society, 1984.

———, ed. *Humor and the Individual.* Los Angeles: California Folklore Society, 1984.

Ottenberg, Simon, ed. *African Religions, Groups and Beliefs: Papers in Honor of William R. Bascom.* Delhi: Archana Publications, 1982.

Paredes, Américo, and Ellen J. Stekert, eds. *The Urban Experience and Folk Tradition.* Austin: University of Texas Press, 1971.

Pocius, Gerald L. "Hooked Rugs in Newfoundland: The Representation of Social Structure in Design." *Journal of American Folklore* 92 (1979): 273–84.

Quimby, Ian M. G., and Scott T. Swank, eds. *Perspectives on American Folk Art.* New York: W. W. Norton, 1980.

Radcliffe-Brown, A. R. *The Andaman Islanders.* 1922. Reprint. New York: Free Press, 1964.

———. "The Interpretation of Andamese Customs and Beliefs: Myths and Legends." In *Studies on Mythology,* edited by Robert Georges, pp. 46–71. Homewood, Ill.: Dorsey Press, 1968.

Redfield, Robert. *The Little Community and Peasant Society and Culture.* Chicago: University of Chicago Press, 1967.

Richmond, W. Edson, ed. *Studies in Folklore: In Honor of Distinguished Service Professor Stith Thompson.* Bloomington: Indiana University Press, 1957.

Roberts, Warren E. *Tale of the Kind and Unkind Girls, Aa-Th 480 and Related Tales.* Berlin: De Gruyter, 1958.

Sebeok, Thomas A., ed. *Myth: A Symposium.* Bloomington: Indiana University Press, 1965.

Senn, Harry A. "Proust and Melusine: From Fairy Magic to Personal Mythology." *Southern Folklore Quarterly* 43 (1979): 267–75.

Smith, Moira, and Regina Bendix, eds. *Conversational Folklore.* Special Issue of *Folklore Forum,* vol. 17, no. 2, 1984.

Smith, William Robertson. *The Religion of the Semites: The Fundamental Institutions.* 1894. Reprint. New York: Schocken Books. 1972.

Stahl, Sandra K. D. "The Personal Narrative as Folklore." *Journal of the Folklore Institute* 14 (1977): 9–30.

Sullenberger, Tom E. "Ajax Meets the Jolly Green Giant: Some Observations on the Use of Folklore and Myth in American Mass Marketing." *Journal of American Folklore* 87 (1974): 53–65.

Taylor, Archer. *The Proverb.* Cambridge: Harvard University Press, 1931.

Thompson, Stith. "The Star Husband Tale." In *The Study of Folklore,* edited by Alan Dundes, pp. 415–74. Englewood Cliffs, N.J.: Prentice-Hall, 1965.

Turner, Victor. *The Forest of Symbols: Aspects of Ndembu Ritual.* Ithaca, N.Y.: Cornell University Press, 1967.

———, ed. *Celebration: Studies in Festivity and Ritual.* Washington, D.C.: Smithsonian Institution Press, 1982.

Vance, Lee J. "Ghost Stories: A Study in Folk-Lore." *Open Court* 2 (1888): 1247–51, 1259–63, 1273–78.

Vincent, George. "A Retarded Frontier." *American Journal of Sociology* 4 (1898): 1–20.

Vlach, John Michael. *Charleston Blacksmith: The Work of Philip Simmons.* Athens: University of Georgia Press, 1981.

———, and Simon J. Bronner, eds. *Folk Art and Art Worlds.* Ann Arbor, Mich.: UMI Research Press, 1986.

Vogt, Evon Z. "Water Witching: An Interpretation of a Ritual Pattern in a Rural American Community." In *Reader in Comparative Religion: An Anthropo-*

logical Approach, edited by William A. Lessa and Evon Z. Vogt, pp. 327–41. Evanston, Ill.: Row, Peterson, & Co., 1958.

———, and Ray Hyman. *Water Witching, U.S.A.* Chicago: University of Chicago Press, 1959.

Wilson, Thomas. "Primitive Industry." In *Smithsonian Institution Annual for 1892,* pp. 521–34. Washington, D.C.: Smithsonian Institution, 1893.

Wilson, William A. "On Being Human: The Folklore of Mormon Missionaries." *New York Folklore* 8 (1982): 5–28.

Yoder, Don, ed. *American Folklife.* Austin: University of Texas Press, 1976.

Young, Frank W. "Folktales and Social Structure: A Comparison of Three Analyses of the Star–Husband Tale." *Journal of American Folklore* 91 (1978): 691–99.

Young, James Harvey. "Folk into Fake." *Western Folklore* 44 (1985): 225–39.

COMMENTARIES

Abrahams, Roger D. "On Meaning and Gaming." *Journal of American Folklore* 82 (1969): 268–70.

———. "Alan Dundes and the State and Fate of Our Discipline." *Folklore Forum* 10 (1977): 31–34.

———, and Susan Kalčik. "Folklore and Cultural Pluralism." In *Folklore in the Modern World,* edited by Richard M. Dorson, pp. 223–36. The Hague: Mouton, 1978.

Ashton, J. W. "The Vitality of American Folklore." *Hoosier Folklore* 6 (1947): 81–87.

Azzolina, David. "Scholarly Communication among Folklorists: Issues and Prospects." *New York Folklore* 9 (1983): 5–12.

Bascom, William. "Perhaps Too Much to Chew?" *Western Folklore* 40 (1981): 285–98.

Bauman, Richard. "Folklore and the Forces of Modernity." *Folklore Forum* 16 (1983): 153–58.

Bayard, Samuel P. "The Materials of Folklore." *Journal of American Folklore* 66 (1953): 1–17.

Benedict, Ruth. "Anthropology and the Humanities." *American Anthropologist* 50 (1948): 585–93.

Brunvand, Jan Harold. "On Abrahams' Besom." *Journal of American Folklore* 83 (1970): 81.

Coffin, Tristram Potter. "Folklore in the American Twentieth Century." *American Quarterly* 13 (1961): 526–33.

Cothran, Kay L. "Participation in Tradition." In *Readings in American Folklore,* edited by Jan Harold Brunvand, pp. 444–48. New York: W. W. Norton, 1979.

Culin, Stewart. "The Road to Beauty." *Brooklyn Museum Quarterly* 14 (1927): 41–50.

Dégh, Linda. "Is the Study of Tale Performance Suspect of Aggressive Nationalism? A Comment." *Journal of American Folklore* 93 (1980): 324–27.

Dorson, Richard M. "Standards for Collecting and Publishing American Folktales." *Journal of American Folklore* 70 (1957): 53–57.

———. "Should There Be a Ph.D. in Folklore?" *American Council of Learned Societies Newsletter* 14 (1963): 1–8.

———. "Is Folklore a Discipline?" *Folklore* 84 (1973): 177–205.

———. "Folklore vs. Fakelore—Again and Again." *Folklore Forum* 7 (1974): 57–63.

———. "Editor's Comment: We All Need the Folk." *Journal of the Folklore Institute* 15 (1978): 267–69.

———. "The America Theme in American Folklore." *Journal of the Folklore Institute* 17 (1980): 91–93.

Farrand, Livingston. "The Significance of Mythology and Tradition." *Journal of American Folklore* 17 (1904): 14–22.

Fiske, John. "Curtin's Myths and Folk-Lore of Ireland." *Atlantic Monthly* 66 (Oct. 1890): 568–72.

Glassie, Henry. "Meaningful Things and Appropriate Myths: The Artifact's Place in American Studies." In *Prospects 3,* edited by Jack Salzman, pp. 1–49. New York: Burt Franklin, 1978.

———. "The Moral Lore of Folklore." *Folklore Forum* 16 (1983): 123–52.

"Guidelines for the Evaluation of Folklore Scholarship and Service." *Journal of American Folklore* 95 (1982): 209.

Halpert, Herbert. "Problems and Projects in the American-English Folktale." *Journal of American Folklore* 70 (1957): 57–62.

Herskovits, Melville J. "Folklore after a Hundred Years: A Problem in Redefinition." *Journal of American Folklore* 59 (1946): 89–100.

Jackson, Bruce. "Folklore and the Social Sciences." In *Papers on Applied Folklore,* edited by Dick Sweterlitsch, pp. 14–21. Folklore Forum Bibliographic and Special Series, no. 8, 1971.

———. "Dorson's Farewell." *New York Folklore* 10 (1984): 99–112.

Jansen, William Hugh. "Ethics and the Folklorist." In *Handbook of American Folklore,* edited by Richard M. Dorson, pp. 533–39. Bloomington: Indiana University Press, 1983.

Jones, Michael Owen. "Organizational Folklore and Corporate Culture." *American Folklore Society Newsletter* 12 (Oct. 1983): 3–4, 6.

Kahn, Ed. "Folklore: A Sub-discipline of Media Studies?" *John Edwards Memorial Foundation Quarterly* 6 (1970): 2–5.

Keil, Charles. "Who Needs 'the Folk'?" *Journal of the Folklore Institute* 15 (1978): 263–66.

McCarl, Robert S. "Reply to Michael Owen Jones." *American Folklore Society Newsletter* 14 (June 1985): 2, 5.

Moller, Helmut. "Aus den Anfangen der Volkskunde als Wissenschaft." *Zeitschrift für Volkskunde* 60 (1964): 218–41.

Newell, William Wells. "Notes and Queries." *Journal of American Folklore* 1 (1888): 79–81.

———. "Review of *The Sabbath in Puritan New England.*" *Journal of American Folklore* 4 (1891); 356–57.

Parsons, Elsie Clews. "Femininity and Conventionality." *American Academy of Political and Social Science* 56 (1914): 47–53.

Powell, John Wesley. "Mythologic Philosophy." *Popular Science Monthly* 15 (1879): 795–808 and 16 (1880): 56–66.

Reuss, Richard A. "On Folklore and Women Folklorists." *Folklore Feminist Communication,* no. 3 (1974), 29–37.

Samuelson, Sue. "Notes on a Sociology of Folklore as a Science." *New York Folklore* 9 (1983): 13–20.

Smith, Marion. "The Importance of Folklore Studies to Anthropology." *Folklore* 70 (1959): 300–312.
State of Folkloristics, The. Special Issue of *New York Folklore,* vol. 9, nos. 3 and 4, 1983.
Taylor, Archer. "Place of Folklore." *Publications of the Modern Language Association* 67 (1952): 59–66.
Thompson, Stith. "Challenge of Folklore." *Publications of the Modern Language Association* 79 (1964): 357–65.
Utley, Francis Lee. "Anthropology and Folklore's Second Century." *Hoosier Folklore* 8 (1949): 69–78,
———. "Conflict and Promise in Folklore." *Journal of American Folklore* 65 (1952): 111–19.
Vance, Lee J. "On the Nature and Value of Folk-Lore." *Chautauquan* 11 (1890): 686–89.
———. "The Philosophy of Folk-Tales." *Open Court* 5 (1891): 2935–37.
Vansina, Jan. "Review of *Folklore and Fakelore.*" *Journal of Interdisciplinary History* 8 (1977): 356–59.

FORECASTS

Dorson, Richard M. "The Academic Future of Folklore." In *Folklore: Selected Essays,* pp. 295–303. Bloomington: Indiana University Press, 1972.
Harrah-Conforth, Bruce. "Whither Goeth Folk Music?" *Folklore Forum* 18 (1985): 76–82.
Harrah-Conforth, Jeanne, and Thomas Walker, eds. *The Future of American Folklore Studies.* Special Issue of *Folklore Forum,* vol. 16, no. 2, 1983.
Herskovits, Melville J. "Some Next Steps in the Study of Negro Folklore." *Journal of American Folklore* 56 (1943): 1–7.
Jacobs, Melville. "A Look Ahead in Oral Literature Research." *Journal of American Folklore* 79 (1966): 413–27.
Jones, Michael Owen. "Two Directions for Folkloristics in the Study of American Art." *Southern Folklore Quarterly* 32 (1968): 249–59.
Kirshenblatt-Gimblett, Barbara. "The Future of Folklore Studies in America: The Urban Frontier." *Folklore Forum* 16 (1983): 175–234.
Rosenberg, Bruce. "The Formula: New Directions?" *Folklore Preprint Series* 6, no. 4 (Aug. 1978).
Thompson, Stith. "The Future of Folklore Research in the United States." *Proceedings of the American Philosophical Society* 93 (1949): 244–47.
———. "The Study of Primitive Storytelling: Its Present Status and Future Directions." *Folk-Liv* 21–22 (1957): 185–90.
Wilgus, D. K. "The Future of American Folksong Scholarship." *Southern Folklore Quarterly* 37 (1973): 315–29.

DEFINITIONS

Abrahams, Roger D. "Personal Power and Social Restraint in the Definition of Folklore." In *Toward New Perspectives in Folklore,* edited by Richard Bauman and Américo Paredes, pp. 16–30. Austin: University of Texas Press, 1972.
———. "The Complex Relations of Simple Forms." In *Folklore Genres,* edited by Dan Ben-Amos, pp. 193–214. Austin: University of Texas Press, 1976.

————. "Genre Theory and Folkloristics." *Studia Fennica* 20 (1976): 13–19.

Balys, Jonas, et al. "Folklore." In *Dictionary of Folklore, Mythology, and Legend,* edited by Maria Leach, 1:398–403. 2 vols. New York: Funk & Wagnalls, 1949.

Bascom, William R. "Folklore." In *Dictionary of Folklore, Mythology, and Legend,* edited by Maria Leach, 1:398. New York: Funk & Wagnalls, 1949.

————. "Verbal Art." *Journal of American Folklore* 68 (1955): 245–52.

————. "The Forms of Folklore: Prose Narratives." *Journal of American Folklore* 78 (1965): 3–20.

Bauman, Richard. "Differential Identity and the Social Base of Folklore." In *Toward New Perspectives in Folklore,* edited by Richard Bauman and Américo Paredes, pp. 31–41. Austin: University of Texas Press, 1972.

Ben-Amos, Dan. "Toward a Definition of Folklore in Context." In *Toward New Perspectives in Folklore,* edited by Richard Bauman and Américo Paredes, pp. 3–15. Austin: University of Texas Press, 1972.

————. "Analytical Categories and Ethnic Genres." In *Folklore Genres,* edited by Dan Ben-Amos, pp. 215–42. Austin: University of Texas Press, 1976.

————. "The Concepts of Genre in Folklore." *Studia Fennica* 20 (1976): 30–43.

————. "On the Final (s) in 'Folkloristics.'" *Journal of American Folklore* 98 (1985): 334–36.

Blehr, Otto. "What Is a Proverb?" *Fabula* 14 (1973): 243–46.

Dégh, Linda. "Reply: Folk and Volk." *Journal of American Folklore* 93 (1980): 331–34.

Dorson, Richard M. "What Is Folklore?" *Folklore Forum* 1 (1968): 37.

Dundes, Alan. "Texture, Text, and Context." *Southern Folklore Quarterly* 28 (1964): 251–65.

————. "What Is Folklore?" In *The Study of Folklore,* edited by Alan Dundes, pp. 1–3. Englewood Cliffs, N.J.: Prentice-Hall, 1965.

————. "Who Are The Folk?" In *Interpreting Folklore,* by Alan Dundes, pp. 1–19. Bloomington: Indiana University Press, 1980.

Foster, George M. "What Is Folk Culture?" *American Anthropologist* 55 (1953): 159–73.

Georges, Robert A. "The General Concept of Legend: Some Assumptions to Be Reexamined and Reassessed." In *American Folk Legend: A Symposium,* edited by Wayland D. Hand, pp. 1–20. Berkeley: University of California Press, 1971.

————, and Alan Dundes. "Toward A Structural Definition of the Riddle." *Journal of American Folklore* 76 (1963): 111–18.

Halpert, Herbert. "Definition and Variation in Folk Legend." In *American Folk Legend: A Symposium,* edited by Wayland D. Hand, pp. 47–54. Berkeley: University of California Press, 1971.

Honko, Lauri. "Genre Analysis in Folkloristics and Comparative Religion." *Temenos* 3 (1968): 48–66.

————. "Genre Theory Revisited." *Studia Fennica* 20 (1976): 20–25.

Hultkrantz, Åke. *General Ethnological Concepts.* Copenhagen: Rosenkilde & Bagger, 1960.

Jackson, Bruce. "Folkloristics." *Journal of American Folklore* 98 (1985): 95–101.

Jacobs, Joseph. "The Folk." *Folk-Lore* 4 (1983): 233–38.

Kagarow. Eugen. "Folkloristik und Volkskunde." *Mitteilungen der schlesischen Gesellschaft für Volkskunde* 30 (1929): 70–77.

Kamenetsky, Christa. "The Uses and Misuses of Folklore Terminology."
    Journal of American Folklore 93 (1980): 327–30.
Keil, Charles. "The Concept of 'The Folk.' " *Journal of the Folklore Institute* 16
    (1979): 209–10.
Ketner, Kenneth L. "A Preliminary Survey of the Grammar of 'Folklore': An
    Introduction to Hominology." *Folklore Preprint Series* 1, no. 5 (Nov. 1973).
Leach, Maria, ed. *Dictionary of Folklore, Mythology, and Legend.* 2 vols. New
    York: Funk & Wagnalls, 1949.
Nicolaisen, Wilhelm F. H. "The Folk and the Region." *New York Folklore* 2
    (1976): 143–49.
Ranke, Kurt. "Einfache Formen." Translated by William Templer and
    Eberhard Alsen. *Journal of the Folklore Institute* 4 (1967): 17–31.
Redfield, Robert. "The Folk Society." In *Sociology Full Circle: Contemporary
    Readings on Society,* edited by William Feigelman, pp. 61–72. New York:
    Praeger, 1972.
Scott, Charles T. "On Defining the Riddle: The Problem of a Structural Unit."
    in *Folklore Genres,* edited by Dan Ben-Amos, pp. 77–90. Austin: Univer-
    sity of Texas Press, 1976.
Simpson, George L. "Notes on a Definition of the Folk for Folk-Regional
    Sociology." *Social Forces* 25 (1946): 31–34.
Taylor, Archer. "The Riddle." *California Folklore Quarterly* 2 (1943): 129–47.
———. "The Problems of Folklore." *Journal of American Folklore* 59 (1946):
    101–7.
Thoms, William. "Folklore." In *The Study of Folklore,* edited by Alan Dundes,
    pp. 4–6. Englewood Cliffs, N.J.: Prentice-Hall, 1965.
Tillhagen, Carl-Herman. "Was ist eine Sage? Eine Definition und ein Vor-
    schlag für ein europäisches Sagensystem." *Acta Ethnographica Acade-
    miae Scientaiarum Hungaricae* 13 (1964): 5–131.
Toelken, J. Barre. "A Descriptive Nomenclature for the Study of Folklore."
    Western Folklore 28 (1969): 91–111.
Utley, Francis Lee. "Folk Literature: An Operational Definition." In *The Study
    of Folklore,* edited by Alan Dundes, pp. 7–24. Englewood Cliffs, N.J.:
    Prentice-Hall, 1965.
———. "A Definition of Folklore." In *Our Living Traditions,* edited by Tristram
    Potter Coffin, pp. 3–14. New York: Basic Books, 1968.
Voigt, Vilmos. "Structural Definition of Oral (Folk) Literature." In *Proceedings
    of the Fifth Congress of the International Comparative Literature Associa-
    tion,* edited by Nikola Banesevic, pp. 461–67. Amsterdam: Universite de
    Belgrade, Swets and Zeitlinger, 1969.
Welsch, Roger L. "A Note on Definitions." *Journal of American Folklore* 81
    (1968): 262–64.
———. "Beating a Live Horse: Yet Another Note on Definitions and Defining."
    In *Perspectives on American Folk Art,* edited by Ian M. G. Quimby and
    Scott T. Swank, pp. 218–33. New York: W. W. Norton, 1980.

STATEMENTS ON PUBLIC AND APPLIED FOLKLORE

Auser, Cortland P. "The Viable Community: Redirections through Applied
    Folklore." *New York Folklore Quarterly* 25 (1970): 3–13.

Barton, Caroline French. "A Year of Club Work: Myths and Folk-Lore."
   Woman's Home Companion 40 (Mar. 1913): 37–38.
Camp, Charles. "State Folklorist and Folklife Programs: A Second Look."
   Folklore Forum 10 (1977): 26–29.
———. "Developing a State Folklife Program." In *Handbook of American
   Folklore,* edited by Richard M. Dorson, pp. 518–24. Bloomington: Indiana
   University Press, 1983.
Carey, George. "State Folklorists and State Arts Councils: The Maryland
   Pilot." *Folklore Forum* 9 (1976): 1–8.
Dorson, Richard M. "Folklore and the National Defense Education Act."
   Journal of American Folklore 75 (1962): 160–64.
———. "Applied Folklore." In *Papers on Applied Folklore,* edited by Dick
   Sweterlitsch, pp. 40–42. Folklore Forum Bibliographic and Special Se-
   ries, no. 8, 1971.
———. "The Lesson of Foxfire." *North Carolina Folklore Journal* 21 (1973):
   157–59.
———, and Inta Gale Carpenter. "Can Folklorists and Educators Work
   Together?" *North Carolina Folklore Journal* 26 (1978): 3–13.
Folklore and the Public Sector. Special Issue of *Kentucky Folklore Record,* vol.
   26, nos. 1 and 2, 1980.
Glassie, Henry, and Betty Jo Glassie. "The Implications of Folkloristic
   Thought for Historic Zoning Ordinances." In *Papers on Applied Folklore,*
   edited by Dick Sweterlitsch, pp. 31–37. Folklore Forum Bibliographic
   and Special Series, no. 8, 1971.
Jones, Louis C. "Folk Culture and the Historical Society." *Minnesota History*
   31 (1950): 11–17.
Jones, Michael Owen. "On Folklorists Studying Organizations." *American
   Folklore Society Newsletter* 14 (April 1985): 5–6, 8.
Loomis, Ormond. *Cultural Conservation: The Protection of Cultural Heritage in
   the United States.* Washington, D.C.: Library of Congress, 1983.
Montell, Lynwood. "Academic and Applied Folklore: Partners for the Future."
   Folklore Forum 16 (1983): 159–74.
Sweterlitsch, Dick, ed. *Papers on Applied Folklore.* Folklore Forum Bibli-
   ographic and Special Series, no. 8, 1971.
Thompson, Stith. "Folklore and Folk Festivals." *Midwest Folklore* 4 (1954):
   5–12.
West, John O. "The Professional-Amateur-Popularizer Feud in Folklore."
   Journal of American Folklore 88 (1975): 299–300.
Wigginton, Eliot. "Comment." *North Carolina Folklore Journal* 26 (1978):
   14–17.

STATEMENTS ON HIGHER EDUCATION

Baker, Ronald L. "Folklore Courses and Programs in American Colleges and
   Universities." *Journal of American Folklore* 84 (1971): 221–29.
———. "The Study of Folklore in American Colleges and Universities."
   Journal of American Folklore 91 (1978): 792–807.
———. "Teaching Folklore in American Colleges and Universities." In *Hand-
   book of American Folklore,* edited by Richard M. Dorson, pp. 470–77.
   Bloomington: Indiana University Press, 1983.

Boggs, Ralph S. *Folklore: An Outline for Individual and Group Study.* Chapel Hill: University of North Carolina Extension Bulletin, Dec. 1920.
———. "Folklore in University Curricula in the United States." *Southern Folklore Quarterly* 4 (1940): 93–109.
Brunvand, Jan Harold. "Crumbs for the Court Jester: Folklore in English Departments." In *Perspectives on Folklore and Education,* edited by Elliott Oring and James Durham, pp. 45–59. Folklore Forum Bibliographic and Special Series, no. 2, 1969.
Dégh, Linda. "Folklore Education at Contemporary European Universities." In *Perspectives on Folklore and Education,* edited by Elliott Oring and James Durham, pp. 32–44. Folklore Forum Bibliographic and Special Series, no. 2, 1969.
Dorson, Richard M. "Growth of Folklore Courses in the United States." *Journal of American Folklore* 63 (1950): 345–59.
———. "Folklore in Higher Education." *New York Folklore Quarterly* 18 (1962): 44–54.
———. "The Study of Folklore and Folklife in American Universities." In *1970 Festival of American Folklife,* p. 45. Washington, D.C.: Smithsonian Institution, 1970.
———. "Teaching Folklore to Graduate Students: The Introductory Proseminar." In *Handbook of American Folklore,* edited by Richard M. Dorson, pp. 463–69. Bloomington: Indiana University Press, 1983.
Jackson, Bruce, ed. *Teaching Folklore.* Buffalo, N.Y.: Documentary Research, Inc., 1984.
Jones, Louis C. "Teaching and Presentation of Folklore." In *Second Folklore Institute of America: Informal Notes on Transactions and Lectures.* Bloomington: Indiana University, 1946.
Ketner, Kenneth Laine, and Michael Owen Jones. "Folkloristic Research as a Pedagogical Tool in Introductory Courses." *New York Folklore* 1 (1975): 123–48.
Leach, MacEdward. "Folklore in American Colleges and Universities." *Journal of American Folklore Supplement* (1958): 10–11.
MacCurdy, George Grant. "The Teaching of Anthropology in the United States." *Science* 15 (1902): 211–26.
Oring, Elliott, and James Durham, eds. *Perspectives on Folklore and Education.* Folklore Forum Bibliographic and Special Series, no. 2, 1969.
Seward, Adrienne Lanier, ed. *The Role of Afro-American Folklore in the Teaching of the Arts and Humanities.* Bloomington: Indiana University, 1979.
Stekert, Ellen Jane. "Folklore: A Vehicle for Teaching Objective Analysis and Cultural Awareness." In *Perspectives on Folklore and Education,* edited by Elliott Oring and James Durham, pp. 4–7. Folklore Forum Bibliographic and Special Series, no. 2, 1969.
Utley, Francis Lee. "The Academic Status of Folklore in the United States." *Journal of the Folklore Institute* 7 (1970): 110–15.
Voegelin, Erminie Wheeler. "Folklore in American Universities." *Journal of American Folklore* 63 (1950): 93.
Winkelman, Donald M. "Folklore in a Small College." *Kentucky Folklore Record* 7 (1961): 17–22.
———, and Ray B. Browne. "Folklore Study in Universities." *Sing Out!* 14 (1964): 47–49.

REFERENCE WORKS

Aarne, Antti. *The Types of the Folktale: A Classification and Bibliography.* 2d rev. ed. Translated by Stith Thompson. Folklore Fellows Communications, no. 184. Helsinki, Finland: Suomalainen Tiedeakatemia, 1964.

Abrahams, Roger D., and John Szwed. *Annotated Bibliography of Afro-American Folklore and Culture.* Philadelphia: Institute for the Study of Human Issues, 1978.

Baughman, Ernest W. *Type and Motif Index of the Folktales of England and North America.* The Hague: Mouton, 1966.

Bronner, Simon J., ed. *American Folk Art: A Guide to Sources.* New York: Garland Publishing, 1984.

Chamberlain, Isabel Cushman. "Contributions toward a Bibliography of Folk-Lore Relating to Women." *Journal of American Folklore* 12 (1899): 32–37.

Clements, William M., and Frances M. Malpezzi. *Native American Folklore, 1879–1979: An Annotated Bibliography.* Athens, Ohio: Swallow Press, 1984.

Coffin, Tristram Potter. *An Analytical Index to the Journal of American Folklore.* Vols. 1–70. Philadelphia: American Folklore Society, 1958.

Collins, Camilla. "Bibliography of Urban Folklore." *Folklore Forum* 8 (1975): 57–125.

de Caro, Francis. *Women and Folklore: A Bibliographic Survey.* Westport, Conn.: Greenwood Press, 1983.

Dorson, Richard M. "American Folklore Bibliography." *American Studies International* 16 (1977): 23–37.

Dundes, Alan. *Folklore Theses and Dissertations in the United States.* Austin: University of Texas Press, 1976.

Flanagan, John, and Cathleen C. Flanagan. *American Folklore: A Bibliography, 1950–1974.* Metuchen, N.J.: Scarecrow Press, 1977.

Folk-Lorist: Journal of the Chicago Folk-Lore Society, The. 1892–93. Reprint. Norwood, Pa.: Norwood Editions, 1973.

Fryer, Judith E. *Twenty-five-Year Index to Pennsylvania Folklife, 1949–1976.* Collegeville: Pennsylvania Folklife Society, 1980.

Georges, Robert A., and Stephen Stern. *American and Canadian Immigrant and Ethnic Folklore: An Annotated Bibliography.* New York: Garland Publishing, 1982.

Green, Archie. "Industrial Lore: A Bibliographic-Semantic Query." *Western Folklore* 38 (1978): 213–44.

Grider, Sylvia Ann. "A Select Bibliography of Childlore." *Western Folklore* 39 (1980): 248–65.

Griffin, William J. "The *TFS* Bulletin and Other Folklore Serials in the United States: A Preliminary Survey." *Tennessee Folklore Society Bulletin* 25 (1959): 91–96.

———. "Indexes to the First Thirty Volumes of the Tennessee Folklore Society Bulletin." *Tennessee Folklore Society Bulletin* 31 (1965): 68–97.

———, and Richard L. Castner. "A Survey of U.S. Folklore Serials." *Tennessee Folklore Society Bulletin* 29 (1963): 42–46.

Haywood, Charles. *A Bibliography of North American Folklore and Folksong.* 2 vols. New York: Dover, 1961.

Hickerson, Joseph C. "A Tentative Beginning toward a Bibliography on the History of American Folkloristics and the American Folklore Society." *Journal of the Folklore Institute* 10 (1973): 109–12.

Hoffman, Frank. *Analytical Survey of Anglo-American Traditional Erotica.* Bowling Green, Ohio: Bowling Green State University Popular Press, 1973.

Kodish, Debora. "A Selected Bibliography on the History of American Folklore Studies." *Folklore Historian* 1 (1984): 6–11.

Lesser, Alexander. "Bibliography of American Folklore, 1915–1928." *Journal of American Folklore* 41 (1928): 1–60.

Mordoh, Alice Morrison. "Analytical Index to the *Journal of the Folklore Institute,* Vols. 1–15." *Journal of the Folklore Institute* 18 (1981): 157–273.

Perkal, Joan Ruman. *Western Folklore and California Folklore Quarterly: Twenty-five Year Index.* Berkeley: University of California Press, 1969.

Randolph, Vance. *Ozark Folklore: A Bibliography.* Bloomington: Research Center for Language and Semiotic Studies, Indiana University, 1972.

Simmons, Merle E. *Folklore Bibliography for 1973.* Bloomington: Research Center for Language and Semiotic Studies, Indiana University, 1975.

———. *Folklore Bibliography for 1974.* Bloomington: Research Center for Language and Semiotic Studies, Indiana University, 1977.

———. *Folklore Bibliography for 1975.* Philadelphia: Institute for the Study of Human Issues, 1979.

Thompson, Stith. *Motif-Index of Folk-Literature.* Rev. ed. 6 vols., 1932–36. Bloomington: Indiana University Press, 1975.

Wildhaber, Robert. "A Bibliographic Introduction to American Folklife." *New York Folklore Quarterly* 21 (1965): 259–302.

STATEMENTS ON HISTORIOGRAPHY

Baker, Ronald L., ed. "The History of Folkloristics: An Exchange of Views." *Midwestern Journal of Language and Folklore* 3 (1977): 41–53.

Ben-Amos, Dan. "A History of Folklore Studies—Why Do We Need It?" *Journal of the Folklore Institute* 10 (1973): 113–24.

———. "The History of Folklore and the History of Science." *Midwestern Journal of Language and Folklore* 3 (1977): 42–44.

Bronner, Simon J. "Publications in Folkloristics: A Review Essay." *Middle Atlantic Folklife Association Newsletter* 6 (1982): 4–7.

Commager, Henry Steele. *The Search for a Usable Past and Other Essays in Historiography.* New York: Alfred A. Knopf, 1967.

Cothran, Kay L. "Meta-Folkloristics and the History of the Discipline." *Midwestern Journal of Language and Folklore* 3 (1977): 44–47.

de Caro, Francis A. "Folklore as an 'Historical Science': The Anglo-American Viewpoint." Ph.D. diss., Indiana University, 1972.

Diggins, John Patrick. "The Oyster and the Pearl: The Problem of Contextualism in Intellectual History." *History and Theory* 23 (1984): 151–69.

Dorson, Richard M. "Afterword." *Journal of the Folklore Institute* (special issue on American folklore historiography) 10 (1973): 125–28.

———. "Comments on the History of Folkloristics." *Midwestern Journal of Language and Folklore* 3 (1977): 50–53.

———. "The Reception of the British Folklorists, Or Have You Read the Great Team?" In *Folklore Studies in Honour of Herbert Halpert,* edited by Kenneth S. Goldstein and Neil V. Rosenberg, pp. 145–55. St. John's: Memorial University of Newfoundland, 1980.

Grobman, Neil R. "Conceptual Problems in Writing a History of the Develop-
   ment of Folkloristic Thought." In *Conceptual Problems in Contemporary
   Folklore Study,* edited by Gerald Cashion, pp. 56–63. Folklore Forum
   Bibliographic and Special Series, no. 12, 1974.
Hallowell, A. Irving. "The History of Anthropology as an Anthropological
   Problem." In *Readings in the History of Anthropology,* edited by Regna
   Darnell, pp. 304–21. New York: Harper & Row, 1974.
Handler, Richard. "Ruth Benedict, Margaret Mead, and the Growth of Ameri-
   can Anthropology." *Journal of American History* 71 (1984): 364–68.
Hymes, Dell. "On Studying the History of Anthropology." In *Readings in the
   History of Anthropology,* edited by Regna Darnell, pp. 297–303. New
   York: Harper & Row, 1974.
Knapp, Peter. "Can Social Theory Escape from History? Views of History in
   Social Science." *History and Theory* 23 (1984): 34–52.
McNeil, W. K. "Telling Facts: Some Thoughts on the Art of Writing a History of
   American Folklore Studies." Paper read at the American Folklore Society
   meeting, San Diego, Calif., 1984.
Matthews, Fred. " 'Hobbesian Populism': Interpretive Paradigms and Moral
   Vision in American Historiography." *Journal of American History* 72
   (1985): 92–115.
Oring, Elliott. "The Gratifications of History: A Folkloristic Example." *Mid-
   western Journal of Language and Folklore* 3 (1977): 47–50.
Reuss, Richard A. "Introduction." *Journal of the Folklore Institute* (special issue
   on American folklore historiography) 10 (1973): 3–5.
Scott, Anne Firor. "On Seeing and Not Seeing: A Case of Historical Invis-
   ibility." *Journal of American History* 71 (1984): 7–21.
Stocking, George W., Jr. "The History of Anthropology: Where, Whence,
   Whither?" *Journal of the History of the Behavioral Sciences* 2 (1966):
   281–90.
————. "On the Limits of 'Presentism' and 'Historicism' in the Historiography
   of the Behavioral Sciences." In *Race, Culture, and Evolution,* by George W.
   Stocking, Jr. Rev. ed., pp. 1–12. Chicago: University of Chicago Press,
   1968.

Index